MW01413543

WITTGENSTEIN'S
TRACTATUS LOGICO-PHILOSOPHICUS

A Critical Guide

EDITED BY

JOSÉ L. ZALABARDO

University College London

CAMBRIDGE
UNIVERSITY PRESS

CAMBRIDGE
UNIVERSITY PRESS

Shaftesbury Road, Cambridge CB2 8EA, United Kingdom

One Liberty Plaza, 20th Floor, New York, NY 10006, USA

477 Williamstown Road, Port Melbourne, VIC 3207, Australia

314–321, 3rd Floor, Plot 3, Splendor Forum, Jasola District Centre, New Delhi – 110025, India

103 Penang Road, #05-06/07, Visioncrest Commercial, Singapore 238467

Cambridge University Press is part of Cambridge University Press & Assessment,
a department of the University of Cambridge.

We share the University's mission to contribute to society through the pursuit of
education, learning and research at the highest international levels of excellence.

www.cambridge.org
Information on this title: www.cambridge.org/9781316512548

DOI: 10.1017/9781009067690

© Cambridge University Press & Assessment 2024

This publication is in copyright. Subject to statutory exception and to the provisions
of relevant collective licensing agreements, no reproduction of any part may take
place without the written permission of Cambridge University Press & Assessment.

First published 2024

A catalogue record for this publication is available from the British Library

Library of Congress Cataloging-in-Publication Data
NAMES: Zalabardo, JoséL., editor.
TITLE: Wittgenstein's Tractatus logico-philosophicus : a critical guide / edited by José L. Zalabardo,
University College London.
DESCRIPTION: New York, NY : Cambridge University Press, 2024. | Series: Cambridge critical guides
| Includes bibliographical references and index.
IDENTIFIERS: LCCN 2023040886 (print) | LCCN 2023040887 (ebook) | ISBN 9781316512548
(hardback) | ISBN 9781009066938 (paperback) | ISBN 9781009067690 (epub)
SUBJECTS: LCSH: Wittgenstein, Ludwig, 1889-1951. Tractatus logico-philosophicus.
CLASSIFICATION: LCC B3376.W563 T73867 2024 (print) | LCC B3376.W563 (ebook) |
DDC 192–dc23/eng/20231206
LC record available at https://lccn.loc.gov/2023040886
LC ebook record available at https://lccn.loc.gov/2023040887

ISBN 978-1-316-51254-8 Hardback

Cambridge University Press & Assessment has no responsibility for the persistence
or accuracy of URLs for external or third-party internet websites referred to in this
publication and does not guarantee that any content on such websites is, or will
remain, accurate or appropriate.

WITTGENSTEIN'S
TRACTATUS LOGICO-PHILOSOPHICUS

Published just over a century ago, Wittgenstein's *Tractatus Logico-Philosophicus* is the only book-length work to have been published during his lifetime, and it continues to generate interest and scholarly debate. It is structured as a series of numbered propositions dealing with central philosophical issues, but ends by declaring that the way to learn from the book is to recognise its propositions as nonsensical. This volume brings together eleven new essays on the *Tractatus* covering a wide variety of topics, from the central Tractarian doctrines concerning representation, the structure of the world and the nature of logic, to less prominent issues including ethics, natural science, mathematics and the self. Individual essays advance specific exegetical debates in important ways, and, taken as a whole, they offer an excellent showcase of contemporary ideas on how to read the *Tractatus* and its relevance to contemporary thought.

JOSÉ L. ZALABARDO is Professor of Philosophy at University College London. He is the author of *Introduction to the Theory of Logic* (2000), *Scepticism and Reliable Belief* (2012), *Representation and Reality in Wittgenstein's Tractatus* (2015) and *Pragmatist Semantics* (2023).

CAMBRIDGE CRITICAL GUIDES

Titles published in this series:

Kierkegaard's *Either/Or A Critical Guide*
EDITED BY RYAN S. KEMP AND WALTER WIETZKE
Cicero's *De Officiis*
EDITED BY RAPHAEL WOOLF
Kierkegaard's *The Sickness unto Death*
EDITED BY JEFFREY HANSON AND SHARON KRISHEK
Nietzsche's *Thus Spoke Zarathustra*
EDITED BY KEITH ANSELL-PEARSON AND PAUL S. LOEB
Aristotle's *On the Soul*
EDITED BY CALEB M. COHOE
Schopenhauer's *World as Will and Representation*
EDITED BY JUDITH NORMAN AND ALISTAIR WELCHMAN
Kant's *Prolegomena*
EDITED BY PETER THIELKE
Hegel's *Encyclopedia of the Philosophical Sciences*
EDITED BY SEBASTIAN STEIN, JOSHUA WRETZEL
Maimonides' *Guide of the Perplexed*
EDITED BY DANIEL FRANK, AARON SEGAL
Fichte's *System of Ethics*
EDITED BY STEFANO BACIN, OWEN WARE
Hume's *An Enquiry Concerning the Principles of Morals*
EDITED BY ESTHER ENGELS KROEKER, WILLEM LEMMENS
Hobbes's *On the Citizen*
EDITED BY ROBIN DOUGLASS, OHAN OLSTHOORN
Hegel's *Philosophy of Spirit*
EDITED BY MARINA F. BYKOVA
Kant's *Lectures on Metaphysics*
EDITED BY COURTNEY D. FUGATE
Spinoza's *Political Treatise*
EDITED BY YITZHAK Y. MELAMED, HASANA SHARP
Aquinas's *Summa Theologiae*
EDITED BY JEFFREY HAUSE
Aristotle's *Generation of Animals*
EDITED BY ANDREA FALCON, DAVID LEFEBVRE
Hegel's *Elements of the Philosophy of Right*
EDITED BY DAVID JAMES
Kant's *Critique of Pure Reason*
EDITED BY JAMES R. O'SHEA
Spinoza's *Ethics*
EDITED BY YITZHAK Y. MELAMED
Plato's *Symposium*
EDITED BY PIERRE DESTRÉE, ZINA GIANNOPOULOU
Fichte's *Foundations of Natural Right*
EDITED BY GABRIEL GOTTLIEB

Aquinas's *Disputed Questions on Evil*
EDITED BY M. V. DOUGHERTY
Aristotle's *Politics*
EDITED BY THORNTON LOCKWOOD, THANASSIS SAMARAS
Aristotle's *Physics*
EDITED BY MARISKA LEUNISSEN
Kant's *Lectures on Ethics*
EDITED BY LARA DENIS, OLIVER SENSEN
Kierkegaard's *Fear and Trembling*
EDITED BY DANIEL CONWAY
Kant's *Lectures on Anthropology*
EDITED BY ALIX COHEN
Kant's *Religion within the Boundaries of Mere Reason*
EDITED BY GORDON MICHALSON
Descartes' *Meditations*
EDITED BY KAREN DETLEFSEN
Augustine's *City of God*
EDITED BY JAMES WETZEL
Kant's *Observations and Remarks*
EDITED BY RICHARD VELKLEY, SUSAN SHELL
Nietzsche's *On the Genealogy of Morality*
EDITED BY SIMON MAY
Aristotle's *Nicomachean Ethics*
EDITED BY JON MILLER

Continued after the Index

Contents

List of Contributors		*page* ix
	Introduction *José L. Zalabardo*	1
1	Wittgenstein's Impatient Reply to Russell *Cora Diamond*	11
2	Modality in Wittgenstein's *Tractatus* *Juliet Floyd and Sanford Shieh*	24
3	Clarification and Analysis in the *Tractatus* *Sébastien Gandon*	50
4	The Fish Tale: The Unity of Language and the World in Light of TLP 4.014 *Hanne Appelqvist*	69
5	That Which 'Is True' Must Already Contain the Verb: Wittgenstein's Rejection of Frege's Separation of Judgment from Content *Colin Johnston*	90
6	Solipsism and the Self *Michael Potter*	110
7	The *Tractatus* and the First Person *Maria van der Schaar*	125
8	Arithmetic in the *Tractatus Logico-Philosophicus* *Mathieu Marion and Mitsuhiro Okada*	145
9	'Normal Connections' and the Law of Causality *Joshua Eisenthal*	166

| 10 | The Ethical Dimension of the *Tractatus*
Ilse Somavilla | 187 |
| 11 | 'Obviously Wrong': The *Tractatus* on Will and World
Duncan Richter | 203 |

References 219
Index 231

Contributors

HANNE APPELQVIST is Docent of Theoretical Philosophy and Director of the Helsinki Collegium for Advanced Studies, University of Helsinki.

CORA DIAMOND is University Professor and Kenan Professor of Philosophy Emerita at the University of Virginia.

JOSHUA EISENTHAL is Research Assistant Professor of Philosophy at the California Institute of Technology.

JULIET FLOYD is Professor of Philosophy at Boston University.

SÉBASTIEN GANDON is Professor of Philosophy at Université Clermont Auvergne.

COLIN JOHNSTON is Senior Lecturer in Philosophy at the University of Stirling.

MATHIEU MARION is Professor of Philosophy at Université du Québec à Montréal.

MITSUHIRO OKADA is Professor Emeritus at Keio University.

MICHAEL POTTER is Professor of Logic at Cambridge University and Life Fellow of Fitzwilliam College.

DUNCAN RICHTER is Charles S. Luck III' 55 Institute Professor of Philosophy at the Virginia Military Institute.

MARIA VAN DER SCHAAR is Senior University Lecturer at Leiden University.

SANFORD SHIEH is Professor of Philosophy at Wesleyan University.

ILSE SOMAVILLA is Wittgenstein Researcher and Editor at the Brenner Archives, Innsbruck University.

JOSÉ L. ZALABARDO is Professor of Philosophy at University College London.

Introduction

José L. Zalabardo

Ludwig Wittgenstein's *Tractatus Logico-Philosophicus* was published just over a century ago. Wittgenstein was in his early thirties at the time. The *Tractatus* was the only philosophy book of his to be published in his lifetime. It is widely regarded as one of the most important works of philosophy of the twentieth century. The *Tractatus* is a small book, around eighty pages, but it covers a huge range of philosophical topics. Its core consists in three inter-related accounts of the structure of reality, of how we represent the world in thought and language and of the nature of logic. The ideas he presents in these areas are firmly rooted in the work of Bertrand Russell and Gottlob Frege, even more so than Wittgenstein's explicit references to these authors would suggest.[1] This is followed by more concise discussions of other philosophical issues, including mathematics, natural science, the self, ethics, the will and 'the problem of life'. In this material, Wittgenstein draws on a more diverse and less straightforward range of philosophical influences.

Wittgenstein's presentation of these ideas is notoriously hard to interpret. The prose is terse, making few concessions to the reader. Claims are often made without explicit argumentative support or discussion of the advantages that might derive from their acceptance. And the difficulty of interpretation is massively compounded by the fact that Wittgenstein's stated goals are fundamentally different from what one would expect from the author of a work of philosophy. This is explained in the last few sections of the book, and to some extent in the Preface. For readers who have reached the end of the book under the impression that its goal is to present Wittgenstein's views on the philosophical issues it covers, the penultimate section will come as a complete shock:

---

[1] See Zalabardo (2015) for my interpretation of these Tractarian ideas.

> 6.54 My propositions serve as elucidations in the following way: anyone who understands me eventually recognizes them – as nonsensical, when he has used them – as steps – to climb up beyond them. (He must, so to speak, throw away the ladder after he has climbed up it.)
>
> He must transcend these propositions, and then he will see the world aright.

If we take this section seriously, as we should, we have to conclude that, contrary to all appearances, Wittgenstein does not see his book as putting forward philosophical doctrines. He does not think that the sentences of the book express philosophical doctrines. They do not express anything – they are nonsensical, and what Wittgenstein expects from his readers is that we come to recognise this fact. This will enable us "to see the world aright". As the Preface suggests, seeing the world aright will involve the realisation that the problems of philosophy should not be posed. Wittgenstein appears to see the urge to pose these problems as a disease, and the *Tractatus* as a programme of therapy that will cure its readers of this disease.

If we accept this account of the goal of the *Tractatus*, we need to see the sentences of the book that appear to put forward philosophical doctrines as aiming instead at promoting the realisation that they are nonsensical. Hence, interpreters of the book face the task of articulating the ways in which the *Tractatus* seeks to achieve this.[2] Some of the best Tractarian scholarship in the past few decades has focused on questions in this area. The issue still plays a major role in contemporary approaches to the book, as demonstrated by several chapters of the present volume.

It might seem, in addition, that on this account of Wittgenstein's intentions, there is no scope for engaging with the book as a piece of philosophy – for treating its sentences as expressing philosophical doctrines and assessing them in this light. There are at least two reasons why this is not so.

First, if Wittgenstein saw his book as a programme of therapy, he would expect his readers to be afflicted by the disease, possessed by the urge to pose philosophical problems. Furthermore, he could not expect us to come to the book with the intention of overcoming this urge, like smokers who

---

[2] I have argued elsewhere that one of the ways in which Wittgenstein seeks to promote the realisation that the problems of philosophy cannot be posed is with an argument for the conclusion that we are not capable of producing the kind of propositional representation that would be required for posing these problems – on the account of propositional representation advanced in the *Tractatus*. See the Introduction to Zalabardo (2015) and the first section of Zalabardo (2018b). Cora Diamond has attacked this view (Diamond 2018). See Zalabardo (2018a) for my reply.

choose to enrol in a smoking cessation programme. He would have expected his readers/patients to come to the book still convinced that philosophical problems are worth posing and seeing his book as a work that poses these problems and attempts to solve them. He would have intended the book to produce in us the experiences that we would describe as understanding, assessing and accepting philosophical doctrines. Following Wittgenstein's therapy for the disease of philosophy can only consist, in the first instance, in treating the book seriously as a work of philosophy – trying to understand and assess the doctrines expressed by its sentences.[3] If the therapy succeeds, these attempts to engage with the book as a piece of philosophy will eventually produce the realisation that there are no philosophical doctrines expressed by its sentences and no actual cognition involved in the experiences that we describe as philosophical understanding. But readers cannot be expected to know in advance that this is the right way of looking at things. We must climb up the ladder before throwing it away. Interpreting and assessing the doctrines expressed by the sentences of the book (or the activities that we are inclined to describe in these terms) is precisely what we need to do if we want to follow Wittgenstein's therapeutic programme.

The second reason for thinking that this account of Wittgenstein's intentions is compatible with engaging with the book as a piece of philosophy arises from the contrast between accepting (a) that Wittgenstein thought that the sentences of the *Tractatus* are nonsensical and that the experience of philosophical understanding has no cognitive value and accepting (b) that Wittgenstein was right about this. Accepting (a) is perfectly compatible with rejecting (b). If we hold this view, we will maintain that Wittgenstein's therapeutic programme fails to produce the intended result or that, when it succeeds, what it does is to produce the *false* impression that perfectly meaningful sentences are nonsensical.[4] This opens the way to the project of trying to understand and assess the doctrines expressed by the sentences of the *Tractatus*, not as a means to a therapeutic end but as an end in itself, while accepting that in doing so we are not being faithful to Wittgenstein's intentions.

---

[3] I have argued elsewhere that in order for Wittgenstein's therapy to work, he needs the reader to accept the sentences of the *Tractatus* as expressing the only viable solutions to the philosophical problems they address. See the Introduction to Zalabardo (2015).

[4] There may be room for arguing that if the therapeutic programme succeeds in producing the intended result, there is no further question as to whether the impression it generates is true or false, since the experience of finding the sentences of the *Tractatus* nonsensical has no more cognitive value than other experiences that we think of as philosophical understanding.

One might wonder whether we are likely to find anything of interest in this project. If the sentences of the *Tractatus* were designed to produce an illusion of sense and to promote a certain psychological effect in the reader, it would be surprising if they turned out to express significant contributions to the enterprise they were meant to undermine. But the surprise disappears when we realise that Wittgenstein did not always have the disparaging conception of philosophy that the *Tractatus* ultimately intends to promote. He once regarded philosophy as a meaningful enterprise, and he thought he was making important contributions to it. Some of the ideas he developed at that time are among the central doctrines of the *Tractatus*.[5] He may have later retooled this material as therapeutic props, but it was originally conceived as containing bona fide philosophical insights. On the view I am describing, he was right then, and wrong later, when he formed the mistaken impression that the sentences that express these insights are nonsensical. If we take this approach, we might have to see ourselves as interpreting the views not of the author of the *Tractatus* but of an earlier Wittgenstein who, unlike his later self, would see the sentences that figure in the book as expressing important philosophical thoughts.[6]

These are some of the complexities of the conceptual landscape that contemporary interpreters of the *Tractatus* need to navigate, and the background against which the chapters of the present volume seek to improve our understanding of some important aspects of Wittgenstein's fascinating book. The rest of this introduction is devoted to a brief summary of each chapter.

The starting point of Cora Diamond's chapter is Wittgenstein's claim, in a letter to Russell, that the theory of what can be expressed by propositions and what cannot be expressed by propositions, but only shown, is the cardinal problem of philosophy. Diamond argues that what Wittgenstein is presenting as the cardinal problem of philosophy is the problem of making completely clear the limit of the expression of thoughts, so that it is clear that everything that can be said lies within this limit, and so that it is also clear how what shows itself shows itself in what

---

[5] For example, we find in the "Notes on Logic" of 1913 the central insight of the picture theory of propositional representation: "Propositions [which are symbols having reference to facts] are themselves facts: that this inkpot is on the table may express that I sit in this chair" (Potter 2009b: 276).

[6] This is not to deny that Wittgenstein had long been aware of problems relating to the expressibility of the features of reality that philosophical reflection focuses on. Thus, in the "Notes dictated to Moore" of 1914 we read: " In order that you should have a language which can express or *say* everything that *can* be said, this language must have certain properties; and when this is the case, *that* it has them can no longer be said in that language or *any* language" (Wittgenstein 1979: 108).

lies within the limit. What shows itself, according to Diamond, is not something thought-like that cannot be expressed by propositions because it fails to meet some necessary condition for expressibility. There's nothing thought-like beyond the limit – nothing thought-like that propositions cannot express.

The goal of Juliet Floyd and Sanford Shieh's chapter is to provide an account of the remarks in the *Tractatus* involving modality. They maintain that these remarks have their source in Wittgenstein's criticism of Russell's multiple-relation theory of judgment. They argue that modality in the *Tractatus* finds its place within a search for a coherent conception of the distinction between truth and falsity, spelling out how in the transition from the *Prototractatus* to the *Tractatus* the notion of possibility is incorporated internally into the very idea of a sentence as a picture. Floyd and Shieh use the resulting modal conception of picturing to explain how non-elementary propositions can be pictures in the same sense as elementary propositions. They defend this treatment of modality against a rival approach, according to which modal claims are grounded in our intuitions about what may or may not hold in other possible worlds. They maintain that possibility in the *Tractatus* cannot be represented pictorially in language or thought, not a matter of "what is the case". Instead, it shows forth *in* our intuitive talk about truth and falsity and negation, which permeates our thinking and speaking about what is the case. On this view, modality cannot receive a theoretical representation, and it cannot be used to draw the limits to possible experience or imagination.

Sébastien Gandon takes as the starting point of his chapter the tension between passages of the *Tractatus* that seem to suggest that philosophical clarification requires the construction of a logically perfect language and those according to which the propositions of everyday language are in perfect logical order. Gandon proposes to understand Wittgenstein's position in terms of a distinction he finds in Russell between a completely analysed language and a weakly logical language, with the former used for the analysis of everyday language and the latter for its clarification. He maintains that, for Wittgenstein, everyday language contains logically unclear expressions that are the source of philosophical problems, but it does not follow from this that Wittgenstein sees analysis as a tool for the solution of philosophical problems. According to Gandon, the philosophical method Wittgenstein propounds is more akin to Russell's clarification in terms of a weakly logical language. Gandon offers two arguments for this reading. First, he maintains that Wittgenstein's peculiar conception of logical analysis renders it unsuitable for the kind of clarification that would provide a treatment of philosophical problems, as he is not in a position to say much about the form of the completely analysed language. Second, he finds in the 3.32s a conception of the task of clarifying expressions of everyday language that does not involve translating them into a different language but simply the recognition of differences between symbols that are not reflected in differences in signs.

Hanne Appelqvist's chapter focuses on the reference at 4.014 to the fairy tale *The Gold-Children* by the Brothers Grimm, with which Wittgenstein seeks to illustrate the depicting relation that holds between language and the world. Appelqvist argues that the reference should be taken as supporting the attribution to Wittgenstein of a form of transcendental idealism. In the tale, the oneness of the youths, their horses, and lilies arises out of their common origin: a golden fish. The fish, Appelqvist argues, stands for the metaphysical subject, as that which grounds the unity of language and the world, even if it cannot be found *in* the world. She also defends a literal reading of the claim at 4.014 that in music we find a manifestation of the essential relation that holds between language and the world. For Appelqvist, musical thoughts are mere spatio-temporal structure without any empirical content. In this respect, their role is similar to the role the *Tractatus* assigns to logical and mathematical propositions – they mirror the spatial and temporal forms of reality without latching on to any material content.

Colin Johnston discusses Wittgenstein's criticisms of Frege's views on the relationship between content, on the one hand, and judgment or assertion, on the other. For Frege, propositional content is prior to and independent of acts of judgment, whereas for Wittgenstein content can only be explained with judgment. Johnston's chapter focuses on the interpretation of the argument Wittgenstein offers, at 4.063, against Frege's position on this point. Johnston maintains that the key to understanding this argument is Wittgenstein's view that a sense is fundamentally a correctness condition for judgment and assertion. This differs from Frege's position, according to which propositional sense is independent of any matter of correctness in judgment and assertion. Wittgenstein's complaint, according to Johnston, is that this view of Frege is incompatible with the thought that it is internal to judgment that it aims at truth.

Michael Potter starts his chapter by placing Wittgenstein's attitude to solipsism in the context of Russell's discussion of the issue. According to Potter, Russell accepted that atomism would have a solipsistic consequence, by making communication about the external world impossible, and concluded that our linguistic representations of the world cannot be

Introduction 7

rendered in atomistic terms. Wittgenstein, Potter argues, rejected this conclusion, maintaining instead that we sometimes say things that can be rendered in atomistic terms. Wittgenstein's version of solipsism, according to Potter, amounts to the claim that the range of objects I can quantify over coincides with the range of objects that have names in my language. Expressing this thought would require an identity sign, and the formal language of the *Tractatus* does not have one. This is the reason why Wittgenstein maintains, on Potter's reading, that what solipsism says, although correct, cannot be said.

Potter goes on to describe a second route to Wittgenstein's solipsism, taking this time the picture theory as a starting point. Language must have logical form in common with the world in order to represent it. It follows that every language capable of representing the world must have the same logical form, and, in this sense, there's only one language – one perspective from which the world can be represented.

Potter links this point with Wittgenstein's rejection of the subject that thinks and entertains ideas. If there is only a single language, then there is no role for the notion of a perspective to play in anchoring my representation of the world, and hence no role for the thinking subject to play.

The chapter ends by considering Wittgenstein's attitude towards solipsism in his middle period, especially in the *Blue Book*. Potter argues that Wittgenstein here does not aim to refute solipsism but to show that the adoption of the view would be bound to seem disappointingly empty.

Maria van der Schaar's chapter provides a wide-ranging argument for the claim that the philosophical method employed in the *Tractatus* is thoroughly first-personal. This marks a major departure from Russell's approach. Russell approaches the analysis of judgment from a third-person point of view – what is it for someone else to judge. Van der Schaar traces in the pre-Tractarian manuscripts Wittgenstein's transition from this approach to an essentially first-personal treatment of judgment (what is it for me to judge), and ultimately of all questions concerning logic, language and metaphysics. She argues that Wittgenstein was aware of the threat of psychologism that came with his first-personal approach and that he sought to avoid this danger by embracing transcendental ideas, although with important differences with both Kant and neo-Kantian philosophers. This move, van der Schaar argues, is the source of the attraction Wittgenstein felt towards solipsism. Additionally, according to van der Schaar, first-person engagement is also expected from the reader of the *Tractatus* – *we* need to *do* something as philosophers when reading the book. She also argues that the first-person perspective informs in important ways Wittgenstein's approach to ethics and to internal relations.

The goal of Mathieu Marion and Mitsuhiro Okada's chapter is to provide an interpretation of the passages of the *Tractatus* that present an account of the natural numbers and arithmetical operations. Marion and Okada take as their starting point Wittgenstein's rejection of logicism, specifically of Russell's attempt to derive the basic concepts of arithmetic within the ramified theory of types, spelling out Wittgenstein's objections to the axioms of infinity and reducibility, as well as his fundamental rejection of the use of classes in the foundation of arithmetic.

According to Marion and Okada, Wittgenstein proposed an alternative, logic-free account of arithmetical concepts, based on equations, conceived as pseudo-propositions, and the method of substitution. They highlight the central role played in Wittgenstein's proposal by the notion of operation, with natural numbers defined as indices of the repeated applications of an operation. They highlight the fact that Wittgenstein's procedure departs from systems of primitive recursive arithmetic, in that multiplication is not defined in terms of addition, and they outline the similarities between Wittgenstein's approach and Church's λ-calculus. They explain that, according to Wittgenstein, the correctness of an equation can be *seen*, and therefore not asserted by the equation. They connect this position with the claim that equations do not express thoughts. Marion and Okada highlight a conflict between this aspect of Wittgenstein's position and the rejection by resolute readers of the idea that there might be some features of the world that show themselves but could only be expressed in propositions that are "nonsense".

The chapter ends by considering how Wittgenstein's views on these topics changed after he returned to philosophy, when he gradually replaced his approach in terms of operations with a more standard treatment in terms of recursion, and introduced a counterpart to mathematical induction in the form of a rule for the uniqueness of a function introduced by recursion.

Joshua Eisenthal's chapter deals with Wittgenstein's treatment of natural science in the 6.3s. More specifically, Eisenthal focuses on the interpretation of a single section, 6.361, where Wittgenstein, mentioning Heinrich Hertz, asserts that only normal connections (in Eisenthal's favoured translation of the original) are thinkable. Eisenthal approaches the passage by looking at the role that the concept plays in Hertz's *Principles of Mechanics*, where normal connections figure prominently. Eisenthal first applies the connection with Hertz's work to the interpretation of an analogy Wittgenstein presents at 6.341–6.342 involving three different nets that are used to describe a picture formed by black spots on a white surface. He argues that a satisfactory interpretation of these remarks is possible only with reference to Hertz's discussion of the different formulations of mechanics. Eisenthal then interprets the reference to "normal connections" at 6.361 in terms of nearby passages about the "law of causality". On Eisenthal's reading, Wittgenstein maintains that abnormal connections are unthinkable because their abnormality places them outside the realm of "causal descriptions" and a fortiori outside the realm of descriptions *simpliciter*.

In her chapter, Ilse Somavilla explores the ethical dimension of the *Tractatus*. Although it is only towards the end of the book that Wittgenstein is explicitly concerned with ethics, Somavilla argues that his treatment of language throughout the book is an ethical one, as is his very use of language. Somavilla concentrates on four main themes. First, she emphasises the importance for Wittgenstein of the view *sub specie aeternitatis*, in aesthetics, ethics, religion and other spheres of life, including his own writing. Second, she demonstrates the importance for Wittgenstein of the attitude of wonder towards the world, as a silent and devout attitude towards the cosmos without the effort to explain. In the ethical sphere, Somavilla argues, the attitude of wonder enables us to experience that which cannot be said. Third, Somavilla considers the importance for Wittgenstein of the attitude of silence, as deployed in the notorious last section of the *Tractatus*. She argues that the attitude of silence in Wittgenstein should not be seen as something negative, involving resignation, but as a path to further insight – into fields like ethics or art, which are "limited from within" by the attitude of silence. Fourth, Somavilla considers the role that the mystical plays for Wittgenstein. She argues that he regarded mystical experience as the only possible approach to the ineffable, including the ethical realm.

Duncan Richter's chapter focuses on Wittgenstein's contention at 6.43 that the exercise of the will cannot alter the world but only the limits of the world. He sets out to assess Elizabeth Anscombe's verdict that this part of the *Tractatus* is the most obviously wrong. Richter's main contention is that Anscombe is right to reject the view of the will that she calls wrong, but it is at least possible that Wittgenstein intends his readers to reject it too – to reject the way of thinking that gives rise to these problems – the way of thinking that treats the subject, value and the will as objects or phenomena in the world. Such thinking, Richter suggests, might be part of the ladder that is to be climbed and then discarded. If we think of the subject as an object, we will not find it in the world. If we think of good and evil as absolutes in the world, we will not be able to make sense of them. And if we think of the will as something that might give rise to good or evil actions, then we will struggle to say anything intelligible about it. Hence, on Richter's reading, Wittgenstein would be urging us to give up the problematic view of the will as a phenomenon or something somehow within the world, linking ethics and events in the world.

English Translations of the *Tractatus*

The *Tractatus* was first published in 1921, under its original title, *Logisch-philosophische Abhandlung*, in Wilhelm Oswald's *Annalen der Naturphilosophie* (Wittgenstein 1921), but this edition was riddled with errors. In 1922 it was published in England by Routledge & Kegan Paul (Wittgenstein 1922). This is generally regarded as the first satisfactory edition of the *Tractatus*. This edition includes the German text and an English translation *en face*, signed by C.K. Ogden but principally the work of Frank Ramsey (Monk 1991: 205; McGuinness 2005: 298). In 1961 Routledge & Kegan Paul published a second English translation of the *Tractatus*, by David Pears and Brian McGuinness, this time without the original German text (Wittgenstein 1974b). Both these translations have been widely used by anglophone scholars, with no clear consensus on the superiority of one over the other.

There are now two other major English translations of the *Tractatus* in preparation, one by Michael Beaney for Oxford University Press and another by David Stern, Joachim Schulte and Katia Saporiti for Cambridge University Press. Both have been circulated among scholars.

The contributors to the present volume make free use of these four translations and in some cases provide translations of their own. This diversity is unavoidable, and probably beneficial. Passages of the *Tractatus* are always cited by section number. Hence, the identity of the passage being cited is never in doubt, independently of which translation is used.

CHAPTER I

Wittgenstein's Impatient Reply to Russell

Cora Diamond

Russell to Wittgenstein, 13 August 1919

I am convinced you are right in your main contention, that logical props are tautologies, which are not true in the sense that substantial props are true.

Wittgenstein to Russell, 19 August 1919

Now I'm afraid you have not really got hold of my main contention, to which the whole business of logical props is only a corollary. The main point is the theory of what can be expressed (gesagt) by props – i.e. by language – (and, which comes to the same, what can be *thought*) and what cannot be expressed by props, but only shown (gezeigt); which, I believe, is the cardinal problem of philosophy. (McGuinness and von Wright 1995: 121–126, emphasis in original)

There are remarks of Wittgenstein's that one might try to take as *tips* on how to understand him – but readers may be left wondering how to understand the tips. Think, for example, of 4.0312, some – or all? – of which sets out what Wittgenstein speaks of as his fundamental idea. Or think of his remark, in a letter to C.K. Ogden, about 4.112, where he had said that the aim of philosophy was the logical clarification of thoughts. Intending to help Ogden with the translation, Wittgenstein wrote, "It cannot be the RESULT of philosophy 'to make propositions clear': this can only be its TASK. The *result* must be that the propositions *now have become clear* that they ARE clear" (Wittgenstein 1973: 49, emphasis in original). This is a great remark to try to make sense of, and thinking about it can help one in one's reading of the *Tractatus* – but the remark *sets a task* for anyone trying to understand 4.112.

My chapter is about a remark of Wittgenstein's from his reply to the letter Russell wrote to him after first reading the *Tractatus*. Two sentences in Wittgenstein's letter reply directly to Russell's saying that he thinks Wittgenstein is correct in his main contention, that logical propositions are tautologies. Like 4.0312 and Wittgenstein's remark to Ogden about the result of philosophy, Wittgenstein's remark in the letter to Russell is a great stimulus to thought about the *Tractatus*. It sets a task, as they do – but a task more likely to leave one baffled.

I will be looking at Wittgenstein's statement of the supposed main contention of the book, since it certainly is not obvious how it should be understood. I also want to consider what the relation is between his main contention and what he describes in the book as his fundamental idea – which I'll put this way: In a proposition, objects have proxies, but the logic of the facts is not something capable of being represented. It has no proxy. The "logical constants" aren't representatives. – And I also want to consider a question raised by Michael Kremer: what does Wittgenstein mean when he says that what he calls his main contention and his main point is what he takes to be the cardinal *problem* of philosophy?

Starting with the third issue: what is the *problem*? I think the sentence in the letter to Russell is one of the most compressed things Wittgenstein ever said. It's a devil to uncompress. You could say that the question that Wittgenstein sets there is: what IS he saying is the cardinal problem of philosophy? What does it even mean to say that the theory of what can be expressed by propositions and what cannot be expressed by propositions but only shown is the cardinal problem of philosophy? – One way to approach this would be to pick out some problem that you think would be dealt with by laying out what can be expressed by propositions and what can only be shown, and you can then say that that's what Wittgenstein really meant – that there was a main philosophical problem that you could resolve through talking about saying and showing. This is what Oskari Kuusela does: he reads Wittgenstein as meaning that there is a central philosophical problem about whether necessities can be the object of genuinely true or false sentences, and then he says that what Wittgenstein meant in the letter to Russell is that that problem can be dealt with by what he is referring to as the theory of what can be expressed by propositions and what cannot be expressed by propositions but can only be shown. So Wittgenstein is read as *not* actually holding that the business about saying and showing is the cardinal problem; it's the *solution* (Kuusela 2011).

I mentioned that it was Michael Kremer who drew attention to Wittgenstein's saying that the theory of what can be expressed by propositions and what cannot be expressed that way but only *shown* – that this is the cardinal *problem* of philosophy. Kremer himself has tried to explain this. He emphasizes that there are various ways of expressing what Wittgenstein took to be *the single great problem* with which he was concerned. Giving the nature of the proposition is *one* expression of the single great problem; giving the limits of what can be expressed in language is another; and there are still others. But Kremer argues that Wittgenstein meant to get us to see that the very idea of such a single great philosophical problem is meant to be revealed as an illusion. Kremer, that is, gives us a kind of *deflationary* understanding of the supposed cardinal problem of philosophy; and he also has a deflationary account of what is meant by *showing*. Briefly, he thinks we can take Wittgenstein's talk of *showing* to be *either* a way of gesturing at a realm of superfacts *or* alternatively a bringing out of practical abilities – for example, those we exercise in making inferences (Kremer 2007).[1] The trouble here is that Kremer sees those two possible understandings of *showing* to be the only two, and so, since he rejects the first, he accepts a deflated understanding of what Wittgenstein meant.

There is an important and complex issue here – and I'll mention two discussions of what *showing* means in the *Tractatus*, which illuminate in very different ways the complexity of the issue. One, that of Gilad Nir, is about Wittgenstein's reference to "the cardinal problem of philosophy" in his reply to Russell, and the other, that of Jean-Philippe Narboux, is a far-ranging essay on *showing* and its significance in the *Tractatus*.

Gilad Nir discusses Wittgenstein on "the cardinal problem of philosophy" in an essay on philosophical riddles and their relevance to Wittgenstein's conception of philosophy in the *Tractatus* (Nir 2021). In explaining the connection that Wittgenstein makes between the "cardinal problem of philosophy" and the "theory" of what can be expressed by propositions and what cannot be expressed by propositions but can only be shown, Nir gives two examples of passages in the *Tractatus* where Wittgenstein speaks of something as showing itself: 5.62, where Wittgenstein says that what the solipsist *means* shows itself, and 6.36, where Wittgenstein speaks of there being laws of nature as something that shows itself. If you were going to look for places where Wittgenstein's talk of what shows itself looks as if he means some kind of superfact, these two passages would be perfect. But they are not at all the kinds of cases that Wittgenstein brings up when he is explaining what he means by speaking of something as showing itself. Compare 4.1211. Here Wittgenstein is spelling out what he had been speaking of at 4.121 as what expresses itself in language. It is important that Wittgenstein chooses examples of what is supposedly *seeable*, and what he thinks his readers will be able to take in as seeable. The two examples that Nir cites can be connected with Wittgenstein's favoured kind of examples, but they contrast with the

---

[1] See also Kremer (2004).

kinds of case that Wittgenstein himself uses in explaining *showing* and what supposedly *expresses itself* in language (4.124, 4.125). The character of Wittgenstein's examples has philosophical significance; and Nir's use of examples that are quite different from Wittgenstein's can make it harder to see what Wittgenstein means.

Narboux rejects Kremer's interpretation of *showing* as merely the illustrating of practical possibility – and very centrally, he rejects Kremer's idea that there are just two basic ways of understanding what *showing* means in the *Tractatus* (Narboux 2014). If there were just two ways of understanding what *showing* means in the *Tractatus*, then if you rejected the Kremer interpretation of *showing* as an essentially practical notion, you'd be committed to the idea of unsayable superfacts as what is supposedly shown by the propositions of the *Tractatus*. But it's that conception of what the alternatives are that Narboux rejects.

I will be setting out a very different view from Kremer's and Nir's, though I agree with them about not just junking Wittgenstein's talk of the cardinal problem of philosophy. I strongly disagree with Kremer's and Nir's deflating of the notion of showing, and I will also be disagreeing with Kremer about whether the idea of *the fundamental problem of philosophy* is an illusion. One further thing about which I think I'm in disagreement with Kremer and possibly Nir as well is the significance of proposition 6 of the *Tractatus* and proposition 6.001: "What [proposition 6] says is that every proposition is a result of successive applications to elementary propositions of the operation $N(\bar{\xi})$". N is the operation that negates all the values of the propositional variable written as $\bar{\xi}$. (This is explained at 5.5 and 5.501.) My disagreement with Kremer about how to read the *Tractatus* is basically about the importance of the idea of propositions as forming a kind of series – and this is the idea you get at 6.001, the idea of propositions as what can be given in the series constructed by the application of joint negation to elementary propositions. So that's what I will be heading towards, but I'm nowhere near that yet. I'm still trying to see the problem situation that we are confronting.

At one point in the *Notebooks* Wittgenstein says that his difficulty is only 'an – enormous – difficulty of expression' (Wittgenstein 1979: 40). In the letter to Russell, I think that that difficulty of expression is indeed surfacing. You can try in various ways to put the problem Wittgenstein took himself to be confronting, and I will not stay with the first formulation, but to start with, we could try something like this: the cardinal problem is: "How can one make clear the logical concept of what a *proposition* is, and, in doing so, also make plain what is supposed to show itself in propositions?" This goes right back to Wittgenstein's fundamental thought, his *Grundgedanke*: in the proposition objects have proxies, but the logic of the facts is not something capable of being represented. So what I'm suggesting now is that when you look at the expression of Wittgenstein's fundamental thought at 4.0312 and you also read the letter to Russell, there is a connection. Both the letter to Russell and the statement of Wittgenstein's fundamental thought involve what supposedly shows forth in propositions. This may sometimes be easy to see, but one thing that philosophy is supposed to do is to enable us to see clearly what the proposition has supposedly shown all along. (The sections of the *Tractatus* that I have particularly in mind at this point go from 4.01 to 4.06, and then into the 4.1s.)

I want to try to get further into the issues here by going in a sense backwards, back from the *Tractatus* passages on what can be said and what cannot, to the remarks in the Notes that Wittgenstein dictated to Moore in 1914, where he begins with a whole page about logical propositions and what they show. He says that logical propositions do not *say* anything, but that merely by looking at them, you can see the logical properties of language that these propositions show; and then later on the page, he says that by merely looking at fa, fa ⊃ ψa, ψa, you can see that the third proposition follows from the other two. This talk of what you can see merely by looking is very striking. It's connected with the passage in the *Tractatus* I mentioned earlier (4.1121), and it's connected with 3.1432. What Wittgenstein says there is: "Instead of, 'The complex sign "*aRb*" says that *a* stands to *b* in the relation R', we ought to put, 'That "*a*" stands to "*b*" in a certain relation says *that aRb*'." This is supposed to be something you can *look at*. What is supposed to be doing the saying is a two-term relation between two signs, and what *the fact that those two signs stand in that relation SAYS is that the two things stand in a relation*. So you can just look and see dual relationality *in* what is doing the saying *and in* what is being said. This is a good example of what Wittgenstein means in saying that the logic of the facts cannot be represented: dual relationality is not represented, it is present in the saying and in what is said to be so. – Wittgenstein's fondness for this sort of example is present also in 4.012, where Wittgenstein says that a relational proposition like "aRb" strikes us as a picture. The sign here is "obviously a likeness of what is symbolized". – But it is essential to Wittgenstein's understanding of what philosophy *does* that what we have here is only a particular case. In the particular case, we can see clearly how the logic of what we are saying is present in our signs. In the particular case, this is open to view, but this is a special case. It's a very revealing case, but not the general case. Hence, you have room for a conception of *philosophical activity as making logical showing perspicuous*, because only exceptionally is this straightforwardly describable as easy to see.

Although I am talking about the *Tractatus*, I want to pause and mark a significant connection with Wittgenstein's later criticism of his earlier way of thinking – the criticism at *Zettel* §444:

> We now have a *theory* ... of the proposition ... but it does not present itself to us as a theory. For it is the characteristic thing about such a theory that it looks at a special clearly intuitive case and says: "*That* shows how things are in every case..." We have arrived at a form of expression that *strikes us as obvious*. But it is as if we had now seen something lying *beneath* the surface. (Wittgenstein 1967, emphasis in original).

Both 4.012 and 3.1432 illustrate the particular importance of relational propositions in furnishing such intuitively convincing cases.

Getting back now to my overall argument, I want to get further into Wittgenstein's understanding of philosophy in the *Tractatus*, by moving to a *later* example and then going *back* to the *Tractatus*. There is an idea Wittgenstein had in the *Tractatus* that he never gave up, but the later example is simpler and can help us to see more clearly one of the basic ideas in the *Tractatus*. My later example comes from his 1939 *Lectures on the Foundations of Mathematics* (Wittgenstein 1976), Lecture 9. Wittgenstein is considering an example in which we have a method for constructing polygons, using ruler and compasses. The method is very narrowly limited in that the compasses have a pre-set radius. You can use a ruler and pre-set compasses to draw a circle, then draw a diameter of the circle, and then construct a square by drawing a diameter at right angles to the original diameter. You then can go on drawing arcs and bisecting the angles created by the intersection of previously drawn lines. So you can go from drawing a *square* to drawing an *octagon*, and then you can go on and draw a polygon with sixteen sides, and so on. Wittgenstein imagines someone who is trying to draw a polygon with a hundred sides, using this method; and the person is slow to catch on that you cannot do this by going on bisecting angles and constructing polygons using the ruler and the set compass. The person keeps on trying and does not succeed. Then you give him a proof that shows him that what you can construct with this method is a series of polygons in which the number of sides is a power of 2, and *then* he sees that the polygon with a hundred sides is *left out*. It is not in the series of polygons you can construct. And this leads him to give up what he had been trying to do. He now has a clearer idea of what he is trying to do, and so he leaves off trying to construct a polygon with a hundred sides. He's willing to accept that he now sees more clearly what it was he wanted. Juliet Floyd has written about the great importance of this sort of persuasion in philosophy as Wittgenstein understands it (Floyd 1995, 2000).

Back to the *Tractatus*. I said Wittgenstein had an idea that he used in the *Tractatus* that also comes up later, the idea of someone being able to see that something *is not going to turn up* in a certain series, and the person can thereby get clearer about something that she was previously unclear about. The way Wittgenstein sets up the *Tractatus*, we are meant to get clear about *what a proposition is* partly by seeing propositions as having a place in a series of propositions constructed from elementary propositions. Heaven knows it is not easy to see how exactly this is supposed to work, and people can differ about what Wittgenstein's idea of the construction of propositions as members of a formal series is supposed to be. But, if you have a way of constructing propositions using the operation of negating all the values of a propositional variable, you are going to be able to see *what you are going to be able to get that way*, and you'll also be able to see *what that construction will not* give you. This is something Wittgenstein says about this general method of constructing propositions at 5.503. Logical methods of construction anticipate what you can construct. Just as the method of bisection of angles *anticipates*, you could say, all the polygons with a number of sides equal to a power of 2, a logical method of construction of propositions *anticipates* a series of propositions. And there are things the series passes by, just as the series of constructible polygons with the ruler and fixed compasses bypasses the construction of a polygon of a hundred sides. But we need to note here that the construction of propositions as a formal series depends on what the elementary propositions are, and Wittgenstein did not think we knew what they were. (I also want to add here that the idea of a method of construction of signs as anticipating what you are going to get by the method is significant later in Wittgenstein's discussion of rule-following.)

I am going to get back to this, but I want first to look further at the ideas reflected in Wittgenstein's letter to Russell. I suggested earlier that the letter itself and the statement of Wittgenstein's fundamental idea are connected with the understanding of philosophy as making perspicuous what is internal to our propositions. When Wittgenstein writes about philosophy as logical clarification of thoughts, you get the rather puzzling idea that the thoughts are in some sense clear already, but their clarity is clouded over in our view of them, and philosophizing should turn our thoughts into ones whose clarity is open to view. This idea is in a letter of Wittgenstein's to Ogden, about how to translate the *Tractatus* remark at 4.112 about philosophy as an activity of clarification (Wittgenstein 1973: 49). This comes right before passages on drawing the limits on what can be thought by presenting clearly what can be said, and before the passages on what propositions show. I want to look briefly at a couple of examples of this business of making perspicuous, making open to view, what is internal to our thoughts.

My first case is based on remarks by Brian McGuinness, which bear on 4.44 to 4.461 (McGuinness 2005: 308–309). This part of the *Tractatus* is where Wittgenstein introduces truth-tables as a way of writing a propositional sign. We often in philosophy talk about the truth-table "for" a proposition, but this is not what Wittgenstein is doing. The truth-table gives a notation in which we can construct propositional signs. Thus, the sign that Wittgenstein has at 4.442 (with the Ts and Fs) is *a propositional sign* for the same proposition we might write instead with the material implication sign. In the TF notation what shows up clearly is the *range* that is left open to the facts by the proposition. This is what Wittgenstein says at 4.463. The truth-table for a tautology shows that reality is in no way determined by the proposition; it leaves everything open. If we go back to 4.05 and 4.06, where Wittgenstein connects a proposition's being a picture and its being something with which reality gets compared, you can see in the truth-table representation of the tautology that there is no such comparison for the tautology. So what shows up in the truth-table notation for propositions is the logical contrast between propositions, which do determine how things are if the proposition is true, and tautology and contradiction, which do not do that.

The second case I want to mention is that of seeing inferential relations. I will not go into details here, but I did want to point out the image that Wittgenstein uses at 5.1311. He suggests a way of writing the premises and conclusion of a familiar form of argument, and then says that, before the suggested rewriting of the premises, the internal relation between the propositional forms is *masked* (verhüllt). The new way of writing is a kind of *unmasking* of the internal relation between propositional forms.

The last thing I want to get to is a pair of very familiar remarks from the Preface to the *Tractatus*:

> The whole sense of the book might be summed up in the following words: what can be said at all can be said clearly, and what one cannot speak of, one must keep quiet about.

The book will therefore draw a limit to thought, or rather – not to thought but to the expression of thoughts: for in order to draw a limit to thought, we should have to find both sides of the limit thinkable (i.e., we should have to be able to think what cannot be thought). The limit can, therefore, only be drawn in language, and what lies on the other side of the limit will be simply nonsense.

Those remarks from the Preface are also connected with what I said about Wittgenstein's claim that his theory of what can be said and what cannot be said but can only be shown is the cardinal problem of philosophy. I said that what is meant by the cardinal problem is the problem of how to make clear the logical concept of a proposition – to make clear, that is, what it is for something to be included in what we can think, what we can say – and through *that* to make plain the showing forth of what shows itself. This is what is at stake in what Wittgenstein speaks of in the Preface as *drawing the limits of the expression of thoughts* from *within* language. To get clear about this we need to keep in mind the idea I mentioned earlier: that producing a series of constructions, or a series of propositions, can help someone see what is *not* going to be in the series. A very crucial proposition in the *Tractatus*, for the issues here, is 6.001, about the general form of a proposition. This is about a recipe for constructing propositions, a recipe for constructing a series of propositions as truth-functions of elementary propositions. Even if we do not know what elementary propositions there are, this recipe for constructing propositions was supposed by Wittgenstein to make clear the general kind of way a series of propositions can be produced, and this would make clear what it is for signs to be included in the series we will get – and also what it is for signs not to be included. Anscombe described in *An Introduction to Wittgenstein's Tractatus* how this was supposed to work. She also explained why it would work only if the number of elementary propositions was finite; and she also argued that Wittgenstein had not been aware of the problems (Anscombe 1971: 132–137). Here I shall discuss how it was supposed to work, ignoring the issues about the infinite number of elementary propositions. I shall be assuming that TLP 6 and 6.001 do give us a series of propositions generated from elementary propositions; and that we are thereby given a clarification of "the expression of thoughts". What then comes out in this clarification is that "the expression of thoughts" has a limit. We can construct propositions from elementary propositions, and there are some signs that will not come up. If we say they aren't within the limits of the sayable, what does that mean? That's what I'm now trying to get to.

I'll give two conflicting answers, using two examples.

One example of something we will not get to is "$(\exists x).x = a$", "There is an object a". This is the kind of proposition that Russell thought would go into a catalogue of what there is in the world. But the identity sign in that would-be propositional sign has not been given any meaning, and the sign therefore is nonsense. (See remarks in the *Tractatus* beginning 5.53, on the identity sign.) You can say that "$(\exists x).x = a$" is on the "far side" of the limits of what can be said, but this means only that it's a sign-construction, which could be given a use as a propositional sign, but which contains a sign to which no meaning has been given. Putting this another way: you are given clarity about what it is to say something by proposition 6.001, which is a recipe for constructing propositions. And thereby what is made clear is what *is not going to be got to* by constructing propositions using that recipe, that is, *what are merely signs without meaning*. "There is an object a" is then one example of such a sign, a sign with no meaning.

The other example I want to consider is one discussed by Roger White in his book on the *Tractatus*. I want to get to his answer to the question about what lies beyond the limits, because he does not take it that what lies beyond the limits is merely signs with no meaning. He is considering the propositions of the *Tractatus* itself, like "A proposition is a truth-function of elementary propositions". He says that propositions like that one "appear to be presented as necessary a priori truths, and therefore to fall outside the scope of the general form of proposition, and hence to be nonsense" (White 2006: 116–117). He also says that the propositions that Wittgenstein used in seeking to establish the limits of language "constantly transgressed the limits they were establishing, and thus fell on the wrong side of the limits, and hence were nonsense" (White 2006: 125). What comes to the surface here is a question about what Wittgenstein means by talking about "limits". This question is important for us now, but it is also at the centre of how we can understand Wittgenstein's letter to Russell, and his remarks in that letter about what cannot be said and what shows itself. And it is also absolutely essential to how we think about the propositions in the *Tractatus* itself, like the one I mentioned, "A proposition is a truth-function of elementary propositions".

Roger White's account is very helpful to us, I think, in enabling us to see that there are two *alternative conceptions* of *being outside the limits*. These are two alternative understandings of what Wittgenstein means in his talk of limits. I'm going to draw on how Peter Sullivan has explained the two conceptions: he speaks of *limits* in the one case and *limitations* in the other. Unfortunately, the easier conception to grasp is the one that is not Wittgenstein's. Here now is Peter Sullivan on this.

> In both his early and his later work Wittgenstein is concerned with understanding the limits of thought. By this notion of a *limit* here is meant something set by, so essentially equivalent to, the essential nature or form of what it limits. It is the notion used when one says that a space is limited by its geometry. ... This notion of a limit is not a contrastive one. There is nothing thought-like excluded by the limits of thought for lacking thought's essential nature, just as there are no points excluded from space for being contra-geometrical. But thinking in general is contrastive: in general, that is, thinking something to be the case is thinking it to be the case rather than not. That is the broadest reason ... why thought about limits is apt to portray them instead as *limitations*, boundaries that separate what has a certain nature from what does not. (Sullivan 2011: 171–172, emphasis in original)

The most important point in Sullivan's attempt to explain Wittgenstein's understanding of limits is his remark that "there is nothing thought-like excluded by the limits of thought for lacking thought's essential nature." There is nothing excluded except what is simply nonsense. I think we can be helped to see what is at stake here by seeing Roger White's account of Wittgenstein on limits because it involves exactly the understanding of limits that Sullivan argues we tend to fall into when we do not grasp what Wittgenstein means by limits.

Moving on now to White's account. White argues that the propositions of the *Tractatus* fall outside of a boundary, which has on one side of it propositions that are constructed truth-functionally from elementary propositions and thus have the general form of propositions, while on the other side of the boundary, there are propositions like those of the *Tractatus*, about which White says that they appear to be presented as necessary a priori truths, and *for that reason*, then, they are on the far side of the limit that they help to establish, and hence are nonsense. It is then part of White's reading of the *Tractatus* that what there is on the far side of the limits are *thought-like constructions*, which are excluded *because they lack what counts as the essential nature of thought*. On White's reading, those proposition-like signs on the far side are not mere constructions that can be anticipated not to turn up when we construct propositions by the recipe given at 6.001. On the *alternative* view to White's, the reason these proposition-like signs do not turn up on the right side is not that they lack the essential nature of thoughts. It's rather that they can be shown to contain one or more signs with no meaning in the particular context. In the case of many of these propositions, the meaningless signs are signs that can in some contexts be used for formal concepts, but in their

Tractarian contexts they do not have that use, and there is no other kind of meaning that they have been given.

This then connects directly back to Wittgenstein's letter to Russell and what he says is his main contention. A reading like Roger White's has at its heart the idea of what cannot be said as something that *is thought-like*. So on that sort of reading, the idea would be that "there is an object a" is not *merely* something with no sense. The Roger White view involves our continuing to think of "There is an object a" as quasi-propositional, as something thought-like, which lacks what Wittgenstein counts as the essential nature of thought. And the idea then is that that's why "There is an object a" counts as nonsense. But Wittgenstein's view is that what shows in the uses of "a" as a name is not a matter of some quasi-propositional content that cannot be put into a genuine proposition. When we think of it as a sort of quasi-propositional content, it appears to be something out of reach of saying, as opposed to being something that is already expressed on *this* side of the limit, in the ways we use all the propositions that say something about *a*.

I want to end by getting back to Wittgenstein's letter telling Russell that he had misread the *Tractatus* and had missed Wittgenstein's main contention. I have a couple of points.

One is that Wittgenstein does not in that letter speak of the "*distinction between saying and showing*". Jean-Philippe Narboux has discussed the way that the expression, "*the distinction between saying and showing*" can be misleading. Here I will just note that talking of *the distinction* between saying and showing encourages the idea that what shows itself is something that is thought-like but which lacks the essential nature of thought, and that *that is why* it is unsayable. It encourages the idea that we are drawing a distinction between genuine expressions of thought and what are thought-like but not genuinely thoughts. This involves the idea of limits as limitations, not as limits. Anyway, I think it is worthwhile to note that Wittgenstein himself does not speak in terms of such a distinction in his letter to Russell.

The last thing I wanted to get to was the business about what the cardinal problem of philosophy is, how to formulate that. My idea was that we could see better how to formulate the problem after reading through some of the paragraphs I've focused on. So here is my reformulation. What Wittgenstein means by the cardinal problem is the problem of making completely clear the limit of the expression of thoughts, so that it is clear that everything that can be said lies within the limit thus drawn, and so that it is also clear how what shows itself shows itself in what lies within the limit. The problem will be thus to delimit at the same time what cannot be thought, by making clear what can be thought. The problem, that is, is that of making clear how what can be thought can be thought clearly, and to determine in that way what is not included. – If this is a formulation of the cardinal problem of philosophy, the Preface statement of the "whole sense of the book" can be read as announcing that the problem has been solved: what can be said can be said clearly; and, as for what is not included in the sayable, darüber muss man schweigen.

CHAPTER 2

Modality in Wittgenstein's Tractatus

Juliet Floyd and Sanford Shieh

2.1 Introduction

What is one to make of the remarks concerning possibility, and modalities in general, in Wittgenstein's *Tractatus*? Even a casual reader of the *Tractatus* may be struck by this. Here is a very small sample:[1]

2.15[2]   This connection of the elements of a picture is called its structure, and the possibility of this structure its form of depiction.
3.11   We use the sense-perceptible sign ... of the proposition as a projection of a possible situation.
4.4   A proposition is the expression of agreement and disagreement with the truth-possibilities of the elementary propositions.
5.473[2]   Everything that is possible in logic is also permitted.
6.33   We ... know a priori the possibility of a logical form.

In an *Abhandlung* qualified as *Logisch*, "every possibility" is said to be the "concern of logic," and "all possibilities" are said to be "its facts" (2.0121).

In what follows, we investigate some of the "concerns of logic" that lead to these remarks. We shall take them not to lead to what Cora Diamond (2018) has usefully called a "fell swoop" reading of the *Tractatus*: one that purports to find one main vein of argument in the book in order to show or to resist the global view that all (traditional?) philosophical problems are nonsense. Instead, we will sketch a view of Wittgenstein's remarks on modality, taking them to instantiate part of an activity aimed at clarifying and transforming *in logic* difficulties that are proper to logic.

Our thanks are due to José Zalabardo for his patience and support. Also to Martin Pilch, whose tremendous editorial work on the manuscript and typescript bases of the *Tractatus* (Pilch 2016) has made the path of analyzing the book so much richer and easier.
[1] References to the *Tractatus* are by remark number only; square brackets refer to a line number within a paragraph. Our English translations depart in small ways from the two standard ones, and we are much indebted to Michael Beaney for sharing a version of his forthcoming translation.

Modality in Wittgenstein's Tractatus

Among the first thinkers to have paid serious attention to the *Tractatus*'s remarks on modality are two leading members of the Vienna Circle, Moritz Schlick (1930) and Rudolf Carnap (1930). They drew from the *Tractatus* a conception of logic and mathematics that conjoins coherently with empiricism. These opponents of traditional metaphysics certainly had no truck with traditional metaphysical views of possibility and necessity. Carnap in particular found in the *Tractatus* an *explication* of the contrast between necessity and contingency as at bottom the contrast between logically and non-logically true propositions.

This anti-metaphysical orientation is elaborated differently in more recent "resolute" approaches to the *Tractatus*.[2] These interpretations take Wittgenstein's apparent appeal to modality not as a reduction of necessity and possibility to logical truth, but instead a thinking through of any such reduction as something to be overcome, something nonsensical. Cora Diamond, for example, takes Wittgenstein to consistently oppose conceptions of "necessity imaged as fact," as what is "*the case*" in all possible worlds (Diamond 1991b: 195). She takes Wittgenstein's characterization of "[l]ogical necessity [a]s that of tautologies" to imply that "sentences about necessity ... really are ... entirely empty" (Diamond 1991b: 198). Another example is Warren Goldfarb, who argues that Wittgenstein intends the reader of the *Tractatus* to see that the metaphysical conception of "possible states of affairs" appearing in the 2's lands in "incoherence" and "implode[s]" (Goldfarb 1997: 65-6, 70). This kind of "logical-activity-first" or "purely logical" reading faces the challenge of reinterpreting the substantial and metaphysical *sounding* language in the *Tractatus* as a gambit designed to get the reader to work through metaphysics and surrender it, acquiescing in logical analysis as a philosophical activity. The key question for us in what follows is what this acquiescence looks like in Wittgenstein's remarks using modality.

There is an opposed tradition that takes the *Tractatus* to rest on modal notions. Stenius (1960) reads the *Tractatus* in a Kantian vein, elaborating a particular critical view of necessity and possibility in terms of transcendental deductions of forms of thought.[3] Wolfgang Stegmüller claims that "the *Tractatus* is 'saturated' ['*durchtränkt*'] with intensional concepts," so that the notion of picturing relies on a "conceptual framework of a class of possible worlds" (Stegmüller 1966: 181, 184). G. H. von Wright also holds that "[t]he notion of propositional significance in the *Tractatus* is itself a modal notion" (von Wright 1982: 188, emphasis in original).

---

[2] For a survey of these, see Engelmann (2021).   [3] See Stenius (1960: chapter XI).

More recently, Raymond Bradley claims that the *Tractatus* contains "sketchy anticipations of" Kripke (Bradley 1992: xvii); in particular, like Kripke, Wittgenstein's "view of possible worlds" rests on a "highly plausible intuition" (Bradley 1992: 134). On this view, the *Tractatus* is a work *grounding* logic in intuitions of necessity and possibility about relations and properties.

We read the *Tractatus*'s conception of logic as ungrounded. Our interpretation differs from reductive accounts of the "merely linguistic" character of logical necessity that are to be found in the positivists, as well as Kantian ideas about mentality's transcendentally deduced form as internal to our capacity for human judgment. We also reject the idea that in the *Tractatus* "being possible" means being true, the case, or a fact in some other possible world.

Our plan is this. First, we show how Wittgenstein's remarks involving modality arise, specifically out of his criticisms of Russell's multiple-relation theory of judgment (MRTJ): They are, to use Diamond's phrase, philosophically *responsive* (Diamond 2018: 281). Second, we reconstruct some key parts of the *Tractatus* in a way that coheres with resolute, antimetaphysical readings. This yields an important contrast. Whereas modality in the *Tractatus* finds its place within a search for a coherent conception of the distinction between truth and falsity, in more recent metaphysics modality is justified by intuitions about essential and contingent properties holding or not holding in other possible worlds. The security of justifications based on modal intuitions, in comparison to the security of justifications *in* logic, is doubtful. Wittgenstein's handling of modality is, to this extent at least, logically speaking preferable to the metaphysicians', even if, as Wittgenstein himself was to see, his treatment of logic in the *Tractatus* was too simple and schematic, and had to be revised and adjusted in his subsequent philosophizing.

In agreement with the resolute perspective on Tractarian modality, we hold that possibility in the *Tractatus* is not depictable, not a matter of "what is the case." Instead, it shows forth *in* our intuitive talk about truth and falsity and negation, which, as the *Tractatus* moves us to see, runs through all of our thinking and speaking about what is the case. In this particular way of working with modality, there is no *perspective* (philosophical or otherwise) from which we see this, no theoretical representation or "deduction" of necessity and possibility, and no way of regarding what is happening as a drawing of limits to possible (philosophical?) experience or imagination with a prior theory of meaning. Seeing our talk of necessity and possibility for what they are is not to grasp a range of thoughts but to acknowledge and recognize fundamental logical features of thought and reality that relate to one another in a host of different ways, ways that we may, in developing a logically perspicuous notation, come to see.

2.2 Russell's Troubles with Judgment and Truth

When Russell and Moore turned against British idealism, they came to hold a theory of propositions as basic entities. On this theory, a proposition is the "*object* of a belief" or a judgment (Moore 1901: 717). (Moore and Russell did not differentiate judgment from belief.) A proposition is not a thought or a sentence, not a mental or linguistic entity that represents a purported fact in the world. Rather, propositions are complex entities the constituents of which are parts *of* the world.

Moore and Russell also reject correspondence conceptions of truth. Truth is not correspondence to reality but rather an indefinable property of propositions. The same holds for falsehood: This is not the absence of correspondence with reality but a primitive property of propositions. In addition, as Russell puts it, "a fact appears to be merely a true proposition" (Russell 1904: 523): that is to say, the notion of fact, or of the obtaining of a state of affairs in reality, is explained in terms of the truth of a proposition.

Starting around 1906, Russell began to doubt this Moore–Russell theory of propositions, especially the idea that there are propositions with a primitive property of falsity. The problem may be formulated thus, following Russell in taking *Othello* to be history rather than fiction. A false proposition like that expressed by the statement:

Desdemona loves Cassio

consists of an entity in which the relation of *love* unites Desdemona to Cassio, with the unanalyzable property of falsehood. But if the relation of *love* unites Desdemona to Cassio, does this not mean that Desdemona loves Cassio? Does this not amount to the existence of a fact or state of affairs *consisting* of Desdemona–loves–Cassio? Here, recall, a "fact" is a true proposition.[4]

By 1910, Russell concludes that there are no Moore–Russell propositions. He formulates the MRTJ to account for belief. Judgment or belief is now a state consisting of a subject standing in the belief relation to the

---

[4] For more on this problem, see Cartwright (1987, 2003) and Sullivan and Johnston (2018).

objects of her belief. This belief state is true if the objects are indeed connected as the subject believes them to be and is false if the objects are not so connected. So, when Othello has the false belief that Desdemona loves Cassio, there is no entity in the world consisting of Desdemona standing in the relation *love* to Cassio. Truth on the MRTJ is correspondence between beliefs and the existence of facts – which Russell calls *complexes* – *in* the world. Complexes are what Russell's earlier "propositions" became. In accordance with a doctrine he had held since *Principles of Mathematics* (Russell 1903) (hereafter *PoM*), Russell holds that complexes are not mere lists or classes of entities but are constituted by a relation relating the remaining constituents. This "relating relation" is a key object of judgments; Russell calls it the "subordinate verb" (Russell 1919b: 59–61); we will call it the *object-relation*. A judgment ("Desdemona loves Othello") is true just in case its object-relation (x *loves* y) relates its remaining objects (Desdemona and Othello) to constitute a complex, which we will call its corresponding or truth-making complex.

The MRTJ raises a problem of which Russell was aware. What, on the MRTJ, explains the difference between, for example,

(1) Othello believes that Desdemona loves Cassio

and

(2) Othello believes that Cassio loves Desdemona?

These beliefs are about the same three objects, but they are different beliefs, since belief (1) is false while (2) is true.[5] This is known as the "direction problem."[6]

Between 1910 and 1913, Russell addressed the direction problem using a long-standing doctrine held since *PoM*: Non-symmetrical relations, including the relation of believing, have *sense*, like a vector, which means that if such a relation relates some terms, it relates them in a specific *order*, and if such a relation relates the same terms in distinct orders, distinct complexes result. Thus, belief (1) differs from (2) because believing relates Othello to Cassio and Desdemona in different orders in them, and the

---

[5] Mihaela Fistioc pointed out to us that, taking *Othello* as history, it is not clear that belief state (2) is true. Following Russell, we accept this bit of "fictionalized" "history."

[6] See Griffin (1985: 219). In the secondary literature, the problem is generally taken to be one of individuating beliefs with the same objects. In our view, it also encompasses a problem of individuating truth-conditions arising from a single set of objects of belief, and a further problem of determining which truth-condition goes with which belief. See Shieh (2022, in press-b) for further discussion.

complexes the existence of which make these beliefs true are constituted by the object-relation *love* relating "*objects* of the belief, in the *same order as they had in the belief*" (Russell 1912: 200) (hereafter *PoP*; first emphasis Russell's).

In 1913, Russell advanced a significantly different MRTJ in a manuscript entitled *Theory of Knowledge*, published in its entirety only in 1984 (Russell 1984) (hereafter *TK*). One salient difference is that according to *TK*, in every belief the subject is also acquainted with the *general form* of complexes of some fixed number of constituents (e.g., dyadicity may be expressed by "xRy"). Another is that relations do not have sense or direction so that the direction problem requires a new solution, based on the new idea of *position relations* (to be explained later in the chapter).

Russell's correspondence with Lady Ottoline Morrell and Wittgenstein shows that while Russell was working on *TK* in the summer of 1913, Wittgenstein twice criticized the MRTJ that Russell was formulating, eventually "paralyzing" Russell and possibly leading him to abandon the manuscript.[7]

We do not have room here for a full discussion of this fascinating episode of philosophical history. We will merely sketch one perspective on what Wittgenstein's paralyzing criticism might have been based, which dovetails with Wittgenstein's "Notes on Logic" (Wittgenstein 1979) (hereafter *NL*; references to *NL* are in the form $x - y$, for manuscript x, remark y; Russell's summary for x is hereafter "S").[8]

As noted, in *TK* Russell gives up order *in* relating.[9] This poses a problem for making sense of the phenomena that motivate taking relations to have sense. The sentences

(3) Desdemona loves Cassio

and

(4) Cassio loves Desdemona

describe different complexes. Each complex is constituted by *love* relating Cassio and Desdemona. What accounts for the difference, if not different orders in which *love* relates? Russell's answer in *TK* is that if a non-symmetrical relation such as *love* relates two objects to form a complex, there are two positions, in this case call them the "lover" and "beloved"

---

[7] Wittgenstein wrote "paralyses," see McGuinness (2008: 42).
[8] See Shieh (in press-b) for a fuller account of Wittgenstein's criticism(s).
[9] See Ricketts (1996) and Shieh (in press-b) for accounts of how Russell reached this position.

positions, that each object "has in" that particular complex. Russell takes "having a position in" a complex to be, fundamentally, standing in a position relation *to* that complex. So (3) is a complex γ such that Desdemona stands in the position relation C_{lover} to γ and Cassio stands in the position relation $C_{beloved}$ to γ, while (4) is a complex γ′ such that Cassio stands in C_{lover} to γ′ and Desdemona stands in $C_{beloved}$ to γ′. Henceforth, we write "*xRy*" for "*x* stands in relation *R* to *y*."

Russell then claims that if Othello has belief (1), "whose objects appear verbally to be" *love*, Desdemona, and Cassio, "there are *really* other objects" and what Othello is "*really* believing is" (*TK*, 148, our emphases) specified by the sentence

(5) There is a complex γ in which Desdemona C_{lover} γ and Cassio $C_{beloved}$ γ.

Othello's "real" belief corresponding to (2), then, would be specified by the existence of its particular truth-making complex, namely,

(6) There is a complex γ′ in which Cassio C_{lover} γ′ and Desdemona $C_{beloved}$ γ′.

Now, Russell holds that for *x* to stand in a position relation *C* to a complex γ is for the relation *C* to constitute a complex δ by relating *x* and γ, in which δ is *different* from γ. Thus, each of sentences (5) and (6) describes a "molecular" complex, whose "atomic constituents" are, respectively, the converse pairs of atomic complexes

(7) Desdemona C_{lover} γ, Cassio $C_{beloved}$ γ

and

(8) Cassio C_{lover} γ′, Desdemona $C_{beloved}$ γ′.

Russell thus holds that the "real" objects of these "real" beliefs (5) and (6) are, respectively, atomic complexes (7) and (8). The original belief ascriptions (1) and (2) make it seem that both beliefs have the same objects, Desdemona, Cassio, and *love*, which raises the question of how they differ. But the "real" beliefs (5) and (6) have different objects by means of which the beliefs are distinguished. (5) is true if the molecular complex constituted by the logical relation of conjunction relating atomic complexes (7) exists; (6) is true if the molecular complex constituted from (8) exists. This seems to solve the direction problem.

Very quickly Russell realizes, however, that this purported solution dissolves. For the atomic complexes (7) and (8) *themselves* have constituents. Russell calls these "ultimate constituents" (*TK*, 120). The ultimate constituents of (7) are

(9) Desdemona, Cassio, C_{lover}, $C_{beloved}$, and γ,

but from these ultimate constituents, a set of atomic complexes distinct and converse from (7) may be constituted:

(10) Cassio C_{lover} γ, Desdemona $C_{beloved}$ γ.

If the "real" objects of belief (1) are the ultimate constituents (9), what does Othello "really" believe? Is it the existence of the molecular complex described by (5), namely (to repeat)

(11) There is a complex γ in which Desdemona C_{lover} γ and Cassio $C_{beloved}$ γ,

or is it the existence of the conversely ordered molecular complex described by

(12) There is a complex γ in which Cassio C_{lover} γ and Desdemona $C_{beloved}$ γ?

There is no unique belief determined by the mere *collection* of objects (9). Thus, Russell is back to the drawing board with the direction problem.

What if Russell insists that the real objects of Othello's beliefs are atomic complexes rather than ultimate constituents? In this case, if the "real" objects of belief (1) are (7), then, unless these atomic complexes both exist, Othello fails to have this belief. But if these complexes exist, then the complex described by (5) exists, contrary to the facts of *Othello*. Russell would then be committed to the objective falsehoods – just what he adopted the MRTJ to avoid.

What is happening is a kind of rifling in the drawer for the determinacy of beliefs and their truth-values. *Something* must determine, that is, fix and constitute, what a belief or judgment *is* and what makes it true. If it cannot be one complex, then it must be another.

It is critical to notice that this Russellian strategy for solving the direction problem runs aground unless Russell admits complexes constituted by object-relations *relating* other objects of belief. That is to say, the downfall of this strategy points toward taking belief to be a relation to a single complex entity that is something like a Moore–Russell proposition.

And thus the question remained unsolved for Russell and Wittgenstein: How are we to make sense of such a conception of judgment without being committed to false objectives (facts)?[10]

---

[10] MacBride (2013) and Lebens (2017) think that it would be easy for Russell to dodge these troubles, by insisting that relations have sense. We think otherwise. See Shieh (in press-b) for reasons to hold that analogous problems arise even on the assumption that believing orders its relata, provided that beliefs have truth-values.

2.3 Propositions as Facts and the Truth-Problem

In *NL* Wittgenstein formulates a conception of propositions intended to avoid commitment to false objectives and escape his criticisms of Russell's MRTJ. Wittgenstein *reinstates* propositions as elements of judgment. Propositions are *facts* that represent facts in the world. (This is not the whole truth, as we shall soon see.) A fact is an *aspect* of a collection or a composite, showing itself through an analysis revealing a complex. Facts have *forms*, something that they have in common with other facts.

Consider the English sentence:

(13) Desdemona loves Cassio.

The sentence is not itself a proposition, for a proposition *expresses*, involving many facts about the sequence of Latin alphabet letters and blank spaces that is (13). One such fact is

(14) "Desdemona" occurs to the left of "loves" and "Cassio" occurs to the right of "loves."

And this fact consists of two syntactical entities, the words "Desdemona" and "Cassio" standing in a complex spatial relation, which we may roughly indicate, in Fregean fashion, as

ξ occurs to the left of the word "loves," and ζ occurs to the right of "loves."

Wittgenstein specifies the *form* of this fact with

xRy (*NL* 4 – 8).

His allusion to Russell's specification of the form of dual complexes (*TK*, 98) leaps to the eye. We thus may take Wittgenstein to have understood his specification to convey

Something has some relation to something (*TK*, 114).

This form is something fact (14) about sentence (13) shares with indefinitely many other facts, for instance, the fact consisting of two people, Desdemona and Cassio, standing in the relation we indicate as

ξ loves ζ.

Fact (14) can be used to represent or "symbolize" any fact with this form (*NL* 4-8). The symbolization requires *conventionally adopted* or *stipulated rules* (for "convention" see S-15, 3-14; compare "laying down" in 4-8). These rules fix:

- What entities "Desdemona" and "Cassio" stand for, the "*meanings*" of these words (2-17, 3-15, 4-8).
- What fact about these meanings are "of like sense" with the syntactic fact (14), that is, what fact about these meanings makes (14) *true* (4-8).
- What fact about these meanings are "of opposite sense" with fact (14), that is, makes (14) *false* (4-8).

For example, one could stipulate:

- "Desdemona" stands for Aristotle.
- "Cassio" stands for Plato.
- The fact that Aristotle is younger than Plato makes (14) true.
- The fact that Aristotle is not younger than Plato makes (14) false.

Call these stipulations (*). These rules specify the definite *way* [*Art und Weise*, 2.031, 2.14ff] in which a propositional fact is compared with facts, or as Wittgenstein puts it, "A proposition is a standard to which facts behave" (S-18, 4-8). Propositions are not only facts; they are facts together with rules of comparison. The proposition that consists of fact (14) together with stipulations (*) we'll call *p*.

Note that what is stipulated to make (14) false is the fact that Aristotle is not younger than Plato. This is an instance of what Wittgenstein calls a "negative fact" (S 1-7, 8, 3-1). Negative facts are also involved in Wittgenstein's account of negation in *NL*:

> [W]e *can* mean the same by "*q*" as by "not-*q*," [this] shows that neither to the symbol "not" nor to the manner of its combination with "*q*" does a characteristic of the denotation of "*q*" correspond. (*NL* 1-9)

This account foreshadows *Tractatus* 4.0621[1] and [3]. If one interchanged the positive fact stipulated in (*) to make fact (14) true with the negative fact stipulated to make (14) false, the result is a different set of stipulations for (14), call them (*'). The proposition that consists of fact (14) together with stipulations (*') is the negation of *p*.

The *NL* theory is coherent, provided that the notion of negative fact is. From the first of Wittgenstein's wartime notebooks (Wittgenstein 1979) (hereafter *NB*, cited by date of entry alone), we see that he had by late 1914 come to realize that he did *not* have a coherent account of negative facts, and thus also no coherent accounts of falsity and of negation. He calls this the "truth-problem (*Wahrheits-Problem*)" (September 24, 1914). It is a version of an ancient problem of falsity as posed, for example, by Plato: How is it possible to "say, speak, or think *that which is not* …

correctly . . .?" (*Sophista*, 238c; emphases ours).[11] We note in passing that the so-called picture theory of propositions often associated with Wittgenstein's early philosophy has its origin in the truth-problem, for Wittgenstein begins his consideration of it with the idea that propositions may be taken to be *pictures* or *models* (September 29, 1914).

Negative facts cannot be false Moore–Russell propositions. So,

(15) Catiline did not denounce Cicero

is not an existing false complex constituted by denouncing relating Cataline and Cicero. Is it then the fact that such a complex is *absent* from the world? But then, how is it different from the absence that is the negative fact that

(16) Iago does not love Cassio?

The difference cannot just be that absence (15) concerns Catiline, *denounce*, and Cicero, while absence (16) concerns Iago, *love*, and Cassio. After all, it is plausible that the sets {Iago, *love*, Cassio} and {Cataline, *denounce*, Cicero} exist. So, what is it for there to be distinct *non-existences of facts* involving these entities?

Wittgenstein takes up this issue early in his struggles with the truth-problem. He tries out the idea that picturing the non-existent requires that each fact in the world has a "logical structure" and a picture has "form," something in the picture that is "identical with reality" (October 20, 1914). The idea derives from the *NL* view that propositional facts symbolize facts with the same form. What, in the first instance, corresponds in the world to a proposition is a structure or form, the very same as the structure of the proposition. The truth or falsity of a proposition is then determined by whether there exists a fact with that structure.

Wittgenstein soon raises doubts, however, about this common form solution to the truth-problem:

> How can there be the form of *p*, if there is no fact of this form? And in that case, what does this form really consist in?! (October 29, 1914)

This worry comes from Wittgenstein's remaining allegiance to Russell's ideas. For Russell, form is the way in which entities are connected to constitute complexes, so if some entities are *not* connected into a complex, then there's no form of their connection. If a fact is absent, surely its

---

[11] See Narboux (2009) for an illuminating discussion of the relations between Plato's discussion of not-being and falsity in *Sophista* and the *Tractatus*.

would-be constituents are not connected. But then, *a fortiori*, there is no particular way in which they are connected, so there is no such thing as their form of connection to correspond to the false picture.

Just a few days later, Wittgenstein entertains a new idea. A proposition taken as a *picture* or "model" consists of names representing things and "connected ... like a *tableau vivant*," and this "logical connection must of course be *possible* for the represented things" (November 4, 1914; emphasis ours). With the hindsight afforded by the *Tractatus*, we see Wittgenstein here on the verge of taking a *possible* connection, that is, *possible* structure, rather than an *existing* structure, to be what corresponds to a picture, just at the point where he raises the vivid analogy between pictures or models and sentences. Moreover, this leaves an opening for form itself to be regarded as nothing but the *possibility* of a certain structure, pictured according to conventions of picturing we lay down.

2.4 Possibility in the *Tractatus*

The wartime notebooks yield no decisive evidence that Wittgenstein took the step to possibility, although the truth-problem seems to fade from view in 1915–16. What we do know is that two remarks absent from the *Prototractatus*, together with an addition to a remark in the *Prototractatus*, are among the very last items to make it into the *Tractatus* manuscript, in 1918:

> 2.033 Form is the *possibility* of structure (our emphasis).
> 2.15 That the elements of the picture stand to one another in a determinate way represents [*stellt vor*] things as so standing to one another.
> This connection of the elements of a picture is called its {structure, and the possibility of this structure its} form of depiction [*Form der Abbildung*].
> 2.151 The form of depiction is the possibility that the things stand to one another as do the elements of the picture.

2.033 and 2.151 are not in the *Prototractatus*. 2.15[1] is *Prototractatus* 2.151. The part of 2.15[2] in curly brackets is an addition to the *Prototractatus* remark:

> 2.15101 This connection of the elements of a picture is called its form of depiction.

Through these additions, Wittgenstein crucially and self-consciously distinguishes *structure* from *form*. He thus takes the step merely contemplated in *NB*, which now incorporates the notion of possibility *internally* into his very idea of a sentence as a picture or model.

The significance of the *Tractatus* structure/form is to engender, among other things, a transformation of the meaning of a number of formulations first drafted in *NL* and *NB*:

- Propositions are *facts*.
- Propositions are *pictures* of facts.
- A proposition pictures a fact by having a *form* that the fact also has.
- The truth and falsity of propositions result from a *comparison* of propositional facts with facts in the world that they picture.[12]

In the *Tractatus*, the articulations of these formulations are now inflected with modality, in virtue of the notion of *form's* incorporation of a conception of *possibility*. This conception takes "possibility of structure" as something untheorized and unexplained, something *elucidatory* in Frege's sense: It is designed to aid us in coming to see our logical activities as *logical* through and through but requires us to engage in the very activities of logic and picturing in order to see this.[13]

A key effect of the form/structure distinction is the notion of a state-of-things (*Sachverhalt*):

> 2.031 In a state-of-things objects stand to one another in a determinate way.
> 2.032 The way in which objects hang together in a state-of-things is the structure of the state-of-things.

In view of 2.033, a state-of-things is, as we might first venture, the realization or the obtaining of a possible structure, with form understood as the possibility of a particular structure. A state-of-things "obtains" (*besteht*) just in case a possibility of things standing to one another in a determinate way is realized, that is, shows forth. One could put it in a slightly different way: a fact that pictures are an embodied expression of a possibility for how things are as represented in this mode of picturing. Pictorial possibility is not however a place in a prior "logical space" filled with metaphysically independent "possibilities." Rather, it is a characterization that is revelatory of logical activity and modeling as such, just as an expression of a face directly expresses, through our acknowledgment of it, a possible expression (happiness or sadness). Discernment of pictorial

---

[12] On the idea of transposing philosophical remarks and criticisms, see Floyd (2007).
[13] On elucidations in Frege and the *Tractatus*, see Weiner (2001). Compare TLP 6.54.

possibility is like "our recognition of facial expressions" (Diamond 1991a: 243): We appreciate these possibilities by appreciating a range of variations, and this in turn is appreciated through the activity of rearranging, contrasting, and comparing our depictions and expressions within a particular form of picturing.

Picturing in the *Tractatus* is in this way fundamentally modal but also a matter of logical activity and saying what is the case: as these *are*. A picture is a fact in virtue of its elements standing to each other in a determinate way. As we appreciate through logical analysis, this *obtaining state* of pictorial elements is what we may call, without further ontological commitment, a *realization of a possibility* for those pictorial elements. In this sense – and this sense only – it is a realization of a form.

Wittgenstein's "form/structure" distinction is not exactly Aristotelian, for it is not equivalent to a "form/matter" distinction. Rather, it emerges in the activity of arranging our (admittedly also material) expressions of thoughts in sentences – that is, signs that are used in a particular language in particular ways to express thoughts – so as to display internal (logical) relations among them, that is, the logico-symbolic role of their grammar.

Suppose that the possibility of structure in a language realized by a picturing fact is also a possibility of structure for the things correlated with pictorial elements to be connected in a state-of-things according to that language's conventions. Then the picturing fact can picture or "represent," that is, model, a possible obtaining of a state-of-things involving the objects correlated with the pictorial elements. Such a picture is *true* if the possibility it presents as obtaining is realized by the things whose representatives are the elements of the picture. The falsity of a picture consists of the non-realization by things of the possibility presented by that sentence.[14] Distinct unrealized possibilities individuate distinct falsehoods. This allows Wittgenstein to reinstate *talk* of "negative facts" but transpose it to a wholly logical, that is, formal, that is, non-grounding key: These facts are unrealized possibilities in the above sense.

Note that Wittgenstein can now answer the question posed in *NB*: How can we make remarks about the logical form of a false picturing fact? For if the things pictured are not connected, then there is no structure of their connection that obtains. However, if it is (logically) possible for them to be

---

[14] We set aside here a complication. According to 4.022, "a proposition *shows* how things are [*wie es sich verhält*]," but "how things are" may be that they realize a possible connection, or that they do not realize that possible connection. Truth and falsity have different constitutions in these two cases. For discussion of this complication, see Shieh (2021).

connected in such a structure, then it is possible for them to be connected in that particular way. And this shows through in logical analysis.

If objects are not in fact connected, one may ask, what *grounds* the possibility of their combination in a state-of-things? Wittgenstein's answer is that

> 2.0121[2] If things can occur in states-of-things, this must already lie in them.

Bluntly put: nothing does.

Better put: a *condition* [here expressed by "if" and "can"] for any "ground" of the possibility itself "lies in" the objects but only in terms of logical roles. These are reflected in internal relations among sentences that we can display in language. In this sense – and this sense only – the idea of a disconnected object contains in itself all of the object's possibilities of combining with others. This is reflected in our use of variables in the course of analysis, which we substitute in for names in sentences to indicate logical relations.

We have almost overcome the truth-problem. The modal features of picturing are, in the first place, modal internal features of *thought*, which, according to *Tractatus* 3, is an activity, a logical picturing of facts. Propositions, sentences-in-use, are a subset of logical pictures: those which have possible sense-perceptible expression (structure) in a particular language. In this way – and this way only – Wittgenstein's analogical construal of sentences as pictures blocks the truth-problem by incorporating modality internally into the very idea of a proposition, or thought. In this way modality is recast into something the idea of which is wholly logical, gaining its central place in the *Tractatus* in virtue of its role in helping us articulate a coherent conception of falsity and truth of thought and proposition (6.37).

As we see it, this line of thinking does not rest on "our intuitions" about the existence of counterfactual circumstances in which actual objects occur. The argument is, rather, that unless the presence or absence of states-of-things are realizations or failures of realizations of possibilities that we may analyze through logical analysis of our sentences, there is no coherent conception of thought that is open to falsity as much as to truth.

The most fundamental philosophical issue at stake in understanding the place of Wittgenstein's remarks about modality in the *Tractatus* is thus his question about the *nature* of the logical. Frege and Russell, central figures of early analytic philosophy, rejected modality as philosophically fundamental to logic. See Frege (1879: 5) and Russell (1994: 520). They accordingly also rejected a traditional Aristotelian conception of logical validity that takes logic to study argument forms, that is, conclusions following "out of necessity" from premises (*Analytica Priora*, 24b18–20).[15] Wittgenstein is offering a *responsive* reading when he uses terms like "possibility" and "necessity" (again, see Diamond 2018: 281): He is not simply insisting on brute metaphysical features of reality but instead thinking through what speaking and engaging in logical activity entangle us in, and finding language for *that*, suitably transforming language from its traditional homes. He is making an offer to Frege and Russell, something to help them move beyond their claimed reductions of the logical to a mere way of looking at *what is the case*.

By contrasting form with structure in his remarks concerning logical analysis, Wittgenstein is not merely adjusting his talk of pictures to match or echo his talk about states-of-things.[16] Rather, he draws possibility back into view as part and parcel of our very idea of the logical analysis of thought. In logic we see *through* our activities of affirming and denying propositions to see these entangled with, and realizing, one series of possible affirmations or denials among others. This does not mean that the modal notions *explain* logic. Rather, they figure in ordinary things we may do in arranging our expressions so as to help ourselves appreciate and articulate logical features of thought *as* logical.

The proposition, the *Tractatus* remarks, is a model [*Modell*] in being a "picture" (2.12, 4.01, 4.463). For example, if we use the Playmobil farm toy set to set out a situation in which the farmer is gazing at his corn and cows in a particular way, and we have already set up our rules of correlating figurines with objects in the world (say, with items and students in the classroom), we can vary the spatial structure of the Playmobil objects bit by bit, demonstrating to the class that insofar as we use the Playmobil set to represent situations in the room that are the case, we are immediately, always and already, entangled with a whole space of contingencies of Playmobil figurines – that is, *different* possible situations in which the farmer, his corn, and his cows (and the objects they go proxy for) may find themselves in. Moreover, we can also use the Playmobil structure to represent precisely what is *not* the case, or what we *hope* is not the case, or should not, in our eyes, *be* the case: We "imagine" logical possibilities precisely *by* the activity of structuring. The idea that the farmer could be

---

[15] See Shieh (2014, in press-a). For the story of Frege and Russell's banishment of modality, see Shieh (2019).
[16] This is argued by Zalabardo (2018a: 349) in his reply to Floyd (2018).

here, the corn *there*, and so on *exemplifies* a range of possibilities for us in this way, subject to the rules and constraints of our proxying and representing already set down. Moreover, by moving the structures around, step by step, we may avoid confusing the elements of the Playmobil set with what they represent, and with the necessities and possibilities we bring into view to make their role clear, for we may also *alter* our constraints of proxying and representing with these figures.

The foregoing might suggest that modal remarks in the *Tractatus* are something like the *ground* of a philosophical theory of thought and logic. We want to resist this suggestion. We start from:

> 2.172 A picture cannot depict its form of depiction, however; it shows it forth [*es weist sie auf*].

As we have seen, form is the possibility of structure. A picture embodies a possibility of connection. In this, it thereby depicts things as realizing that possibility. But pictures can be false. The possibility embodied in the picturing fact may in fact not be realized by those things. If a picture is false, then the things proxied are *not connected* in the "same" determinate way that the proxies are connected. There always is a "determinate combination" of pictorial elements. But with falsity, there is *no* determinate combination of things that corresponds to the picturing fact.

We can put the point this way. The consequence of forms not *being* a structure for Wittgenstein is that, contrary to what Wittgenstein had considered in *Notebooks*, what is essential to picturing is not the correspondence of something in reality to something in a picturing fact. A thought is, of course, a logical *structure*, but its representativeness does not lie in its corresponding to a situation with the same logical structure. While truth is correspondence of structure with structure, falsity is not.

Reality, according to 2.06, is the "obtaining and not-obtaining of states-of-things." We read this as saying that in reality there are only things and presence or absence of connections of things. It follows from our above considerations that form, that is, possibility, is not an *aspect* of reality, even if the concept of *reality* with which the *Tractatus* works has a modal character (2.06ff.). If one attempts to think of logical form as that which makes picturing possible, then it is neither in the picturing fact nor in the reality pictured; it is not really a *condition* or state-of-things that could be laid down. Logical form is fundamentally distinct from any pictorial element or manner of connection of pictorial elements.

To take logical form to be "undepictable," and so "unthinkable," is not to take sentences apparently about possibility and necessity to be entirely empty – unless, that is, they are used by a thinker who supposes that she is engaged in making statements about what is the case. There is no depiction of form in this sense; instead, a picture "shows forth," or exemplifies its form.[17] We understand this "showing forth" in terms of our ability to take a pictorial fact to *embody* a possibility within a particular parochial form of representation (spatial or colored). On this view, the form of a picture shows forth in the same way that an expression manifests itself in a face, and our discernment of pictorial possibility is like "our recognition of facial expressions" (Diamond 1991a: 243).

Diamond has argued that Wittgenstein aims at bringing readers of the *Tractatus* to recognize the "self-defeatingness" of some of its sentences, and thereby to "redirect[] our attention" to certain "logical features of the use of ordinary sentences" (Diamond 2002: 270, 259). We suggest logical form and forms of depiction are some of these features. The point of the *apparent* philosophical theory of modality is not the point of a theory at all. Wittgenstein's remarks serve instead as warnings, a form of responsiveness *to* philosophical views that hamper themselves from attending to human activities of structured variation in the forms of expression of thought that they themselves rely on, as if all that activity is inert or irrelevant to logic. The *Tractatus*'s commitment to thinking through the role of our forms of expression in language, which are as complex as the human organism itself (TLP 4.002), is to bring us to a *recognition* of logic's showing forth in our ordinary thought and talk.

2.5 The Nature of Logic, Picturing, and Truth-Functions

A little more than half a year after Wittgenstein first went to Cambridge, he wrote to Russell that logic "must turn out to be a *totally* different kind than any other science" (McGuinness 2008: 30). This strand of Wittgenstein's thinking never moved Russell, who in 1918 wrote, "[L]ogic is concerned with the real world just as truly as zoology, though with its more abstract and general features" (Russell 1919a: 169).

In the *Tractatus* Wittgenstein continues to reject Russellian conceptions of logic that regard logical activity as a sorting of entities or forms into kinds:

---

[17] "Shows forth" in 2.172 is a rendering of "aufweisen." However, it is connected to the "showing" of "zeigen" in 4.121: "A proposition shows [*zeigt*] the logical form of reality. It shows it forth [*weist sie auf*]." For an illuminating discussion of the notions of showing or showing forth in the *Tractatus*, see Narboux (2014).

> 6.111 Theories which make a proposition of logic appear substantial are always false. [A proposition of logic] gets quite the character of a proposition of natural science and this is a certain symptom of its being falsely understood.

A widespread interpretation of Wittgenstein's rejection is this. On his view, the propositions of natural science are made true or false by correctly or incorrectly picturing the world, and this occurs through the use of material concepts and object terms in the expressions of propositions (cf. 5.44). The "propositions" of logic are, by contrast, senseless (*sinnlos*) tautologies and contradictions. Tautologies are not true in virtue of being correct representations but in virtue of mechanisms of propositional representation. Similarly, contradictions are not "false" as incorrect pictures of the world but because of how propositional picturing works.

This common reading is problematic on at least two levels. To begin with, it's not clear that, for Wittgenstein, tautologies are "true" at all, because their internal logical configurations serve to cancel representation out (4.466), and so they say nothing (4.461), take no stand on the possible realization or non-realization of any situation. Similarly, contradictions are not "false"; they also do not picture reality but are "limiting cases" of sign-facts arising from mechanisms of propositional representation.[18]

Moreover, the usual reading makes it seem that Wittgenstein's disagreement with Russell was over what in particular *is* the ground of the truth for the propositions of logic, as opposed to the question of whether logic consists of a special set of propositions, true in some distinct way.

We understand Wittgenstein's rejection of Russell quite differently. We begin from the remark that

> 6.122 [W]e can even [*auch*] do without logical propositions.

And we take this to mean that appreciating the nature of logic has to do neither with coming to see that a certain class of propositions is demarcated by their *kind* of truth – that is, sorted through our prior understanding of "logical truth" – nor with finding the *ground* of their truth.

In order to unfold our reading further, we first address a question that may have already occurred to the reader. We have explained the sense in which propositions picture in terms of the possible realization or non-realization of facts. But it is not clear that our account rules out the view that in logic we picture truth-functions. If so, this would indicate that there is something in common between logic and ordinary science, and

---

[18] Compare the discussion in Dreben and Floyd (1991).

logical truth would be understandable in terms of our "semantic" understanding of the logical connectives.

To clarify what we have said, let us revisit a long-standing puzzle about the distinction between elementary and non-elementary propositions in the *Tractatus*: If the elementary propositions are pictures, then how can non-elementary propositions be pictures in the same sense? Our answer relies on Wittgenstein's modal remarks, suitably used and transposed.

The modal conception of picturing as presenting "contrastive possibilities," that is, possibilities and non-possibilities for things, applies to elementary propositions. And non-elementary propositions are characterized in two ways: along with all propositions, they are truth-functions of elementary propositions (5), and they are also pictures (4.01). It is clear that for a proposition *p* to be a truth-function of other propositions, the truth or falsity of *p* is to be determined entirely by the truth or falsity of these other propositions. However, this characterization does not answer the question of how *p*, if it is logically compound (non-elementary), counts as a picture.

Consider a disjunctive proposition

(17) *p* or *q*

where *p* and *q* are elementary propositions. (17) does not depict

(i) the situation in which *p* holds but *q* does not,
(ii) nor the situation in *q* holds but *p* does not,
(iii) nor the situation in which both *p* and *q* hold.

Any one of these three situations could fail to obtain without (17) being false. So what does (17) picture?

The answer lies in our ability to reflect on and recognize the modal contrasts involved in picturing. A truth-function of elementary propositions counts as a picture because, like an elementary proposition, it presents a possibility-contrast (i.e., a distinct way for things to be that either is or is not the case, either is or is not a situation realized in the world) but not in the direct way presented by an elementary proposition. Each disjunct of (17) presents a possibility-contrast for things that are either realized or not realized. What the disjunction affirms [*bejaht*] is that one of situations (i)–(iii) is realized in the world. That is to say, a disjunction pictures these three situations, but as open *to* being realized, and as perhaps not realized. In addition, the disjunction also

(iv) denies that the remaining situation, in which neither *p* nor *q* is true, is open to being realized,

That is, it pictures (iv) as closed to realization.

Now, p is true if the situation it presents is realized and false if it is not realized, similarly for q. Here note well our "ifs": The whole of our observations is thoroughly "iffy" in a purely logical sense. A disjunction presents a way the possibilities presented by its disjuncts may or may not be realized in the world. Since picturing *is* the presentation of possibilities for ways situations may or may not be realized in the world, it follows that disjunctions – and truth-functional propositions in general – are pictures.

On this view of disjunctions as pictures, a disjunction is not a fully distinct picture from its disjuncts. A disjunction pictures possibilities for the possibilities presented by its disjuncts, so to speak, that is, a disjunction pictures by means of the possibility-contrasts pictured by its disjuncts, which may well involve further possibility-contrasts. In Tractarian terms, Wittgenstein takes a disjunctive proposition to be *internally related* to its disjuncts.

The internal relation between a disjunction and its disjuncts expresses certain (purely logical) necessities and impossibilities of contrast. For example, if R is the disjunction "p or q":

- It is not possible for p to picture correctly at the same time that R pictures incorrectly.
- If R pictures correctly, then it is necessary that at least one of p and q pictures correctly as well.

Do such remarks "picture possibilities," in the end? *Are* they "would be assertions"? We want to say, with (Diamond 2019: 182), No. These are not "models" in the *Tractatus*'s sense, even in the way in which nowadays we regard representations of data sets as "models." Instead, they are intended to help us pursue the activity of clearly formulating the internal relations among possibility-contrasts articulated in our propositions. The character of an apparent proposition is not always evident from its form: We need to "extract" its internal features's relations to one another and to those in other propositions carefully, by attending to our uses of these sentences, in order to appreciate what it does or does not *actually* say.[19] What the string of signs *might possibly* be used *to* say, with different conventions and rules, is something else altogether.

Internal necessities thus govern the picturing of a disjunction and the picturing of its disjuncts, but only in that they are constituted by patterns in the picturing of these propositions. Any "impossibilities" and

---

[19] Compare Diamond (2019: chapter 4, especially p. 182-3n).

"necessities" of logic are impossibilities and necessities of the truth and falsity of the propositions *P*, *Q*, and *R* in relation to one another's contrastive possibilities. All such necessities may equally be conceived of as certain patterns of truth-values of *P*, *Q*, and *R*. Their necessity lies in that

- It is not intelligible for *P* to picture correctly at the same time that "*P* or *Q*" pictures incorrectly.
- We cannot intelligibly take "*P* or *Q*" to picture correctly and yet at the same time take neither *P* nor *Q* to picture correctly.

Such acknowledged patterns are what Wittgenstein means by "rules of logical syntax" (3.334).[20] Obviously, the rules governing single signs might be altered for special occasions, for example, we could imagine that whenever *P* occurs in a disjunction, it is to be understood as *P'*, some other sentence. But, *given the uses of our signs that we actually have*, this one-time jiggering is required if we are not to acknowledge the internal relations between the truth-possibilities for *P*, *Q*, and *R*.

Tractarian patterns of picturing constitute logical "relations" of implication and incompatibility. For example, the patterns displayed above indicate that

- *P* implies *R*
- The falsity of both *P* and *Q* is incompatible with the truth of *R*.

These implications and incompatibilities are shown in the nature of non-elementary picturing, and in the picturing of these propositions *P*, *Q*, and *R*. They would not be the propositions they are without these implications and incompatibilities among them.

The foregoing account of non-elementary picturing points to the nature of logic. Logical syntax constitutes implications and incompatibilities among propositions. These implications and incompatibilities are imbricated in all reasoning that involves us in logic. Thus, logic lies in the natures of propositions involved in any particular line of reasoning. They do not rest in other "purely logical" propositions.

---

[20] For extended discussion and defense of this reading of "logical syntax" and its connection to Wittgenstein's conception of logic in the *Tractatus*, see Shieh (2014, 2015, in press-a). Shieh holds, in particular, that, in addition to rules of logical syntax such as that governing disjunction, there are rules governing the symbolizing of single propositional-signs such as: it is not intelligible for one part of such a sign to function logically as a proper name and the remaining part to function as a second-level concept-expression. The attribution of the latter sort of rules to the *Tractatus* is tacitly acknowledged by resolute interpretation such as Diamond (1991c) and Conant (2002).

Differently put, logic is not concentrated in a special set of propositions but pervades all propositions, drawing out the nature of what propositions are. This is not to deny that there are such things as "propositions of logic" or that these propositions are tautologies. It is, rather, to claim that the so-called propositions of logic are of peripheral interest *in* logic, which explains 6.122's insistence that we have no *need* of propositions of logic. What is instead essential to logic is which pictures of reality there can be, and this in turn determines the ways in which propositions are internally related to one another. The essence of logic is exhibited in the totality of possibilities for elementary and non-elementary picturing, and this is expressible in written form by what Wittgenstein calls the general form of proposition (4.5).

As to this "totality": It is important that the general form of proposition *can* be schematically envisioned in terms of the step-by-step writing out of formal series "in some one sign-language" (4.5): Any proposition may be conceived of as produced through iterated, step-by-step applications of the generalized Sheffer stroke N to sets of elementary propositions (6).[21] At each application in the construction of further propositions by N, all the contrasts between what may and may not obtain at the elementary level are kept track of. This does not mean that the *Tractatus* is committed to a set of elementary propositions that is to be read off our language directly, or a set of propositions or facts that are facts, just not here in this world. Rather, it recommends logical activity, providing a schematic characterization of, or way of looking at, what *in the end* an ultimate analysis of our language would have to look like. A familiar alternative account of logical truth rests upon the idea that logical truths are specified model-theoretically through an "account" of the logical constants. Wittgenstein has replaced this with formal *procedures*: operations on sentences that display contrasts of obtaining and non-obtaining of situations. The generality of formal operations is not that of the quantifier as it is standardly understood.[22]

This constructed, internally related series of possibility-contrasts – that is, our capacity to express and grasp formal series of forms – is inseparable from, and thus necessary for, what it is to think through a purely logical conception of a proposition. For Wittgenstein, it is not just that necessity is intrinsic to logic. It is that necessity is shown *in* the activity of logic, in the formal procedures drawn from language by and in logic, where a balance is found between the possibilities of obtaining and non-obtaining.

---

[21] On the adequacy of this conception to express first-order logic, see Floyd (2001), Rogers and Wehmeier (2012) and Weiss (2017).
[22] See 4.1252, 5.2522, 5.501 and Floyd (2005).

We are, as it were, always already in the grip of logic, if we think at all, if we picture the world at all. Whence

> 5.4731 [L]anguage itself prevents every logical mistake. – That logic is *a priori* consists in this: that nothing illogical can be thought.

This encapsulates the considerations we have just rehearsed. In any expression of thought, there is something arbitrary, and something not. What is arbitrary is the particular form of the language, its alphabet, and its picturing conventions. However, once these are fixed, and understood in terms of the opening and closing and allowing for contrastive possibilities, there is something non-arbitrary, something that shows through any particular language. That is logical syntax, something common to all possible notations (3.3441, 3.342).

Is logical syntax, then, the ground of the nature of logic? Not quite. There is no ground other than what is cashed out in our activities of articulating ordinary sentences, and the activity of logic involves our rendering the logical aspects of such articulations – the "internal relations" among possibilities for the holding and not holding of atomic facts – in a perspicuous logical notation.

These points are reinforced if we look at how Wittgenstein treats logical inference and logical consequence, worked out in terms of his truth-table notation (4.26ff.), which he takes to express agreements and disagreements of "truth-possibilities" with the possibilities pictured by elementary propositions. The "truth-possibilities" of the elementary propositions mean [*bedeuten*] the (contrastive) possibilities of the existence and non-existence of the atomic facts these elementary propositions picture. In a truth-table all possible combinations of possibilities for all the situations pictured by the elementary propositions involved in a proposition are listed in order, in a series of rows, each column headed by an elementary proposition and listing all possible combinations of truth and falsity for that proposition in relation to the possible combinations of truth and falsity for each of the other elementary propositions involved in the proposition.

The whole table expresses a field of internal relations among these contrastive possibilities, setting them forth: It is a sign expressing a proposition, and thus a picture, but a picture *through* its expressing the possibilities for obtaining and non-obtaining of certain situations. A proposition is taken to be "the expression of agreement and disagreement with the truth-possibilities of the elementary propositions" (4.41) and since Wittgenstein calls its "truth-conditions" the proposition's expression of agreement and disagreement with the truth-possibilities of the elementary propositions, he can say that a proposition in general is the expression of its truth-conditions (4.431). However, we must not think of these "truth-conditions" as metaphysical truth-makers, or further logical propositions or laws, but instead possibility-space articulations. There is no concept of a fact "obtaining" without the concurrent concept of its "non-obtaining": These concepts are entangled through exhausting a (particular) space of possibilities so that they are what they are *in* this contrast. In logic, in reflecting on our affirmations and denials of particular propositions in language, we come to see that there is no such thing as just "obtaining" flatly. The conception is analogous to the way Wittgenstein treats probability: He says it gives us, not knowledge of possibilities as *properties* of situations or objects but rather a way of seeing certain general *internal* properties of ungeneralized propositions in relation to one another (5.15ff).[23] No event is simply probable as ½, but instead it can only be probable relative to a set of other possibilities.

A major point in drawing in the idea of an "internal relation" is that such relatedness is *subject to rendition in step-by-step formal procedures or calculations*, as Wittgenstein calls them. This *can be rendered in terms of step-by-step, humanly written formal procedures*, and this notion itself is a central mark of the logical in the *Tractatus*.

As to the very idea of one proposition "logically following from" another, Wittgenstein points out that by fixing the order of truth-possibilities for a collection of elementary propositions we may express the truth-conditions for a proposition canonically and abbreviatively as a single row of agreements and disagreements, transposing the final column of what we today call a truth-table into a single row of Ts and Fs (4.442). This allows him to characterize the notion of logical consequence. The "truth grounds" of a proposition are the truth-possibilities for a proposition in which it is true (5.101), and the truth of a proposition q "follows from" the truth of a proposition p if all the truth grounds of p are also truth grounds of q (5.121).[24] This is exhibited in a formal *procedure*: We may

---

[23] See Floyd (2010: §2) for discussion of the *Tractatus* on probability.

[24] Martin Pilch has pointed out that the *Tractatus* notion of "truth ground" leads Wittgenstein to reject the principle of *ex falso quodlibet* (that all propositions "follow from" a contradiction). Because a contradiction is never true, it has no truth grounds at all. In *NB* (3.6.15) Wittgenstein had concluded that *ex falso quodlibet* does not hold, since a contradiction is never true, and "no proposition asserts it." He slipped, however, into writing that all sentences "follow from" a contradiction in his manuscript draft for the *Prototractatus* (PT). He ultimately crossed this out by hand in the PT manuscript (104, 12): His notion of "truth ground" allows him to do so. See Pilch (2016: PTT_A_3 p. 12) for an analysis of the manuscript basis.

simply inspect the canonical expressions of two propositions to determine when one follows from another. For example, "*p* or *q*" *follows from* "*p* and *q*" as all the truth grounds of TFFF are also truth grounds of TTTF, but "*p* and *q*" does not follow from "*p* or *q*" because there are truth grounds for TTTF that are not truth grounds for TFFF.

CHAPTER 3

Clarification and Analysis in the Tractatus

Sébastien Gandon

3.1 Introduction

Did Wittgenstein, in the *Tractatus* consider, like Frege before him, that the construction of a logical language, free from all the imperfections of ordinary language, was indispensable for philosophical clarification? Or, on the contrary, did he already consider, like the Wittgenstein of the *Investigations*, that ordinary language is not, as it is, logically imperfect? The seeming opposition between 5.5563 ("All propositions of our colloquial language are actually, just as they are, logically completely in order") and 4.002 ("Language disguises the thought; so that from the external form of the clothes, one cannot infer the form of the thought they clothe, because the external form of the clothes is constructed with quite another object than to let the form of the body be recognized") has puzzled many commentators. Among the first generation of scholars, no consensus existed on the issue about the nature of the relationship between logical and ordinary language. For instance, Copi (1958) thought that the picture theory applied only to the propositions of the logical notation, whereas Hacker (1972) estimated that it applied to the statements of all languages, ordinary or ideographic. Anscombe (1971) and Black (1964) claimed that 5.563 did not contradict 4.002 but they do not explain how a language that is logically completely in order can be the source of logical confusion.

More recently, this issue resurfaced. Starting from the opposition between the formal philosophy of language (championed by Carnap) and the philosophy of ordinary language (championed by Strawson), Kuusela (2019: Ch. 7) makes of this difference (and thus of the difference between logical notation and ordinary language) a key to his reading of Wittgenstein's work. His main claim is that the method used in the *Philosophical Investigations* represents a middle path, taking the best of both sides. More precisely, Kuusela considers that, in the *Tractatus*, Wittgenstein agrees with Russell that philosophical clarification requires "a more suitable means of expression than everyday language furnishes" and that, in his later philosophy he "comes to question the postulation of such underlying structures" (Kuusela 2019: 35). I think this description of Wittgenstein's philosophical clarification in the *Tractatus* is seriously wrong. Commenting on 6.53, Kuusela explains:

> The strictly correct method is a method of logical analysis in terms of a symbolic logical notation, whereby the logical, syntactical or formal properties of logically unclear expressions are clarified by translating them into a logically perspicuous notation. Thus, the formal characteristics of logically unclear expressions can be clarified through their transformation into a logically more perspicuous form. (Kuusela 2019: 85)

Kuusela's claim can then be decomposed into three different components:

(C1) For Wittgenstein, ordinary language contains "logically unclear expressions" that are at the source of philosophical nonsense.

(C2) For Wittgenstein, one can devise a "symbolic logical notation" that is free from "logically unclear expressions."

(C3) For Wittgenstein, the philosophical task consists in an "analysis," that is to say, in a translation from ordinary language to a logical language.

I agree with (C1) and (C2). But I claim that (C3) is mistaken and should be replaced by the following claim:

(C1) For Wittgenstein, analysis of ordinary language and philosophical clarification are two different tasks.

To argue for (C4) and against (C3), I will proceed as follows. In Section 3.2, I will distinguish two ways in which ordinary language is said to be imperfect, one originating in Frege and the other in Russell, and I will argue that Wittgenstein in the *Tractatus* follows Russell. In Section 3.3, I explain some consequences, not always understood, of the Russellian outlook. In particular, I argue that a careful examination of what Russell does in *On Denoting* leads us to distinguish two senses in which a notation can be said to be logically in order, and that (C1) and (C2) imply (C3) only when these two senses are confused. Sections 3.4 and 3.5 are devoted to Wittgenstein's *Tractatus* and present two arguments in favor of (C4). As we know, Wittgenstein is opposed to Russell's epistemological conception of analysis, which brings him to reject any attempt to characterize the logical forms of elementary propositions. In Section 3.4, I argue that Wittgenstein's abstract conception of analysis makes it difficult to understand how analysis can be used to solve philosophical problems. In Section

3.5, I claim that the passage 3.32ff (on the distinction between symbol and sign) in the *Tractatus* can be read as the development of a conceptual framework making intelligible the distinction between the two senses of "logical notation" that Russell's practice induces. Section 3.6 summarizes my argument and draws some consequences.

3.2 Frege and Russell on Logical Notation

Frege (1979a) contrasts two sorts of definition: constructive definition, which consists in introducing a new sign in the logical notation to express a sense constructed out of already given signs, and analytic definition (or logical analysis), which consists in identifying the sense of a simple sign with a long-established use with that of a complex expression belonging to the logical notation. Thus:

> Let us assume that A is the [ordinary] long-established sign (expression) whose sense we have attempted to analyze logically by constructing a complex expression that gives the analysis. Since we are not certain whether the analysis is successful, we are not prepared to present the complex expression as one which can be replaced by the simple sign A. If it is our intention to put forward a definition proper, we are not entitled to choose the sign A, which already has a sense, but we must choose a fresh [logical] sign B, say, which has the sense of the complex expression only in virtue of the definition. The question now is whether A and B have the same sense. (Frege 1979a: 210)

To this last question, Frege answers that any logical translation from ordinary language is open to a serious objection:

> The fact is that if we really do have a clear grasp of the sense of the simple [ordinary] sign, then it cannot be doubtful whether it agrees with the sense of the complex expression. If this is open to question, ... then the reason must lie in the fact that we do not have a clear grasp of the simple sign, but that its outlines are confused as if we saw it though a mist. (Frege 1979a: 211)

Ordinary language is intrinsically vague, and this vagueness makes any translation into ideography, that is, any analysis, dubious and questionable. Frege does not dispute the usefulness of the analytical step: The effect of logical analysis is to remove the fog so as "to articulate the sense clearly." It remains however that logical analysis does not "form part of the construction of the system, but must take place beforehand." To the question of whether the ordinary A and the ideographic B have the same sense, Frege's answer is thus no:

> [W]e can bypass this question altogether if we are constructing a new system from the bottom up; in that case we shall make no further use of

the sign *A* – we shall only use *B*. We have introduced the sign *B* to take the place of the complex expression in question by an arbitrary fiat and in this way we have conferred sense on it. (Frege 1979a: 210–1)

No definition in the logical system is then analytic: "if we are constructing a new system from the bottom up," we can bypass the question as to whether the logical and the ordinary notations have the same content altogether, since, in this case, the sign with the long-established use is not supposed to occur anymore. The idea that ordinary language is intrinsically logically defective and then that analysis is not a proper part of the logical system is reflected in Frege's systematic writing, where all the explanations of ideographic notation are put in German.[1] It also provides the argumentative basis in more polemical writings such as "On Concept and Object" (Frege 1980b), where Frege acknowledges that the use of ordinary language prevents him from fully explaining his thought.[2]

Russell explains in *Principia Mathematica* (hereafter PM):

> When what is defined is (as often occurs) something already familiar, such as cardinal or ordinal numbers, the definition contains an analysis of a common idea, and may therefore express a notable advance. Cantor's definition of the continuum illustrates this: his definition amounts to the statement that what he is defining is the object which has the properties commonly associated with the word "continuum," though what precisely constitutes these properties had not before been known. In such cases, a definition is a "making definite": it gives definiteness to an idea which had previously been more or less vague. (Whitehead and Russell 1910: 12)

Thus, Russell accepts that the long-established symbol "continuum" has the same content as the logical complex symbol that corresponds to it in the logical notation: What Cantor (and Russell after him) is defining "is the object which has the properties commonly associated with the word 'continuum.'" Russell does then exactly what Frege refuses to do: identifying the content of a logical symbol with the one of an ordinary expression.

Kuusela acknowledges that there is a difference between the two authors, but he considers it as an insignificant nuance, which does not change anything essential in the approach to the relationship between

---

[1] See Frege (2013).
[2] "By a kind of necessity of language, my expressions, taken literally, sometimes miss my thought, in that I mention an object, when what I intend is a concept. I fully realize that in such cases I was relying upon a reader who would be ready to meet me half-way – who does not begrudge a pinch of salt." (Frege 1980b: 193)

ordinary language and logical notation.[3] Frege holds that the vagueness of our ordinary expressions enjoins us to reject any translation between ordinary language and the logical notation; Russell would not share these scruples, but, after the discovery of the theory of incomplete descriptions in 1905, he would agree with Frege that ordinary language disguises the form of thought. Thus, in his interpretation, Kuusela gives a decisive role to the Russellian theory of incomplete symbols.[4] Let me pause for a moment on this important point.

According to Russell, an incomplete symbol is a symbol that has no meaning in isolation, but that contributes to the meaning of the sentence in which it occurs. Thus, the definite description "the King of France" is not a proper name that designates something, but it contributes to the meaning of the sentence P = "the King of France is bald." Since the incomplete symbol does not mean anything, the sentence in which it occurs does not have the same structure as the propositional content it expresses. Thus, according to Russell in *On Denoting* (hereafter OD) (Russell 1905), the proposition conveyed by P (noted P_{ca} for completely analyzed P) should be rendered as follows ("K(x)" means that x is King of France, "B(x)" means that x is bald):

$$P_{ca} = \exists x(K(x) \wedge \forall y(K(y) \rightarrow y = x) \wedge B(x)),$$

which is clearly not a subject-predicate sentence, as the sentence Q = "Edward is bald" is, for instance. To help see the difference between P and P_{ca}, Russell introduces, in OD, the following abbreviation (noted P_o for ordinary P):

$$P_o = B(\iota x)(Kx),$$

where "$(\iota x)(Kx)$" is the incomplete symbol "the King of France," the iota (which is inversed in PM), followed by the variable corresponding to the definite article in the ordinary expression. P_o has the same typographical form as Q_{ca} ("e" is the name for Edward):

$$Q_{ca} = B(e).$$

---

[3] "From the point of view of present concerns it is important that, despite certain significant differences in their conceptions of logic, Frege's and Russell's views on the methodological significance of logic for philosophy correspond to one another in key respects." (Kuusela 2019: 19)

[4] "[Because of his theory of descriptions,] Russell comes to take the grammatical forms of ordinary language to be logically misleading similarly to Frege, abandoning the more trustful view of the *Principles*. . . . Consequently, it emerges as a central task for logic or logical philosophy to try to pass through the misleading surface structures or forms of language, and to reveal the underlying logical forms of propositions that sentences express. By so doing philosophy then brings to light genuine philosophical distinctions pertaining to reality." (Kuusela 2019: 21)

Both sentences appear as a result of the application of the predicate "B(x)" to a singular entity, designated by "e" in Q_{ca}, and by "(ɩx)(Kx)" in P_o. But grammatical resemblance between the two ordinary sentences is misleading. The logical form of P is P_{ca}, and not P_o – and P_{ca}, a general proposition, is very different from Q_{ca}, a singular proposition.

Kuusela is then right to insist on the fact that the theory of incomplete symbol opens a gap between the sentence written in ordinary language and the logical form of the proposition it expresses. But he is wrong to lump Russell's and Frege's views together: the difference between the logical form of the propositional content and that of its expression in ordinary language is, in Russell, contrary to what happens in Frege, logically controlled. Indeed, it is the very role of the theory of the incomplete symbol to show how logical forms are projected into the forms of ordinary language! Having a perfectly analyzed notation is no longer a prerequisite for doing logic, since a logical theory (i.e., the theory of incomplete symbols) is precisely intended to explain how the forms of the usual language are related to the one of the completely analyzed language. As I will explain in the next section, far from bringing Russell closer to Frege, the theory of the incomplete symbol leads to distinguishing two senses of the term "logical notation" (which are confused by Kuusela): a weak sense, where a notation is labeled "logical" when it avoids any logical error, on the one hand; a strong sense, where a logical notation is identified with a fully analyzed notation (a language that contains only names that refer directly to elements of the content it expresses), on the other.

3.3 Two Senses in Which a Notation Can Be Said to Be Logical

In the *Grundgesetze* (Frege 2013), after having presented the primitive signs, Frege explains in a second section how one can form new names from primitive ones. As he makes clear in his section 28, "correctly formed names must always refer to something," and Frege shows that the constraints he sets on the definition guarantee that the defined names in the concept script are correctly formed and do have a reference (if the primitive names have them). In PM, after section *20, in which Russell introduces the class-symbol (as an incomplete symbol), and section *30, in which Russell introduces the notation for descriptive functions (the notation "(ɩx)(ϕx)" for definite description has already been explained in *14), almost all theorems contain expressions that do not designate anything in isolation. Let me take the example of theorem *110.643:

$$1 +_c 1 = 2$$

Except for the identity sign, each symbol in *110.643 is incomplete, and the complete analysis of *110.643 would transform this "occasionally useful" statement into a very long and very complicated sentence.[5] Kuusela would surely be right to maintain that the grammatical form of theorem *110.643 does not resemble its real logical form. But he would have then to recognize that the fact that the PM notation distorts the deep logical form does not create any logical problem: The PM proofs are written in notations that use expressions that do not name anything, and no logical mistakes are generated by this policy. The PM notation, although not completely analyzed from a logical point of view (since it contains incomplete expressions), does not generate any logical trouble – in this sense, it is, just as it is, "logically completely in order" (5.563). The example of PM, and the theory of incomplete symbols, shows us then that we must distinguish between two notions that Frege mixed: that of analyzed language, in which every expression has a reference, on the one hand, and the weaker notion of logically ordered language, on the other.

At this point, it could be retorted that the context of this distinction is purely "technical" and has no bearing on what concerns Kuusela, namely the use of logic to clarify philosophical problems. One could thus argue that, even if it is perhaps possible to construct a nonanalyzed notation for deducing mathematical theorems from logical principles, such a language, insofar as it hides the logical form of the propositions, would be unsuitable for philosophy. But this is in fact not the case.

In OD, Russell explains that "a logical theory may be tested by its capacity for dealing with puzzles" (Russell 1905: 484), and lists three such "puzzles," the most famous of which concerns the baldness of the King of France:

> By the law of excluded middle, either "A is B" or "A is not B" must be true. Hence either "the present King of France is bald" or "the present King of France is not bald" must be true. Yet if we enumerated the things that are bald, and then the things that are not bald, we should not find the present King of France in either list. Hegelians, who love a synthesis, will probably conclude that he wears a wig. (Russell 1905: 485)

These puzzles are explicitly linked by Russell to Frege's distinction between sense and reference and to Meinong's theory of nonexisting objects (Russell 1905: 483–4), that is, to typical philosophical

---

[5] Thus, according to the definition *52.01, 1 is a class (thus an incomplete symbol) of all unit classes (which is another incomplete symbol, in the definition of which a descriptive function occurs).

Clarification and Analysis in the Tractatus 57

developments. Moreover, Russell's description of the situation is close to the way Wittgenstein characterizes the philosophical problem in the *Tractatus*: All the puzzles result "from the fact that we do not understand the logic of our language" (4.003). Now, Kuusela seems to believe that Russell's solution consists in the translation of the proposition P = the King of France is bald into

$$P_{ca} = \exists x(K(x) \land \forall y(K(y) \to y = x) \land B(x)),$$

which shows us that ¬P corresponds to:

$$\neg P_{ca} = \neg \exists x(K(x) \land \forall y(K(y) \to y = x) \land B(x)),$$

And not to:

$$P_{ca}' = \exists x(K(x) \land \forall y(K(y) \to y = x) \land \neg B(x)).$$

But a close examination of OD shows that Russell actually is not content with this answer.

After the long passage about the Grey's Elegy, Russell returns to the puzzles and announces that he will show how the theory of descriptions solves them.[6] His solution rests on the distinction between primary and secondary occurrence. An incomplete symbol, if it does not have any meaning in isolation, contributes to the meaning of the proposition in which it occurs. Now, the phrase "proposition in which it occurs" is ambiguous whenever the incomplete symbol occurs simultaneously in several propositions. Let us use the abbreviated notation that Russell employs in 1905. In P_o = B(ɿx)(Kx), there is only one propositional context in which "(ɿx)(Kx)" can appear, namely "B(_)," whereas in $P_{o\_}$ = ¬B(ɿx)(Kx), one can consider that "(ɿx)(Kx)" occurs either in the whole context "¬B(_)" or in the context "B(_)." Russell says that the first interpretation corresponds to the case where "(ɿx)(Kx)" has a primary occurrence, while the second interpretation corresponds to the case where "(ɿx)(Kx)" has a secondary occurrence. When the first reading is selected, the expressed content is P_{ca}', whereas the second choice corresponds to the content ¬P_{ca}. But note that the distinction between primary and secondary occurrence itself belongs to the nonanalyzed notation, since it applies to the occurrence of the incomplete symbol.

Russell's goal here is to show that the statement $P_{o\_}$ ("The King of France is not bald") is ambiguous, in a way that the statement P_o

---

[6] "It remains to show how all the puzzles we have been considering are solved by the theory explained at the beginning of this article" (Russell 1905: 488). Note that the theory itself is not a solution to the puzzles.

("The King of France is bald") is not. As it is this ambiguity that is at the root of the puzzles, Russell's solution will consist in removing the indeterminacy. At the end of this development, one finds the following remark:

> The ambiguity as between primary and secondary occurrences is hard to avoid in [ordinary] language; but it does no harm if we are on our guard against it. In symbolic logic it is of course easily avoided. (Russell 1905: 489)

One could think that, by "symbolic logic," Russell means completely analyzed language, and that the clarification he offers is, as Kuusela thinks, to translate P_o and $P_{o\_}$ into P_{ca} and P_{ca}' or $\neg P_{ca}$, respectively. But in PM, Russell adds to his abbreviated notation a scope mark, which delimits the context in which the definite-description symbol occurs. Thus:

$$P_{o\_[\text{primary}]} = [(\imath x)(Kx)]\neg B(\imath x)(Kx)$$
$$P_{o\_[\text{secondary}]} = \neg[(\imath x)(Kx)]\, B(\imath x)(Kx)$$

In this notation, "the ambiguity as between primary and secondary occurrences ... is of course easily avoided" – but still, $P_{o\_[\text{primary}]}$ and $P_{o\_[\text{secondary}]}$ conceal their true logical form, respectively P_{ca}' and $\neg P_{ca}$.

Let me call *weakly logical* the PM notation with the definite-description symbol and its scope mark. It is clear that this symbolism avoids any logical and philosophical trouble by making explicit the boundary of the context in which the incomplete symbol occurs. It is also clear that this notation is not the same as the analyzed one. Should we consider this PM notation as something distinct from ordinary language? The question is difficult. There is a sense in which the two notations are distinct, since in ordinary language one must constantly be on guard against ambiguity between primary and secondary occurrences, which is not the case in the weakly logical language. But there is also a sense in which the PM notation is a simple extension of our ordinary language: The grammatical form of our ordinary sentences is preserved when we switch from one to the other.

Figure 3.1 below represents the relationships between the three types of notations. I have put the box of the PM notation between the two other boxes because Russell does not say if this notation is an extension of ordinary language or if it has to be regarded as an extension of the completely analyzed language. But even if he did not comment on the articulation between the weakly logical notation and the two other symbolisms, Russell clearly distinguished between the translation of the puzzling sentences into the completely analyzed language (represented by the "analysis" arrow) and

Clarification and Analysis in the Tractatus

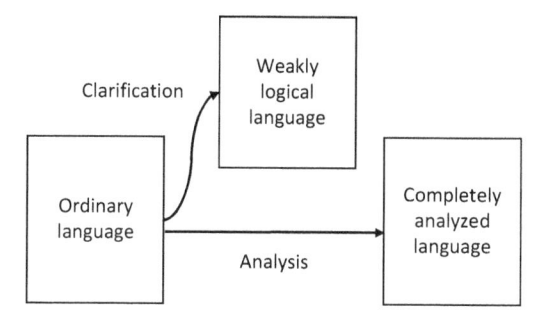

```
                    ┌──────────┐
                    │  Weakly  │
      Clarification │  logical │
                    │ language │
                    └──────────┘
                      ↗
┌──────────┐                        ┌──────────┐
│ Ordinary │                        │Completely│
│ language │───────────────────────→│ analyzed │
└──────────┘        Analysis        │ language │
                                    └──────────┘
```

Figure 3.1   The three notations and the distinction between analysis and clarification in Russell.

the translation into the PM notation (represented by the "clarification" arrow). This is the key point in my discussion: In his treatment of OD puzzles, Russell did not rest content with presenting analyses; he also offered solutions, which I have called clarifications in Figure 3.1. Russell did not explain why he considered that analysis did not suffice to solve the puzzles. But the example he gave to illustrate the distinction between the two types of occurrences, that of the yachtsman's joke, prompts us to suggest the following.[7] The translation into the analyzed language of the exchange between the unpleasant guest and the touchy owner would make the joke unintelligible, as it would cut the link between what the former says and what the latter responds to. On the contrary, the clarification makes visible the fact that the yachtsman is toying, in his reply, with the ambiguity created by the scope of the definite description. In the same way, what remains unsatisfactory in the process of analysis is that, once the translation is done, one no longer understands how one could have been troubled by the puzzles: P_{ca}' and $\neg P_{ca}$ are so different that one does not understand how they could have been confused in the first place. On the contrary, in the weakly logical language that Russell used in PM, one recognizes that $P_{o\_[primary]}$ and $P_{o\_[secondary]}$ are distinct, while at the same time seeing that, if one removes the scope operator, nothing distinguishes the two signs anymore. In other words, the clarification is better than the analysis because it makes us understand at the same time both that the propositions

---

[7] "I have heard of a touchy owner of a yacht to whom a guest, on first seeing it, remarked, 'I thought your yacht was larger than it is'; and the owner replied, 'No, my yacht is not larger than it is'. What the guest meant was, 'The size that I thought your yacht was is greater than the size your yacht is'; the meaning attributed to him is, 'I thought the size of your yacht was greater than the size of your yacht'." (Russell 1905: 489)

are distinct and how easy it is to confuse them (this is precisely what is lost in the analysis).

I will come back to this point in Section 3.5. Let us retain for the moment the content represented in Figure 3.1, and the idea that we can distinguish in Russell between an analyzed language and a logically ordered language.

3.4 Wittgenstein and Russell's Analysis

I do not claim here that the distinction I made between a logically analyzed and a logically ordered notation plays a prominent role in Russell's exoteric writings on philosophy and logical analysis. Indeed, most of the time, Russell oversimplifies his own practices and equates the philosophical task with that of logical analysis.[8] This, however, does not make the distinction I'm bringing forward any less relevant. Regardless of what he says, Russell's actual developments in PM and in OD are different from what we find in Frege, and they force us to distinguish between the move from $\neg P$ to P_{ca}' or $\neg P_{ca}$ (analysis) and the move from $\neg P$ to $P_{o\_[primary]}$ or $P_{o\_[secondary]}$ (clarification). This point is important because it shows that there were, in front of Wittgenstein's eyes, examples of logically ordered, and yet not analyzed, notations, and examples of philosophical clarifications that could not be equated to mere logical analyses.

Let me now come back to Kuusela's interpretation of the *Tractatus*. I do not contest that, for Wittgenstein, ordinary language contains "logically unclear expressions" that are at the source of philosophical problems (C1). Nor do I deny that, for Wittgenstein, a "symbolic logical notation" that is free from "logically unclear expressions" can, and should, be devised (C2). But I do not think that (C1) and (C2) entail that Wittgenstein views analysis as the method for solving philosophical problems (C3). Indeed, Wittgenstein could have endorsed (C1), (C2) and (C4), that is, he could have considered, as Figure 3.1 illustrates, that the "good method of

---

[8] See for instance: "Thus some kind of knowledge of logical forms, though with most people it is not explicit, is involved in all understanding of discourse. It is the business of philosophical logic to extract this knowledge from its concrete integuments, and to render it explicit and pure" (Russell 1914: 53). Note however that, even in his general characterization of the use of logic in philosophy, Russell emphasizes that identifying the logical forms is not the sole way logic and philosophy overlap. Thus: "Mathematical logic, even in its most modern form, is not *directly* of philosophical importance except in its beginnings. After the beginnings, it belongs rather to mathematics than to philosophy. Of its beginnings, which are the only part of it that can properly be called *philosophical* logic, I shall speak shortly. But even the later developments, though not directly philosophical, will be found of great indirect use in philosophising" (Russell 1914: 41).

philosophy" (6.53) consists in clarification, and that clarification is something different from analysis. Taking seriously the difference in approach between Frege and Russell leads us then to see that (C3) is independent of (C1) and (C2) and that the attribution of (C3) to Wittgenstein must be justified for its own sake and cannot rest on his adherence to (C1) and (C2). At this point, I have not established that (C3) is false and that (C4) is true; I have only pointed out the need to find reasons to support one or the other thesis. My main objection to Kuusela is that he provides no argument for (C3) over (C4) – in his book, (C4) is not even considered.

In the rest of the chapter, I will give two arguments for (C4). The first is an indirect one. It aims at showing that Wittgenstein's peculiar conception of logical analysis makes its use in philosophy extremely difficult. If Wittgenstein were to embrace (C3), then some part of 6.53, where Wittgenstein explains what "the right method of philosophy" is, would become unintelligible. The second argument, which will be presented in Section 3.5, holds that the developments around symbol and sign (3.32ff.) provide a natural framework for articulating the relationship between ordinary language and (what we called in Section 3.3) weakly logical language. This shows that Wittgenstein was aware of and used the distinction between the two processes of analysis and clarification depicted in Figure 3.1.

It is well known that Wittgenstein opposed Russell's "epistemic" conception of analysis in the *Tractatus*. While accepting the theory of descriptions, Wittgenstein rejected Russell's idea that logically simple names designate objects with which we are acquainted. There is no "experience" that we could consult to determine if a given expression is analyzed or not.[9] For Wittgenstein, a completely analyzed sentence is a truth-function of elementary propositions, and the only criterion to decide if a given proposition is an elementary one is logical: Elementary propositions are logically independent from each other. Thus, in 6.3751, Wittgenstein explains that the logical structure of color excludes that red and green, for instance, are in the same place at the same time in the visual field – in other words, that the propositions R = "red is in *A* at t" and G = "green is in *A* at t" are contradictory. But R and G are not truth-functions of some mutually incompatible propositions, and their contradiction is therefore not expressed in truth-functional terms. Therefore, R, G or both are not completely analyzed propositions. This example shows how far Wittgenstein is from Russell. From Russell's epistemological point of view,

---

[9] For a short presentation, see Engelmann (2021: 22–3, 30).

both R and G are elementary propositions, since one has an acquaintance with red and green patches, and with positions in our visual field. For Wittgenstein, the only criterion to take into account is logical independence, and the fact of being acquainted does not count for anything. The driving force of analysis in the *Tractatus* is not provided by the determination of the type of entity to be found at the end, as in Russell's case, but by the form the internal relations between propositions must take: In the completely analyzed language, all the logical relations between sentences would be represented in truth-functional terms.

There would be much to say on this point, but the main thing for us is that, given his view, Wittgenstein can say much less than Russell about the form of the completely analyzed language. No epistemic resource can teach us anything about elementary propositions, and logic simply tells us that there are elementary propositions, but not what they are. Wittgenstein calls the process of logical analysis *application of logic*, which "decides what elementary propositions there are" (5.557). And he insists on the fact that this application cannot be bypassed: It makes no sense to anticipate the process of analysis by characterizing in advance, and independently of the process itself, what one is supposed to find at its end. In other words, the logical criterion Wittgenstein uses to define the difference between a completely analyzed and a not completely analyzed language is purely negative: It guarantees the possibility of logical analysis but gives no indication of how to carry it out.

Now, in 6.53, Wittgenstein explains that the right method of philosophy would be this: "to say nothing except what can be said ...; and then always, when someone else wished to say something metaphysical, to demonstrate to him that he had given no meaning to certain signs in his propositions." The advocate of (C3) would see then in logical analysis an answer to someone who wishes to say something metaphysical, a way to delimit for him the boundaries of his language. This answer is relevant when one can propose a particular analysis (this is the case with the analysis of definite descriptions in Russell (1905)), or at least guidelines for an analysis (this is the case with the analysis of physical things in terms of sense data in (Russell 1914)). But Wittgenstein has nothing like that to offer. On the contrary, he seems to be content with having demonstrated the bare possibility of logical analysis and having made clear that the result of analysis can absolutely not be anticipated. How can we consider "there is a logical analysis of language in which all ordinary propositions are truth functions of elementary propositions" as an answer to the metaphysician? By rejecting Russell's epistemic approach, Wittgenstein deprives logical

Clarification and Analysis in the Tractatus　　　　　　　63

analysis of all its concrete content, making it difficult to see how his very abstract notion can be used as a means to solve metaphysical problems.

In reality, it seems that the fact Wittgenstein is content to guarantee the mere possibility of analysis, without engaging himself in any particular analysis, can be interpreted as a willingness to undermine the philosophical importance of analysis. With Russell, Wittgenstein would acknowledge that ordinary language disguises the thought and that logical analysis is required to uncover the logical form of the content expressed by colloquial sentences. But against Russell, Wittgenstein would maintain that the uncovering of the real form of thought is not required to deal with philosophical problems and to draw a limit to language: The demonstration at stake in 6.53 would point to another process, which Wittgenstein would seek precisely to bring out. Let me flesh out this suggestion by turning to sections 3.32ff.

3.5　Symbol and Sign

In Section 3.3, I remarked that Russell did not say anything about the relations between ordinary language, the analyzed symbolism and the in-between notation he introduced in OD. I would like to suggest that the passages in which Wittgenstein distinguishes between the sign and the symbol in the *Tractatus* (3.32ff.) can be read as an attempt to explain this articulation.[10]

In 3.1, Wittgenstein defines a proposition as a sensible expression of a thought. He then explains that a symbol is "every part of the proposition which characterizes its sense" (3.31) and that a sign is "the part of the symbol perceptible by the senses" (3.32). Thus, Wittgenstein starts with the notion of a proposition (3.3: "Only the proposition has sense; only in the context of a proposition has a name meaning"), comes then to the notion of symbol, and finally to the one of sign.[11] This priority given to proposition is in line with both Frege's context principle and Russell's reasoning about incomplete symbols. But the distinction between the parts of a proposition that refer to simple objects (names) and parts that do not (symbols that are not names) more specifically anchors the passage in Russell's thought. Indeed, Wittgenstein claims that, when a proposition is not completely analyzed, then at least one "propositional element signifies a complex" (3.24), and he clearly applies his concept of symbol

[10] I have developed this interpretation in Gandon (2002). See also Kremer (2012).
[11] Thus, the notion of a sign is not primary in the *Tractatus*, as it is the case today, in which we distinguish the syntactic, semantic, and pragmatic levels.

to notation that contains such nonanalyzed propositional parts. A symbol for Wittgenstein (any part of a proposition that contributes to its meaning) is therefore either a name or an incomplete symbol. Now, if this interpretation of the notion of a symbol is correct, then how to explain the distinction between symbol and sign?

Concerning this issue, three lines emerge in the sequence of paragraphs 3.32–3.325. First, Wittgenstein argues that the same sign (or the same kind of sign) can correspond to different symbols (respectively, to different kinds of symbols). Thus, "in the proposition "Green is green" – where the first word is a proper name as the last an adjective – these words have not merely different meanings but they are *different symbols*" (3.323). Second, he explains that, in the "language of everyday life," it often happens that the same sign belongs to different symbols (3.323) and that this is the root of "the most fundamental confusions (of which the whole of philosophy is full)" (3.324). There is thus a connection between the distinction sign/symbol and philosophical nonsense. Third, Wittgenstein argues that "in order to avoid these errors," one needs to use a symbolism that does not apply "the same sign in different symbols" and that does not apply "signs in the same way which signify in different ways" (3.325).

Let me start with this last point. Kuusela sees in this claim evidence that Wittgenstein, aligning himself with Frege and Russell, promotes the idea that it is by translating ordinary language into the logical notation that philosophical problems will be eliminated. But as we saw earlier, close attention to Russell's logical practice leads us to distinguish two different senses in which a notation can be said to be logical. Which sense is used in 3.325? Wittgenstein is quite clear: The "rules of logical syntax" require that differences between symbols (whether complete or incomplete) are reflected in differences between signs ("the same sign [must not be applied in] different symbols"); they do not require that only simple names occur in propositions. In other words, the PM notation, with its scope operator for definite description, in so far as it makes clear the difference between the two symbols that the sign "The King of France is not bald" confuses, "obeys the rules of logical syntax" and is logical in Wittgenstein's sense. Thus, contrary to what Kuusela suggests, the contrast brought forward by Wittgenstein in 3.324 is not the one between ordinary language and completely analyzed language (the two extreme boxes of Figure 3.1); it is the contrast between ordinary language and the two other kinds of notation (the box on the left and the two other ones).

Clarification and Analysis in the Tractatus

With that in mind, let us now turn to the two other features that are put forth in 3.32 ff. At first sight, it seems that what Wittgenstein is denouncing is simply the fact that ordinary language is sometimes ambiguous, that the same word can have different meanings. The examples he gives in 3.323 go in this direction – with the nuance that Wittgenstein stresses that the ambiguity concerns not only words but also their "grammatical categories" (think of the occurrences of the word "green"). There are two problems with this reading, however. The first is that Wittgenstein's symbols are not necessarily names: They do not necessarily have a reference. Assimilating the confusion denounced by Wittgenstein to lexical ambiguity is then difficult because a sign belonging to different symbols may very well belong to symbols that have no meaning in isolation. The second and more fundamental problem is that when we focus on the ambiguity of the signs, we assume that the identification of the signs is self-evident. But this is precisely the point that Wittgenstein rejects. In a notation that does not obey the rules of logical syntax, we no longer recognize which signs occur in our sentences. Let me explain. As I said, in the *Tractatus*, the symbol comes first, and a sign is defined as only a part (the perceptible one) of the symbol. It would therefore be a mistake to believe that we start with the sign "green," for example, which would then, in a second step, be associated with one (or several) symbol(s) – as if signs could be separated from symbols. Strictly speaking, the identity of a sign depends on the identity of the symbol it belongs to, and thus, the sign of the proper name "green" is not the same as the sign of the adjective "green." The two symbols have, of course, their visible parts in common, but these signs must not be detached from the symbolic wholes that contain them, and they should then be distinguished.

The use of the notion of ambiguity leads us to misunderstand the nature of the sign/symbol distinction that Wittgenstein sets up in 3.32ff. Lexical ambiguity directs our attention to the surroundings of the sign (its reference, its context, etc.), making us believe that the identification of signs is never a source of embarrassment. On the contrary, what Wittgenstein tells us here is that in ordinary language the recognition of signs (for what they are, i.e., parts of symbols) is the main source of confusion. The reference to OD is precious precisely because it allows to break with this possible misreading. As I explained in Section 3.3, Russell considers that $P_o = \neg B(\imath x)(Kx)$ is ambiguous. But the ambiguity at stake is not lexical: It is the kind of occurrence of the definite-description sign that is left undetermined. In the first case, the sign "$(\imath x)(Kx)$" is part of the symbol "$[(\imath x)(Kx)] \neg B (\imath x)(Kx)$," where the scope symbol is at the beginning of the sentence, while in the second case, "(ɩx)(Kx)" is part of "¬[(ɩx)(Kx)]B(ɩx)(Kx)." One can, as Russell in 1905, maintain that the same sign "(ɩx)(Kx)" occurs in P_0_, but then, one needs to distinguish between the two sorts of occurrence of this sign. The King of France's baldness puzzle, as the yacht owner's joke, can arise only because English speakers often fail to identify the very symbols that occur in their sentences (or equivalently, the type of occurrences of the component signs of their sentences).

I said above that both the completely analyzed language (left box of Figure 3.1) and the weakly logical language (intermediate box) obeyed the rules of logical syntax (3.324). I propose now to see Wittgenstein's distinction between sign and symbol as a way to better articulate the relationship between ordinary language (right box) and the weakly logical symbolism (intermediate box). In an important sense, the change from ordinary English to the weak logical notation is not a change of language. This contrasts with the way ordinary language relates to the analyzed notation: to go from one to the other, definitions, translation rules, are required. No translation rules are needed to switch from ordinary language to the weak logical notation, because both use exactly the same symbols. This is the reason why Wittgenstein can say that "all propositions of our colloquial language are actually, just as they are, logically completely in order" (5.563). At the same time, however, in ordinary English, the differences in symbols are not always reflected by differences in signs (speakers may fail to recognize their symbols in their signs), and this is why Wittgenstein says that a clarificatory task is needed. From this perspective, clarification is not a translation into a new language; clarification is an attempt to reconcile ordinary language with its misleading appearance – to make visible the logical order that the speaker sometimes loses sight of. I summarize in Figure 3.2 the main tenets of this reading.

Let me conclude by adding a few remarks on Wittgenstein's connection between philosophical problems and the sign-symbol distinction. I said in the previous section that 6.53 is difficult to understand if we stick to (C3): Wittgenstein's abstract notion of analysis cannot provide any answer to the metaphysician's demand. But does clarification, as we have just considered it, help to better understand 6.53? Let me repeat Wittgenstein's words:

> The right method would be this: to say nothing except what can be said ...; and then always, when someone else wished to say something metaphysical, to demonstrate to him that he had given no meaning to certain signs in his propositions [*ihm nachzuweisen, dass er gewissen Zeichen in seinen Sätzen keine Bedeutungen gegeben hat*]."

Clarification and Analysis in the Tractatus

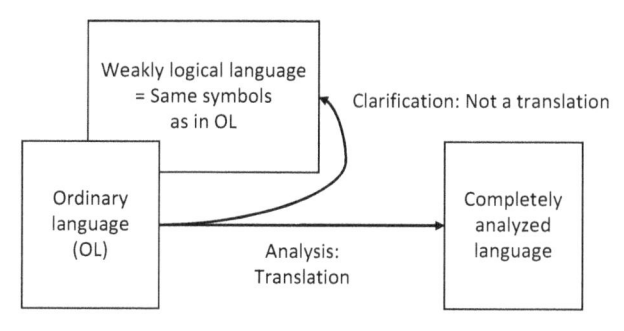

```
┌─────────────────────┐
│ Weakly logical language │
│   = Same symbols    │  ← Clarification: Not a translation
│      as in OL       │
└─────────────────────┘
┌──────────┐                    ┌──────────┐
│ Ordinary │                    │Completely│
│ language │ ─────────────────► │ analyzed │
│   (OL)   │      Analysis:     │ language │
└──────────┘     Translation    └──────────┘
```

Figure 3.2   Analysis and clarification in Wittgenstein.

The first thing to note is that Wittgenstein does not speak about symbols, but only about signs: To demonstrate to the metaphysician that he has given "no meaning to certain signs in his propositions" is thus compatible to Wittgenstein's 3.32ff idea that in ordinary language, some work needs to be done to uncover the symbols hidden in the signs. This is precisely what Russell does to solve the puzzles in OD. But what is really striking in 6.53 is Wittgenstein's recurrent reference to the metaphysician's own point of view: It is required to demonstrate to *him*, that *he* has not given meanings to certain signs in *his* propositions. It is thus the metaphysician who must be brought to recognize that he does not himself understand his own language. The dialogic feature of Wittgenstein's way of meeting the metaphysician's demand is not taken into account in (C3), since the philosophical treatment is then conceived as an analysis, that is, as a change of language. On the contrary, Wittgenstein's emphasis is explained by (C4): Clarification is an activity that takes place within ordinary language, that is, within the language used by the metaphysician.

Wittgenstein, in the *Tractatus*, does not give any examples of analyses of particular propositions. Nor does he give any examples of clarifications of particular philosophical problems. But in our reading, Wittgenstein would manage to state something substantial in 6.53: Contrary to what Russell claims, the correct method in philosophy is not analysis but another process – clarification. The irony is that Wittgenstein would be relying here on what Russell is doing to contest what he is saying.

3.6   Conclusion

Kuusela believes that if (C1) (ordinary language gives rise to philosophical nonsense) and (C2) (one can devise a logical notation free from logically unclear symbol) are true, then (C3) (to solve the philosophical disease, one must abandon ordinary language for the logically analyzed language) is also true. The main goal of this chapter has been to show that this argument is wrong. There is, at the time, in Wittgenstein's immediate environment, a counterexample to Kuusela's reasoning: Russell, in OD and then in PM, endorsed (C1) and (C2), and yet used a notation that was logically in order without being logically analyzed. Therefore, if we want to defend (C3), we must find other justifications than (C1) and (C2). It is not enough to say that ordinary language is not logically clarified and that completely analyzed language is, to warrant (C3).

My second aim, however, has been to show that (C3) is actually false and that (C4) is true. I have claimed that Wittgenstein does not identify clarification with analysis. The case is, however, more delicate than the previous one. I have merely presented here two arguments in favor of the thesis.

The first one has to do with Wittgenstein's criticism of Russell's epistemological notion of analysis. The result of such a critique is to remove the possibility of even a rough characterization of the completely analyzed language (the right box of Figures 3.1 and 3.2). It seems difficult to subordinate the treatment of the philosophical problem to the performance of a task for which Wittgenstein gives no more than general guidelines – and indeed claims that it is absurd to attempt to give any. The solution consisting in distinguishing the task of philosophical clarification from the task of logical analysis seems to me to impose itself more naturally.

The second argument, more direct, is based on the difficult sections 3.32ff. I first showed that Wittgenstein's definition of a notation that "obeys the rules of logical grammar" in 3.325 does not exclude notations containing incomplete symbols, thus unanalyzed notations. I also showed that sections 3.321–4 on the confusion between symbols due to the identity of their signs fit perfectly with what Russell says about the difference between primary and secondary occurrence in OD. What Wittgenstein denounces in this passage is not the lexical ambiguity of certain signs, but the difficulty of identifying our signs and symbols in ordinary language. Consequently, the relation between ordinary language and clarified ordinary language (the two overlapping boxes in Figure 3.2) would not be the relation between two different notations, which would have to be translated into each other, but the relation, within the same language, between a presentation where issues concerning the identification of signs may arise, and a presentation where the differences between symbols are reflected in the signs.

CHAPTER 4

The Fish Tale: The Unity of Language and the World in Light of TLP 4.014

Hanne Appelqvist

> *Music influences the listener not only and absolutely through its own beauty but simultaneously as the sounding picture of the great movements in the universe.*
>
> Eduard Hanslick, *Vom Musikalisch-Schönen*

4.1 Introduction

In 4.014 of the *Tractatus*, Wittgenstein writes:

> A gramophone record, the musical thought, the musical notation, the sound waves, all stand to one another in that internal depicting relation that holds between language and the world.
>
> They all share their logical construction.
>
> (Like the two youths, their two horses, and their lilies in the fairy tale. In a certain sense, they are all one.).[1]

When read literally, the remark says that in music we find a manifestation of the essential relation that holds between language and the world, a relation made possible by the logical form the two share. In the following, I argue that we should adopt the literal reading. This is to say that Wittgenstein's reference to music should not be seen as a mere figurative embellishment of the core claim of the *Tractatus*'s picture theory of language. Instead, Wittgenstein's appeal to music is deliberate, intended to illuminate the character of logical form and how deep into reality that form penetrates.

I argue further that we should take the other reference to the arts in 4.014 equally seriously. This is Wittgenstein's allusion to the fairy tale *The Gold-Children* by Brothers Grimm, given in brackets as an explanation of

---

[1] I am here drawing on the translation by David Stern, Joachim Schulte, and Katia Saporiti, forthcoming from Cambridge University Press.

the oneness of language and the world. Once unpacked, the reference to the fairy tale gives us a reason to doubt Peter Sullivan's seminal argument that the *Tractatus* undercuts rather than embraces the need to offer a philosophical explanation of the unity of language and the world. In the tale, the oneness of the youths, their horses, and lilies arises out of their common origin: a golden fish. The fish, I will argue, stands for the metaphysical subject as that which grounds the unity of language and the world even if it cannot be found *in* the world.

I begin by discussing Wittgenstein's early conception of logical form as the form of reality. I propose that logical form, in Wittgenstein's early sense, incorporates features that for Kant belong to transcendental aesthetic rather than transcendental logic. Next, I connect this proposal to Wittgenstein's appeal to music as a manifestation of the interdependence of language and the world. I then turn to Sullivan's argument according to which the *Tractatus*'s notion of a metaphysical subject – the most plausible candidate as an explanation of the interdependence in question – is the target of Wittgenstein's criticism. I argue that Wittgenstein does not merely set language and reality against each other as "the interdependent notions of formal totalities" but points to an explanation thereof (Sullivan 1996: 209). This explanation accords with Kant's way of explaining the *a priori* connection between thought and empirical reality.

4.2 The Form of Reality

The claim that a musical thought, the recording, the notation, and the sound waves are "in a certain sense one" emerges as an elaboration of the *Tractatus*'s core idea according to which propositions are pictures of reality (4.014). The oneness of the four musical phenomena is said to reside in their having a common logical construction, *der logische Bau*, despite the fact that at the surface level, the notation, say, does not look like a picture of the sounding reality of a music (4.014, see 4.011). The point thus echoes the Tractarian dictum according to which the possibility of picturing requires that the picture and the pictured have the same form, which an analysis of the picture would uncover.

In the beginning of the *Tractatus*, Wittgenstein explains the requirement of shared form for the possibility of picturing by two examples, both drawn from the sensible domain. He writes: "A picture can depict any reality whose form it has. A spatial picture can depict anything spatial, a coloured one anything coloured, etc." (2.171). Language, which consists of pictures of possible states of affairs, is neither spatial nor colored. Yet, Wittgenstein argues, in its "two-dimensional script," language is capable of picturing all of reality, where "reality" stands not just for actual facts but for all imaginable states of affairs (Wittgenstein 1979: 6; see TLP 3.02). For this to be possible, then, that is, for language to be able to picture all possible states of affairs, including spatial and colored ones, it must have the form of reality itself. And this is precisely what Wittgenstein affirms: "What any picture, of whatever form, must have in common with reality, in order to depict it – correctly or incorrectly – in any way at all, is logical form, i.e. the form of reality" (2.18). Like Kant's pure concepts of understanding, the logical forms of language have an internal, *a priori* connection with the forms of empirical reality (Kant 1998: A57/B81; TLP 4.03, 5.4711, 5.4731). However, unlike Kant's categories, Wittgenstein's logical forms are inexpressible. As every meaningful proposition already presupposes logical form, that form cannot be expressed in language. Instead, it is *seen directly*, without the mediation of discursive concepts, in propositions of logic and mathematical equations that have no empirical content (4.041, 4.12–4.121, 6.12, 6.22, 6.2321).

But what is that form of reality? And how does logical form relate to the spatial and colored forms that Wittgenstein mentions as possible, if more limited, pictorial forms? In the *Tractatus*, Wittgenstein famously states that "logic is transcendental" – a statement that some commentators have connected to Kant's transcendental logic (TLP 6.13).[2] Interestingly, the idea of *aesthetics* as transcendental surfaces in the book as well, though it is rarely connected with Kant's account of transcendental aesthetic as the *a priori* investigation of pure forms of sensibility, namely, space and time (TLP 6.421). Insofar as the transcendentality of aesthetics is discussed, this is done in the context of Wittgenstein's early ethics. Indeed, the idea that there could be anything like transcendental aesthetic in Kant's sense in the *Tractatus* is explicitly denied by Hao Tang and Peter Sullivan. According to Tang, "sensibility or anything resembling sensibility is not even a topic for the *Tractatus*" (Tang 2011: 601). Sullivan, in turn, considers the resemblance between Wittgenstein's claim about thinkability as the mark of logical form and Kantian pure intuition of geometry but argues that the seeming similarity is "superficial" and "breaks down all over the place" (Sullivan 1996: 199; see TLP 3.02). But does it? Besides, if nothing resembling sensibility is even a topic for the *Tractatus*, then what should we make of Wittgenstein's repeated references to space, time, and color in

---

[2] See, for example, Stenius (1960), Kannisto (1986), Glock (1992, 1997), Moore (2013), Appelqvist (2016).

the course of the book (see, e.g., 2.0121, 2.013–2.0131, 2.0251, 3.032, 3.1431, 4.123, 6.3611, 6.3751)?

According to Wittgenstein, "[e]very picture is *at the same time* a logical one. (On the other hand, not every picture is, for example, a spatial one.)" (2.182.) I want to suggest that, while not every logical form we encounter in reality is spatial, say, some forms are spatial in essence. This is to say that logical form actually encompasses spatial, temporal, as well as colored forms. One could naturally object by saying that spatiality and the color spectrum need not belong to the *form* of reality. However, in the *Tractatus*, the only available contrast for the form of reality is its *content*. And there are several reasons why space, time, and color (albeit with an important qualification to be discussed below) cannot fall on the side of content.

The distinction between form and content is characteristically Kantian. For Kant, empirical reality and thoughts about it always have form and sensible content. The forms of thought are investigated by transcendental logic, which treats the conceptually mediated *a priori* connection between those forms and empirical reality. But also intuitions providing the sensible content of our thoughts have an *a priori* aspect. In addition to sensory material derived from the senses, intuitions necessarily manifest space and time as *a priori* forms of sensibility itself, investigated in turn by transcendental aesthetic. Moreover, we can abstract away from the material content of intuitions, which is what we do in the case of mathematics. When considering *pure* intuitions independently of material content, our grasp of space and time is unmediated and direct. We can directly "intuit," for example, the correctness of a geometrical truth without subsuming the pure intuitions under concepts (Kant 1977: §12, 1998: A20–21/B34–36). Given that the correctness of geometrical truths is grounded in the *a priori* form of sensibility – indeed, of *imagination* as that aspect of sensibility that is independent of the immediately given sensory material – it is apodictically certain.[3] What is imaginable thus shows what is true *a priori* about empirical reality (see Stenius 1960: 217).

Wittgenstein introduces the distinction between form and content in the context of discussing objects. According to him, states of affairs are combinations of simple objects, which "contain the possibility of all situations" (2.014; see 2.0124). The objects are the world's substance, which subsists independently of what specific states of affairs happen to obtain (2.021, 2.024). This substance, Wittgenstein claims, "is form and

---

[3] For Kant, sensibility incorporates senses as well as imagination; imagination is at play when we represent to ourselves sensible objects in their absence (Kant 1998: B151).

content" (2.025). The forms of objects determine the way in which they can be combined with other objects. The possibilities of combination thus determine the objects' internal properties, properties that could not fail to obtain, as they flow from the logical forms of the objects (see 2.0123–2.0124). By contrast, the actual and hence contingent way in which a given object is combined with others determines the object's external properties. And it is the business of logic to operate with the possibilities embedded in the forms of objects: "Logic deals with every possibility and all possibilities are its facts" (2.0121).

Now, elaborating on the idea of substance as form and content, Wittgenstein states explicitly that "[s]pace, time, and colour (colouration) are forms of objects" (TLP 2.0251)[4]. While the remark is rarely scrutinized by commentators, it certainly seems to affirm that space, time, and color belong to the *form* of reality. Erik Stenius and Heikki Kannisto, who both read the *Tractatus* against the backdrop of Kant's transcendental idealism, are notable exceptions. Both take the remark seriously but refrain from giving space, time, and color the status of *logical* forms, thereby concurring with Kant's distinction between transcendental logic and transcendental aesthetic. Stenius argues that we should not equate the logical forms and the internal qualities of objects, despite the fact that Wittgenstein sometimes seems to use the terms synonymously. Rather, an object may have internal qualities, that is, qualities I "must know" if I know the object, that are not reducible to its logical form (2.01231). As an example of such an internal quality, Stenius mentions the second-order quality of being a color: "[t]o be a colour must … be described as an *internal* quality, and of course this internal quality of a predicate characterizes not only its logical form but also its content" (Stenius 1960: 80; see 77–81, 108–09). Building on Stenius, Kannisto acknowledges Wittgenstein's mention of the Kantian phenomenal forms of space, time, and color as forms of objects but intimates that these forms are not logical forms proper (Kannisto 1986: 133).

Stenius is right to distinguish between logical form and internal, that is, structural, properties of objects and states affairs. After all, Wittgenstein explicitly distinguishes between form and structure, claiming that the former grounds the possibility of the latter (see 2.033, 4.122). However, I find Stenius's explanation of the difference by reference to content

---

[4] Translation changed. The original reads "Raum, Zeit und Farbe (Färbigkeit) sind Formen der Gegenstände." I agree with Pasquale Frascolla that to translate "Färbigkeit" as "being coloured," as Pears and McGuinness do, confuses the point (see Frascolla 2004: 377). It also creates an unnecessary paradox with 2.0232, according to which "objects are colourless [farblos]."

problematic. Granted, the source of the confusion lies in the *Tractatus* itself, in Wittgenstein's suggestion that objects *as* the immutable substance of any imaginable world are *both* form and content. Taken together with his claim that "substance can only determine a form and not any material properties," one might assume that, like Kant, Wittgenstein takes the content of substance to have an *a priori* structure, in addition to its material properties (2.0231). Indeed, something like this seems to be implied by Wittgenstein's "Notes Dictated to G. E. Moore in Norway" in 1914. Discussing the internal relations that obtain between two shades of a color and between two spatially arranged spots, he claims that the "*form* of the latter is part of the *form* of the former" and concludes that we "might thus give sense to the assertion that logical laws are *forms* of thought and space and time *forms* of intuition" (Wittgenstein 1979: 118, emphasis in original).

However, it is difficult to find any clear distinction between transcendental logic and transcendental aesthetic in the *Tractatus*, unless we take Wittgenstein's remark that "[i]n geometry and logic alike a place is a possibility" to be an indication of just that (3.411; see also 3.032–3.05). Rather, it seems that what for Kant belongs to the domain of sensibility in its *a priori* application is contained within the *Tractatus*'s notion of logical form. What makes logic *a priori* according to the *Tractatus* is that the limits of logic and the limits of possible thought coincide (5.4731, 5.6–5.61). And there certainly are limits to what can be thought or imagined about the spatio-temporal domain. Wittgenstein states: "Each thing is, as it were, in a space of possible states of affairs. This space I can imagine empty, but I cannot imagine the thing without the space" (2.013). For Kant, this very point serves to establish the *apriority* of space as a pure form of sensibility: "Space is a necessary representation, *a priori*, which is the ground of all outer intuitions. One can never represent that there is no space, although we can very well think that there are no objects to be encountered in it" (Kant 1998: A24/B38). So if:

(i) "we are quite unable to imagine spatial objects outside space or temporal objects outside time" (2.0121);
(ii) "what is thinkable is possible too" (3.02);
(iii) "logic deals with every possibility" (2.0121);

and

(iv) "the only necessity that exists is *logical* necessity" (6.375);

then

(v) space and time must belong to the domain of logic.

What I am proposing, then, is that while the form of reality is not exhausted by spatial and temporal forms, those forms belong to logic in Wittgenstein's peculiar sense. In other words, when Wittgenstein later claims about the law of causality that "[h]ere, as always, what is certain a priori proves to be something purely logical," we should not read the claim as one that restricts the scope of the *a priori* but rather as broadening the scope of the logical (6.3211; cf. Sullivan 1996: 198).

One obvious complication for the proposal at hand concerns Wittgenstein's inclusion of coloration as a form of objects. After all, Kant stresses repeatedly that in contrast to space and time, colors do not belong to the *a priori* forms of sensibility but only to its material content (Kant 1998: A28/B44). This very point underlies Kant's strictly formalist view that *pure* judgments of taste about painting or music, say, should not be grounded on colors or the timbres of musical instruments but only on the spatial or temporal structures manifest in those artworks (Kant 2000: 5:224–25; see also Kant 2006: 7:241).[5] Importantly, though, Kant notes that while sensations of colors are "given only *a posteriori*... their property of having a degree can be cognized *a priori*" (Kant 1998: A176/B218). And it is precisely *degrees* of color that Wittgenstein mentions in the *Tractatus* as examples of internal properties of objects (2.0131). The same emphasis on degrees of color resurfaces in Wittgenstein's discussion of the formal properties of objects and states of affairs, and the corresponding internal (structural) properties of facts. He writes: "A property is internal if it is unthinkable that its object should not possess it. (This shade of blue and that one stand, eo ipso, in the internal relation of lighter to darker. It is unthinkable that *these* two objects should not stand in this relation)" (4.123).

The reading of phenomenal forms as logical accords with Wittgenstein's later article "Some Remarks on Logical Form," written in 1929. There, Wittgenstein argues that in the "logical analysis of actual phenomena,"

> we find logical forms which have very little similarity with the norms of ordinary language. We meet with the forms of space and time with the whole manifold of spatial and temporal objects, as colours, sounds, etc., etc., with their gradations, continuous transitions, and combinations in various proportions. (Wittgenstein 1993: 31)

---

[5] In the *First Critique*, Kant still assumes that, in contrast to space and time as forms of sensibility, pure judgments of taste (like judgments of beauty) do not warrant a transcendental investigation but are materially grounded. However, he later changes his mind and, in the *Third Critique*, seeks to establish the legitimacy of pure judgments of taste as judgments that have an *a priori* ground (see Kant 1998: A132/B172; 2000: 5:168–70 and "Editors introduction," xiii–xiv).

As examples of phenomena that manifest such gradation, he mentions the length of musical intervals, the pitch of tones, and the brightness or redness of a shade of color, and argues that a "characteristic of these properties is that one degree of them excludes any other" (Wittgenstein 1993: 32). In describing such phenomena, Wittgenstein systematically uses the notion of "logical form" and emphasizes that propositions about the impossibility of, say, a note being a one-lined g and being a one-lined e "do not express an experience but are in some sense tautologies" (Wittgenstein 1993: 32). These examples accord with the *Tractatus*. Indeed, the only examples given about the internal properties of objects are examples drawn from the aesthetic domain, indicating necessities that can be grasped *a priori*. Wittgenstein writes:

> A speck in the visual field, though it need not be red, must have some colour: it is, so to speak surrounded by colour-space. Notes must have *some* pitch, objects of the sense of touch *some* degree of hardness, and so on. (2.0131.)

And

> [T]he simultaneous presence of two colours at the same place in the visual field is impossible, in fact logically impossible, since it is ruled out by the logical structure of colour. (6.3751)

It is difficult to avoid the impression that what is at stake is transcendental aesthetic in Kant's sense. At the very least, it is difficult to agree with the assessment that sensibility is not even a topic for the early Wittgenstein.

4.3 The Form of a Musical Thought

If we now consider 4.014 in light of the proposal that, for Wittgenstein, space and time belong to the form of reality, then the remark about the internal depicting relation that holds between a musical thought, its recording, notation, and the sound waves acquires new pertinence. It no longer looks like a mere illustration or a useful analogy of an abstract claim about the preconditions of representation but brings intuitive tangibility to the otherwise elusive and abstract notion of logical form.

The first point to notice is that music, whether imagined or actually performed, is spatio-temporal structure. It consists of tonal configurations that are in movement in a musical space, to appropriate Eduard Hanslick's famous characterization of music's content as tonally moving forms (cf. Hanslick 1986: 29). This is also why for Kant absolute music was an example of free beauty: as the tonal structure of a composition is based on pure forms of sensibility, it invites free contemplation of the purposiveness of its form independently of concepts (Kant 2000: 5:229, 5:225). If we now bear in mind Wittgenstein's point about the necessity of notes having *some* pitch, which allows the notes to combine together as an articulate musical theme, Wittgenstein's reference to the musical thought follows organically as the best available example of space and time as forms of objects (2.0131, 3.141).

The second, related point is that when Wittgenstein talks about the internal depicting relation that holds between language and the world, only the formal aspect of that relation is at stake. Like Kant's cognitions, propositions with sense always have both (logical) form and (empirical, material) content (see TLP 3.13; Kant 1998: A18/B33; Moore 2020: 38–40). The former is shown in the proposition, whereas the latter is attached to the proposition when the proposition is used to say something about a specific state of affairs: "A proposition *shows* how things stand *if* it is true. And it *says that* they do so stand" (4.022). Yet, a musical thought, which in German aesthetics typically indicates a musical theme or a tune, does not *say* anything.[6] Accordingly, we cannot determine which of the four manifestations of music are supposed to stand on the side of language and which on the side of the world.

We might, of course, take the musical thought to stand for a proposition or thought (TLP 4). In the same vein, we could take the recording and the musical notation to correspond to propositional, spoken or written, signs (cf. 3.11). The sound waves, in turn, could be seen as the state of affairs "pictured" by the musical thought. However, there is something unnatural and forced in such an analysis. As noted by Kannisto, the relation between a proposition and the state of affairs pictured by it is asymmetrical precisely because a proposition with sense always *says* or *asserts* something about a given state of affairs and only by doing that acquires empirical content (see 3.13). By contrast, instead of asserting anything about music, musical notation, the recording, and the sound waves just manifest the spatio-temporal structure of the musical

---

[6] For example, Eduard Hanslick uses "der musikalische Gedanke" in this way, arguing that the theme is the basic, self-standing unit of music (Hanslick 1986: 80). I take Wittgenstein to use "musical thought" in this very sense. In his early work, he compares a theme/melody to a proposition by reference to its articulateness and to a tautology by reference to its completeness (e.g., in Wittgenstein 1979: 40; TLP 3.141). In his later remarks on music, the focus is again on melodies, used as an object of comparison for sentences (Wittgenstein 1969a: 42, 166, 184, 2009: §§527, 531, 2016: 8:66).

thought in different ways. Hence, the relations between the four manifestations of the musical thought are symmetrical (Kannisto 1986: 73–74). The situation corresponds to Wittgenstein's characterization of temporal processes, which he evokes to explain Hertz's fundamentally Kantian idea that "only connexions that are *subject to law* are *thinkable*" (6.361):

> We cannot compare a process with "the passage of time" – there is no such thing – but only with another process (such as the working of a chronometer).
>
> Hence we can describe the lapse of time only by relying on some other process.
>
> Something exactly analogous applies to space: e.g. when people say that neither of two events (which exclude one another) can occur, because there is *nothing to cause* the one to occur rather than another, it is really a matter of our being unable to describe *one* of the two events unless there is some sort of asymmetry to be found. And *if* such an asymmetry *is* to be found, we can regard it as the *cause* of the occurrence of the one and the non-occurrence of the other. (6.3611, emphasis in original)

Here, we might as well substitute "musical thought" for the "process" to bring the point home, which is in fact exactly what Wittgenstein later does. When addressing the question of whether the necessity we hear in music can be explained, he repeatedly states that we can only place the tune side by side with something else that manifests the same structure (see, e.g., Wittgenstein 1969a: 166, 1999: 65, 2009: §527, 2016: 9:39). We cannot objectify or take as our object of comparison the form (space and time) that makes such structures possible, because that would require that we positioned ourselves outside of those forms.[7]

It is impossible to find an asymmetry between the four musical phenomena and hence a clear boundary between language and the world in the example, because a musical thought is mere spatio-temporal structure without any empirical content (save the material properties of sounds). The musical thought or a theme does not say anything; it only displays its constituent notes in determinate relations to one another (cf. 2.14).

---

[7] Incidentally, we could take this to be the point underlying Wittgenstein remark on Kant's problem about the right and the left hand, if we want to avoid deeming Wittgenstein's argument "just awful" (6.36111; see Fogelin 1987: 90). For Kant, the fact that the two cannot be made to coincide in a three-dimensional space entailed that space is transcendentally ideal (Kant 1977: §13). In light of 6.3611, Wittgenstein's claim that this would be possible if the right hand could be turned round in four-dimensional space could be seen as yet another illustration of the impossibility of transcending space as already conditioning the imaginable. This cannot be done any more than we can devise "another language dealing with the structure of the first language" (Wittgenstein 1974b: xxii).

Hence, unlike propositions with sense, the musical thought is not answerable to an external standard with which it could be compared (cf. 2.223, 4.05). In this regard, it is more like mathematical propositions, whose "correctness can be perceived without its being necessary that what they express should itself be compared with the facts in order to determine its correctness" (6.2321; see Kant 1977: §2).[8] For while a musical thought has no empirical content, it is not mere gibberish. In the course of explaining what it means for a proposition to be an articulate fact, that is, a structure made possible by logical form, Wittgenstein notes that a "theme in music is not a blend of notes" (3.141). It is not a blend of notes but a structure that is based on the forms of the notes, that is, their possibilities of combining together. As Wittgenstein puts it in 1915: "A tune is a kind of tautology, it is complete in itself; it satisfies itself" (Wittgenstein 1979: 40; 4.3.15).

The final point concerns the relation between the subject of language and the form of reality. We began from Wittgenstein's central idea that propositions have sense in virtue of being pictures of possible states of affairs and that this presupposes that the two have the same form. An equally central idea of the *Tractatus* is that a picture – whether spatial, colored, or propositional – cannot depict its pictorial form (2.172). In order to do that, one should step outside of the pictorial form in question and depict it from without, as it were. If the form in question is the form shared by language, thought, and reality, this naturally cannot be done. This point is usually treated as the core of Wittgenstein's rejection of synthetic *a priori*. Unlike Kant, for whom the bounds of theoretical reason may be neatly tabulated as categories of judgments, given that for him language and thought can legitimately go beyond the domain of knowledge, Wittgenstein's boundaries for each coincide. We cannot express the *a priori* forms of our thought in language. Instead, the apriority of logic resides in that it is impossible to think illogically, that is, without our thoughts already conforming to that form (5.4731).[9]

---

[8] According to Kant, "we must observe that properly mathematical propositions are always judgments *a priori*, and not empirical, because they carry with them necessity, which cannot be obtained from experience" (Kant 1977: 4:268). Wittgenstein, in turn, notes that "[a] priori knowledge that a thought was true would be possible only if its truth were recognizable from the thought itself (with anything to compare it with)" (3.02). Tautologies meet this description. So do musical thoughts, even if "truth" sounds awkward when applied to music. Wittgenstein himself talks about necessity (Wittgenstein 1999: 65, 2016: 39).

[9] Those who deny that logic is *a priori* for the early Wittgenstein usually appeal to his statement according to which "[t]here is no *a priori* order of things" (5.634). However, as the remark taken as a whole indicates, Wittgenstein is here talking about facts which are, of course, contingent. "Whatever we can describe at all could be other than it is" and hence "[t]here are no pictures that are true a priori" (5.634, 2.225; see Kannisto 1986: 152).

However, as stressed repeatedly by A.W. Moore, Wittgenstein acknowledges modes of "rational engagement with things" that fall outside the scope of meaningful language and thought (Moore 2013: 253).[10] These include, among other things, knowledge of objects, logical inference, and the practice of mathematics – notions that have loomed in the background of my discussion. While Moore includes evaluation and thereby aesthetics among kinds of ineffable knowledge we can find in the *Tractatus*, he claims that the opening bar of Beethoven's fifth symphony is only "*trivially* ineffable*,*" like a sock (Moore 2003: 175, 2013: 253). Unlike the nonsensical sentences of the *Tractatus* that initially look like meaningful propositions, the opening of Beethoven's fifth "clearly [does] not to have content that makes [it] either true or false" (Moore 2003: 175, see 178). In this respect, Moore argues, the musical case differs from cases that Wittgenstein evokes as examples of ineffable understanding. The latter present "illusions that manifest the urge we have, itself ill-conceived, to transcend our limitations: illusions that arise when we try to apply concepts that are adapted to these limitations as though they were not, indeed as though they were not adapted to any limitations at all" (Moore 2003: 189).

While I otherwise admire Moore's analysis of Wittgenstein's notion of ineffability, I am not convinced that a musical phrase is ineffable only trivially, though a single bar may not be enough to bring the point home. In my understanding, a complete musical theme presents an illusion relevantly similar to those nonsensical sentences that express our urge to transcend our limitations – or at least presented such an illusion to Wittgenstein himself. This illusion arises from the cunning similarity between a proposition and a theme, brought up by Wittgenstein already in 1915 and resurfacing repeatedly for the rest of his career (Wittgenstein 1969a: 167, 1979: 40, 2009: §527, 2016: 8:66). It is this very likeness that prompts Wittgenstein to make the following remark in 1935: "'This tune says *something*', and it is as though I had to find *what* it says" (Wittgenstein 1969a: 166. See Wittgenstein (1967: §161, 2009: §531)). But given that the tune is mere structure, there is no answer to this question, which shows the question itself to be nonsensical (see TLP 6.5).[11] The illusion thus lies in the attempt to apply empirical, "determinate" concepts to something

---

[10] See also Moore (2003).
[11] For the same reason, given that it is mere structure, the tune is neither true nor false in the sense in which propositions with sense are true or false. I would be willing to propose, though, that the "completeness" of the tune and the fact that "it satisfies itself," may be treated as a feature relevantly similar to the unconditional truth of a tautology or the correctness of a mathematical equation (Wittgenstein 1979: 40). See 4.461, 6.2321. But that would require another argument.

that is mere structure. This, of course, is the very essence of a transcendental illusion, namely, to confuse the transcendental with the empirical.

As noted above, for Kant, transcendental aesthetics was not only, or even primarily, an investigation of evaluative judgments of beauty but covered our engagement with the domain of sensibility in its *a priori* application in general. The characteristic feature of aesthetics as such is its direct, unmediated character. Geometrical truths are grasped directly in imagination, they are "intuited" or *seen*. In the same way, the validity of judgments about the formal purposiveness of musical structures, which for Kant was nothing but their beauty, depends on their being independent of determinate concepts applicable to empirical reality (Kant 2000: 5:211, 5:339–40). What I am suggesting is that in our grasp of a musical theme as a paradigm example of a direct engagement with the domain of sensibility, we have a model for a "rational mode of engagement with things," which is neither mystical in the pejorative sense of the term nor mere gibberish but exemplifies the ineffability of logical form.

In the *Tractatus*, Wittgenstein explains the form's ineffability as follows:

> Propositions cannot represent logical form: it is mirrored in them.
> What finds its reflection in language, language cannot represent.
> What expresses *itself* in language, *we* cannot express by means of language.
> Propositions *show* the logical form of reality.
> They display it. (4.121)

I find it no coincidence that Wittgenstein uses exactly the same expression in relation to logical form that he later repeatedly employs in relation to music. Moreover, the point is consistently the same: music, like logic and, later, grammar, "expresses itself." As a response to the illusion prompted by its likeness with a sentence Wittgenstein states that a musical theme

> does not say anything such that I might express in words or pictures what it says. And if, recognizing this, I resign myself to saying "It just expresses a musical thought", this would mean no more than saying "It expresses itself." (Wittgenstein 1969a: 166)

In the same context, Wittgenstein compares the musical illusion with another one from the aesthetic domain, namely, our quest to find out what a face expresses when only we give ourselves up to the features before us. So is it a mere coincidence that when, in the *Tractatus*, Wittgenstein discusses internal properties of facts, exemplified by the internal relation between a lighter and darker shade of blue, he claims that these could be called *features* of facts "in the sense in which we speak of facial features" (4.1221, see 4.124)?

Wittgenstein gives propositions of logic and mathematical equations a unique role in his classification of different kinds of propositions. Meaningful propositions do manifest logical form, but since their empirical content invites a comparison with reality to determine the proposition's truth value, that form is not transparently visible. Propositions of logic, on the other hand, are tautologies without empirical content and hence without sense. They are not nonsensical, because they display their own form, which ensures their unconditional truth (4.461). Propositions of mathematics, in turn, are equations and as such nonsensical "pseudo-propositions" (6.2–6.21). But in spite of this difference, tautologies and mathematical equations come together in one important respect. They both reveal the form of reality: "[t]he logic of the world, which is shown in tautologies by the propositions of logic, is shown in equations by mathematics" (6.22). In my reading, musical themes belong to the same camp, and this is the point we should bring home from 4.014. The logical construction of a musical thought mirrors the spatial and temporal forms of reality without latching on to any material content. Accordingly, as Wittgenstein notes in 1915, "[k]nowledge of the nature of logic will . . . lead to knowledge of the nature of music" (Wittgenstein 1979: 40).

4.4 What Lies at the Limit?

If the form of reality expresses itself, covertly, in propositions and more overtly in tautologies, mathematical equations, and musical tunes, then what grounds that relation? Those who read the *Tractatus* as a Kantian work usually see a parallel between Wittgenstein's reasoning and Kant's proposed solution. They take Wittgenstein's argument to begin from the assumption that there are (*de facto*) meaningful propositions that, as articulate pictures of possible states of affairs, have their logical form in common with what they picture. Moreover, they take Wittgenstein to hold that we can investigate that form by investigating the domain of the imaginable. But the question remains on what grounds are we justified (*de jure*) in our application of logical form to empirical reality. This is a question that Wittgenstein himself evokes. After noting that logic is "prior to the question 'How', not prior to the question 'What?,'" he asks: "And if this were not so, how could we apply logic?" (5.552–5.5521). The answers provided in the literature diverge even among the supporters of the Kantian interpretation in accordance with how much weight is placed on the explanatory role of the metaphysical subject that Wittgenstein introduces in the 5.6s.[12]

Following Kant's argumentative framework, there are three available explanations. According to the first, empirical reality imprints its form on our thought. However, leaving the necessities of logic at the mercy of contingent, empirical processes does not fit well with Wittgenstein's view of the strict impossibility of illogical thought, not to mention his view that philosophy and natural sciences are qualitatively different kinds of enterprises (Kant 1998: Bxvi–xviii; TLP 5.4731, 4.111). The second, equally dissatisfying option is to assume that the form of reality and the form of thought are independent of one another, yet (mysteriously) in harmony. This view is hard to square with Wittgenstein's claim that while logic "is prior to the question 'How?,'" it is "not prior to the question 'What?'" (5.552). The third, Kantian explanation is that the forms of thought and reality have a common source. The two have an *a priori* relation, because those forms arise together with the metaphysical subject as their seat and vehicle (Kant 1998: A346–348/B404–406; B137–138). Hence, Wittgenstein's statement that "The *limits of my language* mean the limits of my world" is taken to imply a subject similar to Kant's "I" of the "I think" that accompanies every thought as the formal point to which the world is given (5.6; see Kant 1998: B131–132).

According to Sullivan, the very question of the source of the isomorphism between language and reality should be resisted. In his reading, the *Tractatus* aims at showing that no explanation is needed. In doing so, it takes Kant's transcendental idealism, along with his account of the metaphysical subject, to be a tempting but ultimately misconceived position. For Sullivan, "the requirement for something to be thinkable is not a tightening up of any broader conceptual space. In thought, the requirement excludes nothing, and in language nothing is excluded but straightforward, ordinary nonsense" (Sullivan 1996: 200). The limits of language and of the world do coincide, but unlike Kant's limits of theoretical reason these limits are not limitations, limited by something ineffable. Instead, "the notions of language and world ... are the interdependent notions of formal totalities" (Sullivan 1996: 209). This interdependence finds a crystallized expression in the general form of a proposition "This is how

---

[12] Stenius and especially Kannisto follow the Kantian route to its conclusion by assuming a metaphysical subject as the source of the structural isomorphism, whereas Glock takes the answer to lie in the ineffable metaphysical essence of reality. See Stenius (1960: 218–22), Kannisto (1986: 124–30, 149–52), Glock (1992: 16–20, 1997: 292–97).

things stand," which Sullivan equates with truth-functionality or intrinsic truth-directedness as the characteristic feature of propositions (Sullivan 1996: 197, 209; see TLP 4.5). The metaphysical subject, in turn, is the "inevitable and illusory upshot of the vain attempt to comprehend this feature 'from without'" (Sullivan 1996: 197). It "neither rests on nor brings into play any substantial or determinate conception of the subject" (Sullivan 1996: 211). For Sullivan, something like the *a priori* status of space and time, while *formal*, would be enough to make the conception of the subject substantial.

The main target of Sullivan's criticism is what he calls an "object-centred" reading of the *Tractatus* that gives a "quasi-extensional" character to notions that really are formal in nature, such as language, world, proposition, and object.[13] The object-centered reading takes the isomorphism between language and reality to be grounded in the combinatorial possibilities of objects. However, in doing so it fails to acknowledge that for Wittgenstein objects are "a final logical demand, not a first epistemological anchor" out of which possible states of affairs can be cobbled (Sullivan 1996: 205). Given that notion of an object is a *formal* concept, it is nonsensical to say "There are objects" (4.1272). Accordingly, Sullivan argues, Wittgenstein's remarks about *knowing* objects should not be understood as entailing acquaintance but simply as "having the notion of an object" in general (Sullivan 1996: 207; cf. TLP 2.0123–2.01231, 5.524). In other words, the limits attached to formal concepts are "not to be conceived in any such extensional fashion as the object-centred view recommends; instead grasp of them is equivalent to appreciating the structural features of their instances" (Sullivan 1996: 207).

I agree with Sullivan's rejection of the extensional understanding of the limits of language if this means that we are to think about objects as entities, like sense data, that *exist* in the empirical domain. I also agree that Wittgenstein introduces the notion of an object as a logical requirement, to guarantee the independence of the sense of one elementary proposition from the truth of another (2.0211). Finally, I agree that truth-functionality or bi-polarity is the essential feature of propositions that *have sense*, and hence of language understood as the totality of pictures of states of affairs. However, I do not believe that these points entail that there is nothing more to the grasp of logical form than the appreciation of the structural

---

[13] Sullivan mentions Jaakko Hintikka, David Pears, and Peter Hacker as proponents of the view. Hans-Johann Glock would likely qualify as well (see fn. 10).

features of language and the world. So where is the difference between our views?

First, Sullivan claims that to treat objects as that which determines the limits of language and of the world entails an extensional or "quasi-extensional" understanding of those limits. However, if objects are form and content and if the limit of the world is equated with the *forms* of objects only, irrespective of their material content, then there need not be anything extensional in the account (see, e.g., 2.0123. 2.023–2.0231, 2.024). While it makes sense to talk about the *existence* of states of affairs, that is, facts comprising empirical reality, and thereby imply something about the material content of objects as the constituents of those facts, it is clearly nonsensical to talk about the *forms* of objects as if those forms were existing entities (2, 2.0231).[14] So when Wittgenstein states that "empirical reality is limited by the totality of objects," we should read him to refer to objects only as regards their forms (5.5561).

The second, related difference concerns the distinction between form and structure. As indicated by Sullivan's reminder of objects as the terminus rather than a starting point of our analysis of language, we do not encounter individual objects, let alone individual forms of objects, floating around in isolation of one another. Rather, we encounter the world as a totality of facts (including propositions), the structuredness or articulateness of which Wittgenstein invites us to appreciate (1.1, 2.0122, 2.0271–2.034). The structure of a state of affairs is "the determinate way in which objects are connected" (2.032). Similarly, the "determinate way" in which "the elements of a picture are related to one another" is called the structure of the picture (2.15). And again, the structure of a proposition – just as the structure of a melody – lies in the fact that "its elements (the words) stand in a determinate relation to one another" (3.14, see 3.141). But importantly, in each case, Wittgenstein states that the possibility of structure *depends* on form: "Form is the possibility of structure" (2.033; see 2.151, 4.12). This distinction is undermined by Sullivan's equation between the grasp of the limits of language and the appreciation of its structural features.

---

[14] The notion of existence does not apply to objects any more than it applies to the metaphysical subject or to God. When Wittgenstein writes that "[t]here are two godheads, the world and my independent I", equating "God" with the world as independent of my will, he is zeroing in on necessities (Wittgenstein 1979: 74). It is instructive to read the remark in light Wittgenstein later remark that echoes Kant's position: "God's essence is said to guarantee his existence – what this really means is that here what is at issue is not the existence of something" (Wittgenstein 1999: 94); see Kant (1998: A598/B626), Sullivan (1996: 196).

Max Black questions the very need of the distinction, whereas Stenius correctly notes that the structural properties of facts should not be equated with their logical form (see Stenius 1960: 79 ; Black 1964: 66). As I see it, the distinction is indispensable. This is because it corresponds to the relation between *transcendental* form on the one hand and the *empirical* structures made possible by that form, on the other. Empirical reality is given to us as structured facts: states of affairs, pictures, propositions, thoughts, and musical themes. And what specific structures happen to obtain is entirely contingent (2.0271, 2.225, 5.634). It is quite possible to appreciate the articulateness of such structures without acknowledging the form that makes the structure possible. We can, for example, appreciate the spatial intervals, chords, and cadences or the temporal rhythm, tempo, and agogics of music without giving a thought to spatiality or temporality as the forms that allow the realization of these structural properties. Yet, while the specific determinate way in which a given structure is put together is contingent and *a posteriori*, the possibility of constructing those structures in this or that way depends on the forms that ground those very possibilities. And this just means that the grasp of the *limits* of language and the world on the one hand and the appreciation of their *structural features* on the other are not the same thing, even if the latter, as contingent empirical facts, may lead us to realize the necessity of the former. Indeed, even if the latter may be required for the grasp of the former (5.552–5.5521).

Finally, for Sullivan, the essential characteristic of propositions is their truth-functionality, which he takes to be enough for fleshing out the formal relation between language and reality. Granted, the picturing capacity and hence the expressive power of language reaches as far as our ability to imagine how things might stand. In other words, the limits of language and of reality coincide, when "reality" is taken to mean the realm of imaginable possibilities (2.06, 3.001, 3.02). When conceived in that way, it certainly seems that we cannot draw a limit to either language or reality, for the structural frame of the general propositional form allows us to always imagine new possibilities. It thus seems that the limit of language is no limitation at all – a lesson we are supposed to take home from Wittgenstein's failing drawing of the visual field in 5.6331 (Sullivan 1996: 198).

But while the intrinsic truth-directedness of propositions with sense may articulate their relation with empirical states of affairs, such truth-directedness is not essential for propositions without empirical content. In Sullivan's view, the limit of language, understood in terms of truth-functionality, excludes nothing but "straightforward, ordinary nonsense" (Sullivan 1996: 200). Yet, propositions of logic and of mathematics and, as I have argued, musical tunes, while not meaningful, are not straightforward nonsense either. Propositions of logic are not nonsensical even if they are not bipolar and hence lack sense (4.461–4.4611). Mathematical equations do not express thoughts, yet are used as part of a logical method (6.2). And musical tunes are not mere gibberish, even if "unmusical people" may take them as such (Wittgenstein 1979: 41). In all three, the *form* of reality displays itself independently of *content* that is indispensable for truth-functionality that goes hand-in-hand with *saying* something (cf. 3.13).

For Wittgenstein, showing and saying are strictly mutually exclusive modes of expression (4.1212). And this just means that my relation to tautologies and musical tunes is markedly different from my relation to ordinary meaningful propositions. While meaningful propositions are compared with empirical reality, the form expressed in tautologies, pseudo-propositions, and musical tunes is seen directly, without mediation. While that form does not take us *outside* the world, it reveals that whatever is *inside* the world – contingent structures – is conditioned by a more fundamental, limiting, transcendental principle.

4.5 The Tale

In the beginning, I noted that Wittgenstein's allusion to the fairy tale *Gold-Children* gives us a reason to take seriously the Kantian interpretation according to which the metaphysical subject is ultimately responsible for the *form* of reality, if not for its material content. Wittgenstein claims that the two youths, their horses, and lilies are like the four manifestations of the musical theme, united by their common logical construction. In the tale, the unifying feature across the youths, horses, and lilies is that they are all golden. Moreover, they are golden neither by accident nor because one set of the pairs influences the others, but because they all spring from common origin, a golden fish. The fish, when caught by a fisherman, instructs the man to cut her in six pieces, give two of the pieces to his wife, two to his horse, and bury the remaining two in the ground. The man follows the instructions, and later his wife and horse alike have golden twins and two golden lilies grow out of the ground. As the golden twins grow up, they leave home but are ridiculed over their golden appearance. One of the youths returns home while the other covers himself in bearskins. When the latter is facing death, one of the golden lilies withers, alerting the other twin to go and save his brother's life.

The tale fits the Tractarian account of logical form in more respects than one. First, like logical form that manifests itself in language, thought, as well as reality, the golden fish has multiple realizations. Second, just as the structural isomorphism of the four manifestations of a musical thought is made possible by logical form, so too the shared golden coloration of the youths, horses, and lilies reflects the golden essence of the fish. Third, like the logical form of language is hidden from view by the arbitrary conventions of everyday language, the more adventurous youth covers his golden essence in bear skins while exploring the world (4.002). The implications of these parallels for the interpretation of logical form may not be particularly novel even if the Kantian interpretation informing them is contested. However, if taken seriously, the allusion to the fish adds an important aspect to the reading. This is because it suggests that the unity of language, thought, and the world is underwritten by a more fundamental principle. Just as the shared coloration of the youths, horses, and the lilies depends on their common origin in the golden fish, the formal unity of language, thought, and the world reflect their common origin, the metaphysical subject (5.632, 5.61).

Once the magical fish has been eaten by the fisherman's wife and the mare and absorbed by the earth, it disappears from sight and becomes discernable only in its subsequent manifestations. In this respect, the fish resembles Wittgenstein's characterization of the metaphysical subject that "shrinks into a point without extension," leaving behind only the "reality co-ordinated with it" (5.64). However, Wittgenstein claims that this very coordination, namely that "the world is my world," is why "philosophy can talk about the self in a non-psychological way" (5.641). To talk about something in a philosophical rather than a psychological (or more generally, scientific) way is to talk about the conditions of the world. Such talk has no empirical content and hence, when expressed in language, will inevitably be nonsensical (5.633; Wittgenstein 1979: 80). Yet, the metaphysical subject as a condition of the world shows itself in the fact that the world unified by its form is given to *me*. Like Kant's "I" of the "I think," the metaphysical subject cannot be found in the world, yet its necessity reveals itself in the unique point of coordination to which the world is given as the totality of imaginable states of affairs.[15]

Wittgenstein himself equates the limits of language with the limits of the world (5.6). These limits he aligns with the limits of logic and, further, with the metaphysical subject (5.61, 5.632). According to Sullivan,

---

[15] For an argument for the similarity between Kant and Wittgenstein on this point, see Moore (1987).

Wittgenstein eliminates all metaphysical baggage from these claims by showing that the limits are not limitations, given that the imaginable is not outrun by any "broader conceptual space" (Sullivan 1996: 200). To be sure, there is no transcendent domain outside the limits of language, even if Wittgenstein once, in my view carelessly, mentions the outside of the world (6.41). Rather, the reason Wittgenstein gives for his equation of the limits of logic with the limits of the world is that "logic pervades the world" (5.61). I have argued that logic pervades the world by expressing itself in structured (empirically real) facts, the possibilities of which are grounded in the (transcendental) forms of objects as the substance of the world. But if logic is an all-encompassing feature of the world, so is the metaphysical subject. The limits of the world go no further than my ability to imagine how things might be. Still, given that the "possibility of all imagery … is contained in the logic of depiction," the limits of imaginability in its *a priori* application reveal the sense in which the world is *my* world (4.015).

CHAPTER 5

That Which 'Is True' Must Already Contain the Verb: Wittgenstein's Rejection of Frege's Separation of Judgment from Content

Colin Johnston

5.1 Introduction

Frege presents it as a key advance of his logical theorising that it effects a 'separation of the act from the subject matter of judgment' (Frege 1984: 149). Propositional content is theoretically independent of, and so theoretically prior to, the acts of judgment and assertion. This would-be advance is not endorsed, however, by the Tractarian Wittgenstein, who on the contrary saw a profound misstep. Content, Wittgenstein insists, is explained only with judgment: a propositional content is fundamentally something *to be judged*.

Frege's separation is built into his conceptual notation, and Wittgenstein's contrary position likewise pervades his work, essentially informing the Tractarian treatment of negation and denial, the understanding of logical propositions, the conception of inference, the commitment to bivalence, and more besides. It would be a major project to trace such threads in Wittgenstein. In this essay, I want to take on the more limited task of examining a ground Wittgenstein offers for his position. In the 4.06s, Wittgenstein considers and rejects certain views he ascribes to Frege concerning sense and assertion. Indeed, Wittgenstein appears in 4.063 to offer an argument against these ascribed views. This section has I think been underestimated. Certain commentators have thought that its reasoning is vitiated by serious misunderstandings of Frege. Others have found the reasoning good but held it to target the later Frege's assimilation of propositions to names – something which hardly needs further disproof. As I shall read the section Wittgenstein's basic target is something well worthy of our attention, namely the separation of judgment from content. And the section is of systematic importance, for it contains in seed a compelling argument against this target. Wittgenstein shows Frege's view to be untenable that content is explained independently of judgment.

That Which 'Is True' Must Already Contain the Verb   91

The chapter will have three major parts. The first part will be concerned only with Frege, describing how he renders judgment external to content. Subsequently, I shall consider Wittgenstein's recognition and rejection of Frege's stance, providing interpretations in particular of *Tractatus* sections 4.062, 4.063, and 4.064. Finally, I shall consider a motivation offered by Frege and say something brief about how that motivation may be deflected by Wittgenstein.

5.2 Frege's Separation of the Act from the Subject Matter of Judgment

5.2.1

Frege's first great work, *Begriffsschrift*, sets out a novel script for the representation of judgment. This script is trailed in the book's introduction, where Frege recommends to his reader certain of its key features. First and apparently foremost amongst these is a repudiation of the Aristotelian notions of subject and predicate:

> The mere invention of this ideography has it seems to me advanced logic. … In particular, I believe that the replacement of the concepts *subject* and *predicate* by *argument* and *function* respectively will stand the test of time. (Frege 1972: 7)

This replacement comprises two moves. First, Frege introduces his assertion sign '⊢':

> A judgment will always be expressed by means of the sign '⊢' which stands to the left of the sign, or the combination of signs, indicating the content of the judgment. (Frege 1972: §2)

Second, what indicates the judgment's content is divided into expressions of function and argument. These two proposals are fundamental to his new script and remain untouched throughout his ensuing career. Between them, however, they effect what Wittgenstein will see as a profound mistake.

Frege's assertion sign is on the face of it not terribly hard to understand. The symbol 'A' in a Begriffsschrift formula '⊢A' indicates a propositional content but does not in itself effect an assertion of that content. To do that, to manifest a judgment, we prefix the contentful 'A' with the sign '⊢'. Frege's own explanation of his sign in *Begriffsschrift* section 3 is, however, slightly puzzling. The section begins:

> A distinction between subject and predicate finds no place in my representation of a judgment. (Frege 1972: §3)

Later on, Frege then describes this new representation as follows:

> Imagine a language in which the proposition 'Archimedes was killed at the capture of Syracuse' is expressed in the following way: 'The violent death of Archimedes at the capture of Syracuse is a fact'. Even here, if one wants, subject and predicate can be distinguished, but the subject contains the whole content, and the predicate serves only to present it as a judgment. Such a language would have only a single predicate for all judgments, namely, 'is a fact'. It can be seen that there is no question here of subject and predicate in the usual sense. Our Begriffsschrift is a language of this sort and the symbol '⊢' is its common predicate for all judgments. (Frege 1972: §3)

How, one may however wonder, can this description be apt? If as Frege insists there is *no* place in the Begriffsschrift representation of a judgment for a distinction between subject and predicate, then how can there remain a sense in which Frege's script has a single predicate for all judgments?

To appreciate Frege's explanation here of his script, we need to consider the concepts of subject and predicate he at once rejects, and then also appeals to. These concepts belong as said to an Aristotelian tradition, one which would be familiar to his envisaged reader. And the basic, relevant feature of this tradition is a conception of judgment as *predication*. To judge is to act on a certain object: it is to predicate something of that object. To judge that Jack is tall, for example, is to predicate *tallness* of the man Jack. This conception of atomic judgment integrates with a view also of its linguistic expression. An Aristotelian atomic judgment is expressed by a sentence composed of a subject term and a predicate expression. The subject term introduces a certain object, and the predicate expression expresses an act of predication directed on that object. The judgment that Jack is tall, for example, is expressed by a sentence 'Jack is tall' composed first of 'Jack', a name introducing the object Jack, and second of 'is tall', a predicate expression expressing the act of predicating *tallness*.

Frege rejects this Aristotelian picture. More specifically, he rejects the unity of act and content embodied in the Aristotelian predicate. Within the Aristotelian sentence 'Jack is tall', the words 'is tall' express an act of predicating, and so an act of judging. And this is a *contentful* act. There is, that is to say, a commonality of content among judgments so made. (In this case, they are all judgments of something's being tall.) As Frege sees it, however, this unity is misconceived; the predicate's aspects of act and content should be separated out. To do this, he makes the two moves we noted above. First, he introduces his assertion sign whose role is to express pure, contentless act: it expresses that act common to all judgments no matter their content. And, second, he introduces his function expressions whose role is to indicate actless content: a function expression expresses no act but serves instead to indicate the commonality of content embodied in a traditional predicate. With the Aristotelian predicate dissolved in this way, the judgment that Jack is tall is now represented in Frege's new script by a formula '⊢ Jack is tall' of not two elements but three. The name 'Jack' combines with the function expression 'is tall' to indicate the actless propositional content that Jack is tall. And attaching to this combination is the assertion sign '⊢' by which the content is then represented as judged.

As for the puzzle in Frege's explanation of his new sign, this arises from his desire to explain his representation of a judgment to a reader from the Aristotelian tradition, and so to explain it in Aristotelian terms. Here Frege has two options, depending on whether the traditional predicate is considered primarily as act or primarily as content. Foregrounding matters of content, the composition represented by the subject–predicate division is supplanted in Frege's new account by a force-free structuring into argument and function. And so we have 'the replacement of the concepts *subject* and *predicate* by *argument* and *function*' (Frege 1972: 7). Here we are stripping the essentially contentful predicate of its force and 'flattening it' into a function. We are, as Frege later puts it, 'disassociating assertoric force from the predicate' (Frege 1979b: 185). From a perspective of predicate as force, however, Frege's dissolution is a stripping of the essentially forceful predicate of its content and relocating that content instead with an enlarged subject. And so Frege describes his script as a language in which 'the subject contains the whole content, and the predicate serves only to present it as a judgment' (Frege 1972: §3). Both of these perspectives may of course be helpful, but equally both may mislead, for the Aristotelian predicate is essentially both act *and* content. This being so, the strict truth of the matter is that the subject–predicate distinction 'finds *no* place' (§3, italics added) in the *Begriffsschrift* representation of judgment.

5.2.2

In abolishing as he does the Aristotelian predicate, Frege effects a 'separation of the act from the subject matter of judgment' (Frege 1984: 149). This separation, I want now to underline, is a theoretical reordering. Where for the Aristotelian, propositional content is explained only with the act of judgment, Frege renders content theoretically independent of judgment, and so theoretically prior to it. A Fregean content is by its nature something which may be judged, but it is not something *in* its nature *to be judged*. To appreciate this distinction, let us consider a rather different case.

There are such things as dances: the Viennese Waltz, for example, and the Macarena. These dances may be the objects of various attitudes, or acts. One might revere the Viennese Waltz, say, and detest the Macarena. One might prefer the Salsa to the Rumba. The possibility a dance bears of being detested or preferred is, however, external to the dance itself. The Macarena is a dance, and as such is liable to be loved, but this liability is not constitutive of the dance's basic nature. One does not recognise what the Macarena fundamentally is by recognising it as something one might love. What is not so external to the Macarena, on the other hand, is that it may be *danced*. A dance – any dance – is fundamentally something *to be danced*. (As one might say, the dance has its being as something one may dance.) Or again, a dance is precisely a *manner of dancing*. Where the Macarena is danced, one's dancing does not have an act-object structure. There is not within one's dancing of the Macarena an entity danced discernible separately from one's dancing of it. Rather, the dance one dances is the form one's dancing takes. To dance a certain dance is not to act with a certain object, as one does when one adores the Waltz, say, or eats a cake; rather, it is to dance in a certain manner. In dancing, one *exemplifies* the dance one there dances.

Parallel remarks apply to Aristotelian predicates. The noun 'predicate' is used in the tradition to refer both to the linguistic expression of an act of predication and also to what is predicated in such an act: *tallness*, for example, or *being tall*. To judge that Jack is tall is to predicate a certain predicate, namely *being tall*, of Jack. This predicate is not, however, something which *as it happens* be predicated, as a dance can as it happens be admired. Rather, as a dance is essentially something to be danced, so a predicate is essentially something to be predicated. Or again, as a dance is a manner of dancing, so a predicate is a manner of predicating. To judge that Jack is tall is to predicate *being tall* of Jack, but what is predicated in this judgment is not a second object alongside Jack of an act of predication. There is here no act of 'pure predicating' which takes two objects, *being tall* and Jack. (Predicating *tallness* of Jack is not like introducing Jack to Jill.) Rather, the predicate predicated is the predicating's determinate form.

This claim is simply a repetition of point above that the Aristotelian linguistic predicate expresses a unity of act and content. The linguistic predicate does not play two separate roles: it does not on the one hand express an act of pure predication, and on the other supply an element of the judgment's content, an object for that pure act. (The predicate 'is tall' does not divide into an 'is' and a 'tall'.) Rather, it expresses a unitary, contentful act of predicating. It expresses, that is to say, a manner of predicating, and so a manner of judging. This manner of predicating is, however, precisely what is repudiated by Frege's separation of the act from the subject matter of judgment. Indeed, Frege rejects with his separation all idea of a manner of judging. For the Aristotelian, what is judged – the judgment's content – is a way of judging: it is a way of predicating as directed on a certain object. But this is not so for Frege. In disassociating the act of judgment from all elements of content, and so from content *tout court*, there remains no unitary manner of judging, one which does not divide into act and object. A Fregean content, it follows, is not something to be judged but is, where judged, a theoretically independent object of that act.

5.2.3

An appreciation of the wider significance of this point within Frege's theorising is beyond the scope of this chapter. (It entails, for example, a division in Frege between the prior, descriptive laws of truth and the subsequent, normative laws of judgment (see e.g. Frege 1984: 351). In preparation for Wittgenstein, however, two contextualising comments may quickly and somewhat dogmatically be made, comments which relate to the 'pride of place' Frege ascribes in his theorising to the notion of truth (Frege 1979b: 253).

The first of these comments is that content, whilst prior to judgment, is coeval theoretically with truth. Propositional contents are for Frege the basic truth bearers: for a judgment to be true is for it to have a true content. The notion of truth is thus explained with that of content. And conversely, the notion of content is explained with that of truth. Frege writes: 'I ... introduce a thought as that to which the question 'is it true?' is in principle applicable' (Frege 1979b: 253). Here Frege is not singling out for our attention a certain type of being, namely thoughts, on which we already had a separate grip, a grip independent of truth. Rather, he is introducing the notion of a thought as the notion of that which may be true. A Fregean thought is in its conception a truth or falsehood. (See Frege 1979b: 168: 'the most appropriate name for a true thought is a truth').

Frege's separation of judgment from content is thus at once its separation from truth: if truth and content are coeval, then if content is prior to judgment, so too is truth prior to judgment. Truth is theoretically independent in Frege of the notion of judgment. For the second preparatory comment, we may pause a moment on Frege's conception of a propositional content as at base something true or false. Here, one might think, there is a suggestion that a content is something *for the mind*; for a truth or falsehood, so one might think, is something *to be thought*. Thought here cannot of course mean *judged*, but there are other things for it to mean.

Frege tells us many times that in order to judge, the subject must first *grasp* the thought (see e.g. Frege 1979b: 267). This is not a claim of temporal priority, a speculative assertion about temporal order in human psychology. Rather, it is a claim of act containment. To judge for Frege means to judge something grasped; the subject judges *with understanding*. (Just the same goes for the act of questioning. As the act of judgment contains that of understanding, so too 'in raising the question [the investigator] is grasping a thought' (Frege 1984: 375).) Grasping is strictly prior here in the order of explanation: whilst the act of judgment is set out only with that of grasping – to judge means to judge something grasped – the act of grasping is independent of judgment. What is more, grasping is internal for Frege to that which is grasped. So he writes:

> The being of a thought may ... be taken to lie in the possibility of different thinkers' grasping the thought as one and the same. (Frege 1984: 376)

Thoughts are not in their basic nature entities external to the mind, so that a question might arise of how it is we manage to grasp them. (How do we access the third realm?) Rather, as Frege writes, the task of logic – including centrally that of the explanation of content – 'could be represented as the investigation of *the* mind' (Frege 1984: 369). A thought is not merely something which may be grasped; rather, it is fundamentally something *to be* grasped.

In dancing a certain dance, subjects exemplify the mode of dancing which is the dance. Similarly, where the Aristotelian subject predicates a certain predicate of an object, her predicating exemplifies the mode of judging which is the predicate. And again, the Fregean subject's grasping of a thought is not an act with a certain object but an exemplification of that mode of the understanding which is the thought she there grasps.

5.3 Wittgenstein's Repudiation of Frege

5.3.1

Like Frege, Wittgenstein explains truth with notions of content and explains content with reference to truth. (Indeed, Wittgenstein's endorsement of Frege's conception of logic as an unfolding of the nature of truth is I think his most basic inheritance from Frege.) The sense expressed by a Tractarian proposition, the situation it represents (4.031), is precisely the condition of its truth. What is more, a Tractarian sense is, as a truth condition, something *for the mind*, something *to be thought*. Here, though, the alignment with Frege contains also a divergence, for the act of thought internal to Tractarian content is correlate not to Fregean understanding but to Fregean judgment.

The *Tractatus* does not deploy a consistent and narrowly circumscribed terminology of judgment and assertion, preferring instead a more varied bag which, besides judging and asserting, includes also thinking and representing and saying and picturing. Like Fregean judgment and assertion, however, and unlike Fregean grasping, these are all acts for which *truth is correctness*. So on picturing, we find:

> The picture represents its object rightly or falsely. (2.173)
>
> In the agreement or disagreement of [the picture's] sense with reality, its truth or falsity consists. (2.222)
>
> The picture agrees with reality or not; it is right or wrong, true or false. (2.21)

For the picture, truth is agreement with reality, and so truth is correctness. A true picture is as such a correct picture. And crucially, it is with the act of picturing (representing, saying, thinking) that truth and content are explained for Wittgenstein. It is with an act for which truth is correctness, rather than with an act correlate to Fregean grasping – one for which truth is no correctness – that truth and content are set out in the *Tractatus*. Truth has no understanding in the *Tractatus* separate from its status as correctness in judgment.

Truth is fundamentally correctness in representation. What a picture represents, its sense, is fundamentally a condition of correct representation. That Wittgenstein diverges here from Frege is something of which he is well aware. Indeed, it is something he thematises. This is most explicit and sustained in the 4.06s, a passage headed by the claim:

> A proposition can be true or false – only in virtue of being a picture of reality. (4.06)

A proposition has content – is true or false – only insofar as it is a picture of reality: only insofar, that is, as it is something which agrees or disagrees with reality, something which is correct or incorrect. For Frege this is not so. A Fregean proposition '⊢A' has content in virtue of the content of its component 'A', and this component has content – it expresses a truth or falsity – quite separately from any matter of judgment and assertion, and so quite separately from any matter of agreement or disagreement with reality.

In this second part of the chapter, I want to examine two key moments of the 4.06s. First, I shall consider Wittgenstein's rejection in 4.062 of an idea that we might 'make ourselves understood with false propositions just as we have up till now with true ones'. Here the contrast with Frege is manifest, but there is no argument against Frege, nothing which would demonstrate Frege to be mistaken. For that, we shall move to consider Wittgenstein's 'analogy to illustrate the concept of truth' of section 4.063. In this section, I shall suggest, Wittgenstein offers a forceful argument against Frege's view that content is explained independently of judgment.

5.3.2

Dummett begins his paper 'Truth' with a criticism of Frege's separation of truth from assertion. He makes a comparison between truth and winning: much as 'it is part of the concept of winning a game that a player plays to win' (Dummett 1959: 142), so too 'it is part of the concept of truth that we aim at making true statements' (Dummett 1959: 143). Frege's theory of content, however, 'leaves this feature of the concept of truth quite out of account' (Dummett 1959: 143):

> Frege indeed tried to bring it in afterwards, in his theory of assertion – but too late; for the sense of the sentence is not given in advance of our going in for the activity of asserting, since otherwise there could be people who expressed the same thoughts but went in instead for denying them. (Dummett 1959: 143)

Frege does not deny that judgment and assertion aim at truth. What he does, rather, is bring this in afterwards, as something subsequent to the account of truth and content, so that whilst it is internal to judgment that it aims at truth, it is not internal to truth that it is the goal of judgment. But this is too late, Dummett holds, for if content were theoretically prior to assertion, 'there could be people who expressed the same thoughts but went in instead for denying them' (Dummett 1959: 143).

Dummett is repeating here a consideration of *Tractatus* 4.062. Wittgenstein asks:

> Can we not make ourselves understood by means of false propositions as hitherto with true ones, so long as we know that they are meant to be false? (4.062)

In English, we express a propositional content by means of a sentence '*p*', and in doing so we assert that content. But if, as Frege holds, judgment is external to content, and so assertion is external to the expression of content, this will be a matter simply of convention. It is a convention of

English that a symbol expressing a propositional content – a sentence – effects an assertion of that content. This convention does not operate for Frege's script. In Frege's script, no forceful act is made by the symbol which expresses the thought. To make an assertion, we need to do something more than deploy a symbol with propositional content: we need to prefix that symbol with the assertion sign. Equally, though, one might from Frege's perspective have a convention opposite to that of English, a convention whereby in expressing a certain content one effects not an assertion of that content but a *denial* of it. Instead of deploying sentences intending them to be understood as true, we could deploy sentences intending them to be understood as false.

Dummett does not elaborate on the incoherence of 'people who expressed the same thoughts but went in instead for denying them' (Dummett 1959: 143). This is supposed, it seems, to be evident. Wittgenstein is slightly more expansive, answering his question as follows:

> No! For a proposition is true, if what we assert by means of it is the case; and if by 'p' we mean $\sim p$, and what we mean is the case, then 'p' in the new conception is true and not false. (4.062)

To put a sentence with the content that p forward as false would be to assert that not-p. It would be to make an assertion with the correctness condition that not-p. If by deploying a certain sentence we assert that not-p, Wittgenstein however maintains, then that sentence is true if not-p. The sentence, that is to say, will have as its content not that p, but that not-p.

In this reasoning, Wittgenstein's anti-Fregean position is manifest that a sentence's content, its truth condition, is not separable from the correctness condition of the assertion it effects. Truth is essentially correctness in assertion. It is rather less clear, however, why Frege should not hold the line – why, that is, he should admit that if a sentence is used to assert that not-p, then the sentence is true if not-p. Dummett apparently senses a *reductio*, but Wittgenstein does not write as if he were demonstrating a mistake, and it is clear, I take it, that any such demonstration would require substantial additional support.

5.3.3

Wittgenstein's tone is rather different in section 4.063. Here, he is clearly offering an argument and names Frege as its target. It is less clear, perhaps, what aspect of Frege is being targeted. Wittgenstein speaks specifically of the later Fregean doctrine that propositions designate truth values, and certain commentators have suggested that this doctrine is at the centre of Wittgenstein's sights (see e.g. Sullivan 1994; Ricketts 2002). As I shall read this section, however, what is at basic issue in the argument is something constant throughout Frege's career, something deeper in his thought, and something much more engaging philosophically, namely the separation of judgment from content.

The section is reproduced verbatim from the 1913 *Notes on Logic* (Wittgenstein 1979: 99–100) and could certainly have used a rewrite. Indeed, its final sentence deploys a Russellian notion of a verb, but this notion is obsolete by the time of the *Tractatus* and is found nowhere else in the book. (Where a thought holds good, and is enjoyed by Wittgenstein, he typically does not take the trouble to update its expression.) Let us begin by sketching the section sufficiently to find puzzling a certain attribution it makes to Frege. This puzzle will then provide the initial context for a more thorough review.

The section comprises three paragraphs, the first of which sets up an 'analogy to illustrate the concept of truth'. Here, Wittgenstein compares points of a sheet of paper which are either black or white to sentences '*p*' which are either true or false. Proceeding to a second paragraph, Wittgenstein writes:

> But to be able to say that a point is black or white, I must first know under what conditions a point is called black, and when white; in order to be able to say '*p*' is true (or false) I must have determined in what circumstances I call '*p*' true, and thereby I determine the sense of the proposition. (4.063)

In order to be able to say that '*p*' is true, I must determine when this symbol is called true. And in doing so, I determine its sense. This single sentence paragraph is then followed by a third, again of a single sentence, which begins:

> The point where the simile breaks down is this: we can indicate a point on the paper, without knowing what black and white are; but to a proposition without a sense corresponds nothing at all... (4.063)

Unlike the point on the paper which can be indicated separately from a determination of when it is called black and when white, there is, Wittgenstein holds, nothing meant by '*p*', and so no contentful '*p*' here to recognise, separately from a determination of when '*p*' is called true – separately, that is, from a determination of its sense. In spelling out the simile's breakdown, however, Wittgenstein makes at the same time a puzzling criticism of Frege:

... but to a proposition without a sense corresponds nothing at all, for it signifies no thing (truth-value) whose properties are called 'false' or 'true'; the verb of the proposition is not 'is true' or 'is false' – as Frege thought – but that which 'is true' must already contain the verb. (4.063)

There is a question here of the attribution to Frege of 'the verb of the proposition'. But the more basic puzzle is the criticism of Frege that he fails to recognise the breakdown of the simile. Like a Tractarian sense, a Fregean thought or judgeable content is fundamentally a truth condition (see Frege 2013: §32). So, for Frege as much as for Wittgenstein, there is no meaningful '*p*' to be found separately from a determination of the condition of its truth. What can Wittgenstein mean in suggesting otherwise?

My strategy with 4.063 will be to start at the end, looking first at the attribution to Frege of 'the verb of the proposition' – and for this we shall consider also section 4.064. With that understood, we shall be able to see how, for Wittgenstein, Frege does indeed not recognise the simile's breakdown. Only then shall we turn to the question of what Wittgenstein's *argument* might be, what ground Wittgenstein might provide in this section for *criticising* Frege.

5.3.4

Whilst Wittgenstein did not give 4.063 the rewrite it needed, he does follow it in the *Tractatus* with a section which recasts its final thought:

> Every proposition must *already* have a sense; assertion cannot give it a sense, for what it asserts is the sense itself. (4.064)

Here, one might suspect, Wittgenstein has got Frege plain wrong. It is not Frege's position that a proposition gathers a sense – that is for Frege, comes to express a thought – through an act of assertion. Seeking to decipher 4.063, Ian Proops ascribes to Wittgenstein just this mistake. He writes:

> Let us begin by considering how Frege introduces the assertion sign in *Grundgesetze*. He writes: 'In a mere equation there is as yet no assertion: "2 + 3 = 5" only designates a truth value, without its being said which of the two it is ... We therefore require another sign in order to be able to assert something as true' (Frege 2013: I §5). The point Frege wants to make is that the *thought* expressed by '2 + 3 = 5' does not assert itself; rather, *we* have to intervene by recording our recognition that the proposition is true, and we do this ... by means of the assertion sign.
>
> Frege's point is thus that '2 + 3 = 5' designates a truth value in contrast to expressing a judgment. He is not claiming that '2 + 3 = 5' designates a truth

value in contrast to expressing a sense. I think it likely, however, that Wittgenstein read this passage in the second of these ways. (Proops 1997: 132)

Reading certain passages of Frege, Proops suggests, Wittgenstein comes to the misunderstanding that a Fregean proposition expresses a thought only insofar as it is asserted. By itself, the symbol 'p' in Frege's '⊢p' refers to a truth value but expresses no thought. For that, we need to apply the assertion sign.

This attribution makes easy sense of 4.064. And it provides an explanation also of Wittgenstein's claim against Frege in 4.063 that 'to a proposition without a sense corresponds nothing at all, for it signifies no thing (truth-value)': Wittgenstein is objecting to a view he finds in Frege that a symbol 'p' may refer to a truth value but express no thought. With this attribution, Frege will moreover fail to recognise the breakdown of Wittgenstein's simile, for his symbol 'p' refers to a truth value even though the condition of its truth – the thought it expresses – is not yet set. These benefits granted, Proops's suggestion is nonetheless highly unwelcome. Wittgenstein is doubtless not the most diligent student of other philosophers. And someone could perhaps read selected passages of Frege in the manner Proops suggests. Still, it is surely preferable if at all possible not to interpret Wittgenstein as blundering quite so grossly in his understanding of the philosopher he identifies alongside Russell as his principal influence, the philosopher to whose 'great works' he attributes 'much of the stimulation of my thoughts' (TLP preface).

Avoiding Proops's reading is moreover perfectly possible. To do that, we hold that by 'sense' in 4.064 Wittgenstein means something importantly different from *Fregean* sense. The possession of a sense which for Wittgenstein's Frege is achieved only by assertion is not the expression of a Fregean thought. This option might be hard to navigate, or even to notice, if one's understanding of Tractarian sense is not relevantly different from one's understanding of Fregean thought. For us, however, this is an open door. Unlike a Fregean thought, a Tractarian sense is essentially a correctness condition for judgment and assertion. For a symbol to have a sense is for it to effect an assertion with a certain condition of correctness. And Wittgenstein is quite right that for Frege, a propositional symbol has *such* a sense only in virtue of being asserted. What has a Tractarian sense is something correct or incorrect depending on how things are – a sense is fundamentally a correctness condition – and in Frege's script this is not his symbol 'p' with propositional content (what refers for the later Frege to a truth value) but the composition of such a symbol with the assertion sign.

That a Tractarian sense is fundamentally a correctness condition for judgment and assertion is the key to understanding also section 4.063. Indeed, the final phrase of 4.063 can be seen as making the same, correct attribution as 4.064. In this phrase, Wittgenstein deploys a notion of verb which occurs nowhere else in his book. The term would appear, however, to derive from Russell's *Principles of Mathematics*, where it matches – broadly speaking – the Aristotelian notion of a predicate. A verb is a distinguished propositional element which contains, or gives, the assertion (Russell 1903: §51–52). Here in 4.063, then, Wittgenstein is describing Frege's position in the same way Frege himself describes it when he says in *Begriffsschrift* that his language has 'a single predicate for all judgments, namely, "is a fact"' (Frege 1972: §3). (There is a notable issue that Frege's single predicate 'is a fact' has become not one verb but two, 'is true' and 'is false'. I set this aside here: it has to do with the consequences of Frege's separation for the treatment of negation and denial.) And in so describing Frege's theorising, the ascription is precisely that of 4.064, namely that what has propositional content for Frege – 'that which "is true"' – comes to participate in something with sense – something right or wrong depending on how things are, a (Tractarian) proposition – only with the application of the assertion sign.

Of course, Wittgenstein does not merely ascribe a view to Frege: he simultaneously rejects it. There is for Wittgenstein no propositional content – no expressing a thought, or referring to a truth value – prior to the possession of a sense. Indeed, what is asserted – the propositional content – is nothing less than the sense. ('That which "is true" must already contain the verb'; 'what it asserts is the sense itself'.) And so we can see too how, from Wittgenstein's perspective, Frege fails to recognise the breakdown of the analogy with black and white points. Much as a point may be indicated separately from a determination of the circumstances of its being black or white, so for Frege – as Wittgenstein holds – a propositional symbol is given separately from a determination of the circumstances of its being true or false. This was puzzling, for a Fregean thought is precisely a truth condition. The puzzle goes away, however, when we recognise that by a condition of something's being true Wittgenstein means a *sense*: he means, that is, a *Tractarian* truth condition. And Frege does indeed hold there to be a meaningful '*p*' separate from any matter of correctness in judgment and assertion, and so separate from any determination of Tractarian sense.

5.3.5

We have in place now an understanding of the final paragraph of 4.063: an understanding of the attribution to Frege of 'the verb of the proposition', and also of Frege's failure to recognise the breakdown of the analogy with black and white points. What we do not yet have is any idea of Wittgenstein's *argument*. What reason, if any, does Wittgenstein give us for holding against Frege that that which 'is true' must already contain the verb?

The first paragraph of 4.063 does no more than set up an analogy, and the third does no more in itself than reject Frege's position. If the section contains an argument, then, its basic move must be contained in the second paragraph:

> But to be able to say that a point is black or white, I must first know under what conditions a point is called white or black; in order to be able to say '*p*' is true (or false), I must have determined under what conditions I call '*p*' true, and I thereby determine the sense – of the proposition. (4.063)

There is indeed here, I think, a consideration against Frege. In order to say that a point is black, the subject must know when a point is called black: she must know, that is, when a point is *correctly* called black. Similarly, in order to assert that a sentence '*p*' is true, the subject must determine the circumstances in which this assertion is *correctly* made, the circumstances in which her assertion is *correct*. And in doing so, Wittgenstein says, she determines the correctness condition – the sense – of the sentence '*p*'.

The predicate 'is true' here is Wittgenstein's take on Frege's assertion sign '⊢', so that 'calling "*p*" true' means as much as asserting that *p*. Wittgenstein's thought may thus be recast in terms simply of assertion. In order to assert that *p*, Wittgenstein maintains, the subject must determine the circumstances in which her act is correct: she must determine her assertion's sense. Frege cannot agree with this. To assert a certain Fregean thought, the Fregean subject must have that content in view: she must grasp the content she would assert and express that content with a symbol '*p*'. And the content she grasps and expresses is – as it happens – the correctness condition of the assertion she would make: it is the condition of the assertion's truth, and truth is correctness in assertion. But the content is not grasped or expressed by the Fregean subject *as* her assertion's condition of correctness, for it is not internal to the Fregean truth condition that it is a condition of correct assertion. The Fregean subject grasps a truth condition, and she asserts it, acting on the object grasped. But she does not possess therein a conception of her act's correctness.

The same point may be made also for judgment. In order to judge, Wittgenstein will hold, the subject must determine *as such* the condition under which her act is correct. For Frege, this is not so. In order to judge, the Fregean subject must determine the content of her act. And this content is, indeed, the condition under which her act is correct. But it is not as such that she determines it for her act. Whether the point is framed in terms of assertion or judgment, however, it is here, I think, that Wittgenstein sees Frege as demonstrably mistaken rather than merely divergent. It is plainly true, as Wittgenstein sees it, that judgment and assertion involve a determination of Tractarian sense, that the subject judges or asserts only where she has a conception of her act's correctness.

What is plain to Wittgenstein, however, might for others take a little spelling out. This may be done, I take it, with an idea of *aim*. Consider an act of shooting an arrow at a tree. In order to do this, the subject must have determined in what circumstances her act will be successful. Shooting at the tree, the subject must have a conception of what it is for her to hit the tree. This is because her act is, internally, an attempt at such success. To shoot at the tree is to attempt to hit the tree, and so there is no shooting at the tree without an understanding of what it is to hit the tree. Somewhat similarly, the thought will then be, judgment aims internally at truth. In judging, the subject aims to judge truly. And so it is a condition on the subject's judging that she know what it is for her judgment to be true. Indeed – and this is the crucial point – the judging subject must know the condition of her act's truth, *conceiving that condition as the condition of her act's success*. The understanding of success involved in firing an arrow at a tree is not a grasp of an event the occurrence of which would *as it happens* constitute success in one's act. It is not an understanding of what it would be for the arrow one fires to strike the tree. Rather, it is an understanding of what it would be for one to succeed in one's act – what it would be to *hit* one's *target*, the tree. Similarly, the judging subject who aims at truth therein conceives her act's truth condition as its condition of success. In Tractarian terms, the subject must, in order to judge, determine her judgment's sense.

This requirement is met in the *Tractatus*, for it is simply the requirement that the subject know in judging what it is that she judges. Judgment is a self-conscious act: the subject judging that *p* knows that she so acts, and so she knows the sense of her act, the condition of its correctness. For Frege, by contrast, the subject has no such knowledge. The Fregean subject judges knowing the content of her act. (Indeed, this content is possessed by her in a prior act of grasping.) And this content is as it happens the condition of her act's correctness, for truth is correctness in judgment. But it is not as such that the Fregean subject knows it. The grasp of content implied within Fregean judgment is a possession by the subject of the content's internal nature. It is, however, no part of its nature that the content is the condition of correctness of its own judgment. And so the Fregean subject does not aim in judging at judging truly. It is not internal to Fregean judgment that the subject aims at truth.

5.3.6

The word 'internal' is important here. A Fregean theorist might reply to the Wittgensteinian criticism by saying that their subject, the Fregean subject, will surely acknowledge that truth is in general correctness in judgment, an acknowledgement which will then inform her judging. The subject will judge in the knowledge that the content she judges is the condition of correctness for her act. An appropriate spelling out of this point, the reply would then go, will provide a sense in which the Fregean subject can indeed aim at truth.

Such a reply will not, however, meet Wittgenstein's requirement that in order to assert, the subject must determine the condition under which her act is correct. Compare politeness in eating. It may in general be correct for me to eat politely. And this is something I may know, and so something which may inform my eating. I may, eating my meals, aim to eat politely knowing that I shall thereby act correctly. Politeness remains here, however, an *external* norm for eating, a norm in light of which I shall eat in certain ways, but not a norm without which no eating is possible. It is no part of what it is for the subject to eat that she aims at eating politely. Similarly, there could doubtless be a sense in which the Fregean subject may aim when she judges to 'do the right thing' and judge only truth. But this aim will remain external to the act of judgment itself. Whilst the Fregean subject may judge aiming to judge truly, it will not be constitutive of her act of judgment that she do so – no more than it is constitutive of the act of eating that one aim to eat politely.

In 1904 Russell subscribes with Frege to a dual relation theory of judgment: judgment is a relation to a prior object, the proposition judged. In this context, Russell considers the 'preference ... people ... feel in favour of true propositions' (Russell 1904: 524) when they judge, and concludes that this preference 'must be based ... upon an ultimate ethical proposition: "It is good to believe true propositions, and bad to believe false ones"' (Russell 1904: 524). The striking oddity of this suggestion consists, I take it, in the fact that by considering it an *ethical* matter that people aim to judge truly, Russell sees this aim as unexplained by the act of judgment itself. As I have interpreted *Tractatus* 4.063, Wittgenstein's consideration against Frege is that he is committed to this same view. In separating judgment from truth and content, Frege knowingly rejects that it is internal to truth that it is the aim of judgment. On the other hand, Frege wants – quite properly – to maintain that it is internal to judgment that it aims at truth. Wittgenstein's thought is that these positions are incompatible. There can be a propositional act – call it judgment or representation or picturing or saying – which aims internally at truth only if it is internal to truth that it is correctness for this act.

5.4 Frege's Motivation

Wittgenstein's conception of truth as correctness is of pervasive significance in the *Tractatus*. It plays a fundamental role, for example, in his account of logical operations, logical propositions, and inference. Exploring such matters would however be work for another time. To close, I want to consider instead a key motivation Frege gives for his separation.

As we have seen, Frege believed that his replacement of the concepts of subject and predicate by those of argument and function would stand the test of time (Frege 1972: 7). He does not set out his grounds for this belief in *Begriffsschrift*. Later on, however, Frege offers the following consideration in favour of his separation:

> According to the view I am here presenting, '5 > 4' and '1 + 3 = 5' just give us expressions for truth-values, without making any assertion. This separation of the act from the subject matter of judgement seems to be indispensable; for otherwise we could not express a mere supposition – the putting of a case without a simultaneous judgement as to its arising or not. We thus need a special sign in order to be able to assert something. (Frege 1984: 149)

Here Frege sets out precisely the view which Wittgenstein rejects in sections 4.063 and 4.064, the view that there is propositional content – expression of thought and reference to truth value – independently of the possession of Tractarian sense. With the view comes also, however, the thought that it must be so, for propositional content can in certain contexts be expressed without there being asserted. The context Frege refers to here is that of a supposition, but there are of course others, including in particular that of molecular assertion. Frege writes of conditional propositions:

> Even if the whole compound sentence is uttered with assertoric force, one is still asserting neither the truth of the thought in the antecedent nor that of the thought in the consequent. (Frege 1979b: 185–86)

An assertion 'not-p' or 'p implies q' involves the expression of the content that p without any assertion being made of that content.

Whilst I cannot hope here to give anything like a full Tractarian reply to this thought, a preliminary counter can quickly be sketched in line with recent work by Kimhi (2018). Imagine there to be a play about Frege's life. And imagine that at some point in this play the actor playing Frege writes a symbol '$\vdash \epsilon'f(\epsilon) = \alpha'g(\alpha) \equiv \forall x[f(x) = g(x)]$' on a blackboard. Do we have here, on the blackboard, a token of the famous Begriffsschrift proposition? Well, we surely want to say the following. First, no assertion is made by the actor: the actor does not assert Basic Law V. (And this of course is Frege's own view; see e.g. Frege 1979b: 233; 1984: 164.) Second, there is on the blackboard a token of Frege's assertion sign: the mark '$\vdash$' in chalk is Frege's assertion sign, just as much as the mark '=' in the formula which follows is the identity sign. And third, the essential role of Frege's assertion sign is to effect an assertion. There is of course a tension between these three, but this tension is defused by saying that the context of a play is such that Frege's assertion sign '$\vdash$' does not on this occasion perform its essential role. The essential role is of course still present in a fashion: the context of the play does not simply rub out the sign's assertoric role, leaving the actor merely expressing the thought of Basic Law V. Rather, the context is such that, by this sign, the actor does not assert the thought but *makes as if* to assert it.

What answer do we give, then, to the question of whether we have on the blackboard a token of the Begriffsschrift proposition '$\vdash \epsilon'f(\epsilon) = \alpha'g(\alpha) \equiv \forall x[f(x) = g(x)]$'? Well, we could give either answer. We could say yes: the symbols of the proposition are all tokened here, and they are combined exactly as they are on page 36 of volume I of *Basic Laws of Arithmetic*, so we do indeed have the proposition. Or we could say no: the proposition is tokened only where a certain assertion is made, and there is here no such act. What is important for our purposes, however, is that we *can* say yes, that there is this answer to give. For the first move in defence of Wittgenstein from Frege's motivating consideration will be that in something like the same way in which there is, indeed, a Begriffsschrift proposition on the blackboard even though no assertion is made, so there is indeed the Tractarian proposition 'p' tokened within tokens of the

Tractarian propositions 'not-p' and 'p implies q' – and again in such contexts as 'Suppose p' – even though no assertion that p is made. The occurrence, such as it is, of 'p' in 'not-p' no more requires a separation of judgment from content than the occurrence of the Begriffsschrift proposition '$\vdash \epsilon'f(\epsilon) = \alpha'g(\alpha) \equiv \forall x[f(x) = g(x)]$' on the blackboard of our play requires a separation of judgment from Frege's assertion sign.

CHAPTER 6

Solipsism and the Self

Michael Potter

6.1 Wittgenstein's Early Solipsism

We have it on Russell's evidence that Wittgenstein was already tempted by solipsism as early as 1912.

> I argued about Matter with him. He thinks it is a trivial problem. He admits that if there is no Matter then no one exists but himself, but he says that does not hurt, since physics and astronomy and all the other sciences could still be interpreted so as to be true. (Russell to Ottoline Morrell, 23 Apr. 1912, in Griffin 1992)

The context of the conversation Russell here reports is as follows. At that time Russell's main research project concerned the problem of matter. He had identified the objects I can name with those with which I am acquainted. The problem that then arose was that of deriving our ordinary talk about the external world (or at least an adequate proxy for such talk) from talk about the objects of acquaintance. Russell therefore distinguished three positions. The solipsist claims that the external world can be constructed out of his own sense data as a base. The phenomenalist attempts to construct the world out of the sense data of himself and other conscious beings.[1] The realist holds that these bases are insufficient and therefore posits other entities as part of the constructional base. Russell had been tempted by phenomenalism (although he did not himself use this term to describe the position at this stage), and in 1914 he expressed the hope that the phenomenalist, or even solipsistic, base would be sufficient. However, he conceded in the same paper that he had not been able to make this work. Indeed, the desire he mentioned in this paper to 'render solipsism scientifically satisfactory' reads like the temporary effect of Wittgenstein on him. Once this effect had worn off, therefore, Russell

---

[1] See Russell (1927: 209).

'gave up the attempt to construct "matter" out of experienced data alone' and contented himself instead with 'a picture of the world which fitted physics and perception harmoniously into a single whole' (Russell 1959: 105).

In the original version of his view, the other entities posited were ordinary physical objects. In the later version which he formulated in the autumn of 1913, the other entities are what he called 'sensibilia', i.e. entities of the same kind as sense data, although they may not be data to the senses of any conscious being. The central point to focus on here is the relationship between the matter and the constructional base of experienced data. It was fundamental to Russell's pre-war epistemology to distinguish between two kinds of knowledge – knowledge by acquaintance and knowledge by description – represented in language by two kinds of singular term – logically proper names and definite descriptions. Our ability to think about sense data is explained by the directness of the epistemological link provided by the relation of acquaintance. Our ability to think about matter, by contrast, is to be explained quantificationally by means of the variable.

By the summer of 1912, however, Wittgenstein had begun to be influenced by Frege into rejecting some elements of Russell's views. In particular, he began to hold that the role Russell's project gave to variables was incoherent. Russell illegitimately required a two-level view in which the variable ranges over entities for which I do not have names. In a letter of June 1912, Wittgenstein had told Russell,

> [O]ne thing gets more and more obvious to me: The prop[osition]s of Logic contain ONLY APPARENT variables and whatever may turn out to be the proper explanation of apparent variables, its consequence *must* be that there are NO logical constants.
>
> Logic must turn out to be a *totally* different kind than any other science. (Wittgenstein to Russell, 22 June 1912, in McGuinness 2008, emphasis in original)

It follows from this that the variable cannot have the substantial role that Russell had assigned to it. The variable is only a piece of notation that enables us to collect together propositions in order to apply a quantifier to them. A mere piece of notation cannot do any substantive epistemological work.

The influence of their argument in April 1912 is visible in several places in the development of Russell's own views. The paper he was then trying to write, 'On matter', is notably hesitant and Russell did not attempt to publish it. In the autumn of 1913, he changed tack and abandoned phenomenalism, albeit reluctantly, by positing a world of *sensibilia*, many of them unsensed by any consciousness. And in his 1918 lectures on 'The Philosophy of Logical Atomism' he granted that atomism, if strictly followed through, makes the possibility of communication with other people about the external world inexplicable.

> The meaning you attach to your words must depend on the nature of the objects you are acquainted with, and since different people are acquainted with different objects, they would not be able to talk to each other unless they attached quite different meanings to their words. ... A logically perfect language, if it could be constructed ... would be very largely private to one speaker. That is to say, all the names that it would use would be private to that speaker and could not enter into the language of another speaker. (Russell 1918b: 517–20)

What Russell now granted, that is to say, was that his logical atomism, if interpreted strictly, would have a solipsistic consequence, namely that my language would be capable of referring only to my own experience. Russell's preferred solution to this was to hold that ordinary language is not in fact the precise language dictated by logical atomism.

Plainly, though, Russell's 'solution' is in grave danger of at a stroke making analytic philosophy irrelevant. It is relatively uncontroversial to hold that *some* of the things we say about the world cannot be accurately rendered in the formal language of atomism. But Russell now seemed to be conceding that *none* of them can. Wittgenstein rejected this way out, holding that we do at least sometimes say things that have a completely determinate sense and are therefore amenable to atomistic translation. This conviction of Wittgenstein's that we are capable of saying things about the world that have a determinate sense is plausibly at least part of what he meant by his puzzling claim that 'all the propositions of our everyday language, just as they stand, are in perfect logical order' (5.5563).

If we rule out the possibility that the atomistic language is irrelevant to everyday language, the only other get-out from solipsism would be to concede that communication about the external world is impossible and instead conceive of us as having several essentially incommensurable languages. In the *Tractatus*, however, Wittgenstein rejected this possibility too, insisting instead that the language of atomism is the only language available to me.

For the passage in which Wittgenstein made this claim, Russell offered the translation, 'The boundaries of language (the only language I understand) indicate the boundaries of my world.' His use of 'indicates' suggests that he wished to emphasize the commonality between Wittgenstein's use of the verb *bedeuten* and Frege's. Each name in language indicates (*bedeutet*) an object, and so the boundaries of language (i.e. of what names there are) indicate the boundaries of the world (i.e. of what objects there are). We thus retrieve the version of solipsism that traces its origin to 1912, namely the claim that the range of what I can quantify over coincides with the range of what I can name. According to the usage adopted in the *Tractatus*, indeed, the range of the quantifiers consists of those entities that do in fact have names: Tractarian quantification is, that is to say, narrowly substitutional. In order for this to be plausible, we must evidently allow that there are names that never have been nor ever will be tokened. Wittgenstein did not himself comment on this point. It was left to Ramsey to note that in logic 'it cannot be any concern of ours whether anyone has actually symbolized ... a proposition' (Ramsey 1926: 363). Hence, we should allow the possibility of 'types of which there may be no instances'.[2]

Wittgenstein's solipsism, then, amounts to the claim that the range of objects I can quantify over coincides with the range of objects that have names in my language. So in the case where there are only finitely many names 'a_1', 'a_2',..., 'a_n' in our language, we can express our solipsism as

$$\forall x(x = a_1 \vee x = a_2 \vee \ldots \vee x = a_n).$$

Or rather, we *could* express this if we had a sign of identity in our formal language. According to the *Tractatus*, however, there can be no genuine relation of identity between simple objects, and as a consequence, the formal language of the *Tractatus* has no sign of identity. This explains why 'what solipsism *means* [namely (1)] is quite correct, only it cannot be said, but it shows itself' (5.62). Solipsism therefore emerges as one of those things 'it would be right to call ... "true" if, *per impossibile*, they could be said' (Anscombe 1971: 162, emphasis in original).

Incidentally, the account just sketched explains why Wittgenstein originally numbered the remarks on solipsism so as to make them subsidiary to those on identity. Both his argument for solipsism and his reason for holding this to be unsayable depend directly on the Tractarian account of identity.

The route to Wittgenstein's Tractarian solipsism just sketched very evidently takes Russell's atomism as its starting point but transforms it by rejecting the epistemological basis that underpinned it. It is worth pausing to see how radical this transformation was. First, if there are names

---

[2] This appeal to uninstantiated symbols is discussed further in Potter (2021). On Frege's version of the same idea, see Dummett (1991).

that are never tokened, the link between naming and acquaintance is stretched. But, second, if the criterion for nameability is necessary existence, then the link is broken entirely. What is simple according to Russell is whatever is immediate and indubitable in experience. What is simple according to the *Tractatus* is whatever cannot be conceived not to exist. Third, what is epistemologically simple according to Russell may very well not be structurally simple: it may have internal structure. What is simple according to the *Tractatus*, on the other hand, has no (expressible) internal structure.

One way of putting this point would be to say that Russell's atomism was bottom-up, but Wittgenstein's was top-down. Russell's logically proper names were to be attached to whatever are the immediate objects of acquaintance. Wittgenstein's were to be given to whatever turn out to be the simple entities at the endpoint of analysis. This change of perspective inevitably has a knock-on effect on their respective attitudes to the notion of privacy. Russellian sense data are in practice, if not in principle, private to the senser. Wittgenstein's system makes no such assumption: there is no requirement that in order for an object to have a name I should be acquainted with it.

It follows from this that solipsism is a much less virulent doctrine in the context of the *Tractatus* than it was for Russell. When the latter rejected solipsism as implausible, he had in mind a solipsism of acquaintance according to which the external world is a construction that has my own sense data – the objects with which I am acquainted – as its base. Wittgenstein's solipsism, by contrast, has as its base Tractarian objects – whatever are the simple entities that my senseful discourse about the world presupposes.

6.2 Solipsism from Logical Form

The route to Tractarian solipsism that I have sketched so far has its roots in Wittgenstein's engagement with Russellian atomism. I want now to note another, at least superficially somewhat different, route to the same conclusion, one that has a more obviously Fregean rather than a Russellian origin. This route takes as its starting point the picture theory, which holds that in order for representation to be possible there must be an identity of form between a picturing fact and the pictured fact that has to obtain in order that the picturing fact should be true. Wittgenstein's solipsism attempts to show that there could not be distinct perspectives on the world. All picturing takes place from a single perspective, namely mine.

Solipsism and the Self

There are two ways in which your language – your scheme for representing the world – might in principle differ from mine. It might contain names that mine lacks, or, more radically, it might be based on an altogether different manner of combination of those names to form pictures. The former possibility has already been addressed in relation to Wittgenstein's engagement with Russell. Let us now consider the latter.

Wittgenstein's central claim here is that there is a single form that all representations must share. Wittgenstein expressed this by talking of '*the* language which alone I understand', but he did not trouble to offer any explanation of *why* my language is unique. Why could there not be a different, incommensurable language which represents the same world?

A quick answer to this question would use the world as the anchor to connect different representations. The picture theory requires that my picture should have the same form as the world. And it also requires that *your* picture should have the same form as the world. Therefore, it follows that my picture and your picture must have the same form.

This answer is correct as far as it goes, no doubt, but one might hope for an alternative answer that does not use the world as an anchor to bind our representations together. Wittgenstein does at least sketch an argument of this more direct kind when he speaks of what different sorts of representation have in common.

> The gramophone record, the musical thought, the score, the waves of sound, all stand to one another in that pictorial internal relation, which holds between language and the world.
>
> To all of them the logical structure is common.
>
> In the fact that there is a general rule by which the musician is able to read the symphony out of the score, and that there is a rule by which one could reconstruct the symphony from the line on a gramophone record and from this again – by means of the first rule – construct the score, herein lies the internal similarity between these things which at first sight seem to be entirely different. And the rule is the law of projection which projects the symphony into the language of the musical score. It is the rule of translation of this language into the language of the gramophone record. (4.014–4.0141)

Wittgenstein's thought here is that apparently dissimilar pictures have something in common just because they are inter-translatable. That, though, does not really get us what we were after, since it presupposes inter-translatability. What we need is an argument to show that there cannot be incommensurable – i.e. untranslatable – pictures. In the *Tractatus*, no such argument is presented – not explicitly, at least. I wish to suggest, however, that Wittgenstein's conception of logical form was intended to have this as a consequence. The idea is that logical form is the form that any picture must have merely in order to be a picture at all. So, the language whose form is logical form is maximally general and in that sense unique.

It may seem surprising that Wittgenstein arrived at the sign/symbol distinction from a solipsistic perspective, whereas Frege's argument for the sign/sense distinction alluded to a private/public distinction. In arguing for the notion of sense to explain the informational content of 'Hesperus = Phosphorus', Frege rejected appealing to the signs, because the content is not about language, and rejected appealing to ideas, because the content is not private. We are compelled, he thought, to posit a 'third realm' of senses in order to ground the public nature of what is communicated in language. How could Wittgenstein reach the same conclusion without this contrast?

The answer is that the role of the sign/symbol distinction in the *Tractatus* is to make the picture theory compatible with the obvious fact that we cannot read off the structure of the world from the structure of everyday English (or German) sentences. It can therefore be seen to have its roots in the same difficulty that motivated Frege. Frege's two explorers require the notion of sense in order to have the resources to acknowledge that their language does not match the world, because two distinct names, 'Aphla' and 'Ateb', have inadvertently been given to the same mountain.

Wittgenstein outlawed this procedure by adopting the convention that in his formal language one object should never be given two different names. But he could adopt this convention only because of his atomism. The logical atoms of the *Tractatus* do not have different aspects, so one cannot inadvertently name them twice. The two explorers, by contrast, had done nothing wrong: when we name a real-world object such as a mountain, we have to leave room for the possibility that we may later discover another aspect of it.

6.3 I and We

The self that owns the world is the speaker of the one language that I understand. But if that language is the public language that is shared by all of us, one might well wonder whether it might be better to call this self 'we' rather than 'I'. Indeed, just this way of interpreting the solipsism of the *Tractatus* was proposed by Brian McGuinness (2002b).

In that case, though, one might wonder whether the position really deserves to be called solipsism rather than idealism. In the 1916 notebook, however, Wittgenstein mentioned idealism explicitly in order to contrast it with solipsism:

> This is the way I have travelled: Idealism singles men out from the world as unique, solipsism singles me alone out, and at last I see that I too belong with the rest of the world, and so on the one side nothing is left over, and on the other side, as unique, the world. In this way idealism leads to realism if it is strictly thought out. (Wittgenstein 1979: 15 October 1916)

Yet when he adapted this remark for inclusion in the *Tractatus*, idealism did not even get a mention.

> Here we see that solipsism strictly carried out coincides with pure realism. The I in solipsism shrinks to an extensionless point and there remains the reality co-ordinated with it. (5.64)

It is surely noteworthy, indeed, that idealism is barely mentioned in the *Tractatus* at all. The reason for this omission should now be apparent, namely that there is no space between solipsism and realism for idealism to occupy. If solipsism collapses into realism, as the *Tractatus* claims, then any position intermediate between these two, idealism included, collapses along with it.

So the suggestion that the self of Wittgenstein's solipsism is 'we' *rather than* 'I' seems to me (*pace* McGuinness) to miss the point.[3] To describe the world's owner as 'we' is to suggest that it is simply the community of language speakers, whereas what is notable in the *Tractatus* is that the private/public distinction is simply absent from it.[4] (The words 'private' and 'public' do not occur in the book.) The Tractarian notion of a symbol is the inheritor of Frege's notion of the sense of a word, but not because a symbol is public rather than private. What it inherits is Frege's idea that the sense of a word exhausts its logical significance, because it consists in the word's contribution to the truth-conditions of sentences in which it occurs. To give substance to that idea we need to understand the place of logic as the study of the structure that language must have if it is to represent the world at all. But we can do that, Wittgenstein thought, without invoking language's role in communication. Frege had incorrectly linked objectivity with publicity.

---

[3] Williams (1974) contains some perceptive remarks on the Tractarian 'we'.
[4] For an argument that the *Tractatus* contains a sort of 'private language argument', see Diamond (2000a). For a counter-argument, see Child (2013).

6.4 The Thinking Subject

In fact, the *Tractatus* takes this one step further in order to hold that there is at least one sense in which 'I' is not a referring term at all. In its original 1916 version, that is to say, the passage on solipsism finishes with a blunt denial. 'The subject that thinks and entertains ideas, there is no such thing' (5.631). At this stage, however, Wittgenstein did not offer any argument for his blunt claim. (The various remarks that follow in the final version of the *Tractatus* were added to the passage only later.) There is evidently a degree of speculation involved in offering any argument on Wittgenstein's behalf here. However, what I have said about solipsism earlier is surely consonant with the denial of the thinking subject. For the argument was not that the world is represented from one particular perspective rather than some other, i.e. that my perspective is somehow especially privileged but rather that the notion of different perspectives is dissolved once we realize that logical form is the form that any representation at all must have. If there is only a single language – the language which alone I understand – then there is no role for the notion of a perspective to play in anchoring my representation of the world, and hence no role for the thinking subject.

In the *Tractatus*, then, solipsism can be viewed as merely a staging post on the road to a correct understanding of the relationship between thought and world. What the solipsist intends, namely that the world is my world, comes to seem a disappointingly anodyne claim once we discover how insubstantial is the self who claims ownership.

6.5 The Attraction of Solipsism

Solipsism as traditionally understood is a form of scepticism concerning the world. Specifically, it is scepticism concerning whether other people have private experiences that are parallel to and of the same standing as my own. The solipsist takes his own experiences to be the only ones that are 'real'.

Presented in this way solipsism, like other variants of external-world scepticism, will rightly be viewed as primarily a philosopher's device, a position whose primary role is to test out the defences of our conception of the world. The intended endpoint is not to become a sceptic but to refine our conception so as to bolster our defences against the sceptic.

Most philosophers who bother to mention solipsism at all therefore do so only in passing. Even Schopenhauer, more amenable than many to philosophical lost causes, dismissed solipsism swiftly. Wittgenstein therefore stands out as unusual in the seriousness with which he treated the sceptic. In the *Tractatus* he held that what the sceptic intends is 'quite correct', albeit unsayable. In the *Blue Book*, he no longer gave scepticism any endorsement, but he nonetheless thought it a sufficiently significant position to be worth an extended attempt to defang it.

This suggests that Wittgenstein's sympathy for solipsism went beyond the narrow sense, to be considered shortly, in which the position he adopted in the *Tractatus* can be argued to entail it. Rather few philosophers have taken solipsism at all seriously. Yet Wittgenstein took the trouble to consider it in some detail. Why so? Part of the explanation, no doubt, is that most philosophers have understood solipsism in something closer to the empirical sense to which Russell's famous quip about Christine Ladd-Franklin – that she was a solipsist who was surprised that there were no others – might apply.[5]

What I have said already puts me at odds with an influential interpretation according to which Wittgenstein intended not merely to defang but to deny solipsism. Rhees, for instance, claimed that 'Wittgenstein has never held to solipsism, either in the *Tractatus* or at any other time'. He supported this claim by suggesting that we should translate 'meint' not as 'means' but as 'wants to say' (Rhees 1947: 388). 'What solipsism wants to say is quite correct'. I see no reason to object to this translation, but I fail to see how it supports Rhees's contention. Solipsism is unsayable, but what it 'wants to say' is quite correct.

Reading the 5.6s as an endorsement of solipsism is not only more straightforward than Rhees's alternative, but it makes better sense of the sympathy Wittgenstein expressed for solipsism elsewhere. This sympathy is evident, for instance, in his 1916 notebook, where he repeatedly adopted the solipsist's perspective on the world. 'What has history to do with me?' he wondered. 'Mine is the first and only world. I want to report how I find the world' (Wittgenstein 1979: 2 Sep. 1916). And in the *Tractatus* Wittgenstein did not confine his sympathy with solipsism to the 5.6s. 'At death', he said, 'the world does not alter, but comes to an end' (6.431). Why, then, have commentators been so keen to deny, despite appearances to the contrary, that Wittgenstein was endorsing solipsism? Part of the reason is probably that they agree with Stebbing (1933: 74) that 'any philosophical view which leads to the conclusion that what solipsism

---

[5] Russell was not immune to embellishing a story for the sake of a neat joke. See Trybus (2020) for a discussion of Ladd-Franklin's (and Russell's) actual views on solipsism.

means, or intends, to say is quite correct is ... obviously false'; they therefore suppose that charity requires them to seek an alternative interpretation.

Part of the explanation for Wittgenstein's sympathy for solipsism comes from what he understood by the position. His position on ethics, that all propositions are of equal value, will strike most readers as absurd until they understand that by 'ethics' he does not mean the everyday guide to action that we usually mean but rather something absolute and unsayable that transcends the contingencies of everyday life. In a somewhat similar fashion, Wittgenstein's solipsism is not that of someone denying the reality of the minds of other people he encounters from day to day. Instead, I suggest, it is the solipsism of one who is overwhelmingly struck by the specialness of his first-person perspective on the world.

6.6 The Later Additions

So far, I have focused principally on the solipsism passage as it occurred in the version of the *Tractatus* that Wittgenstein had succeeded in compiling by late 1916.[6] From August 1916 onwards, however, he made further remarks about solipsism and the self in his notebook, and these were incorporated into the book quite soon thereafter. (The exact date is a matter of conjecture.) In its extended form, renumbered as the 5.6s, the principal role of the passage on solipsism is to form a sort of transition to the 6s. There Wittgenstein seeks to show that various putative instances of the synthetic *a priori* are not really such, since they all count as unsayable. The dissolution of the self in the 5.6s is a prolegomenon to this. The general tenor of the added remarks might be characterized as irresolute, since they seem to back away both from Wittgenstein's firm rejection of the thinking subject and from his claim that solipsism is unsayable. (This irresolution is intriguing, not least because those who urge a resolute reading of the *Tractatus* often concede that Wittgenstein may have been irresolute when he started writing it and wish to insist only on his resolution when he finished it.) The principal purpose of the added remarks, then, is as a vehicle for Wittgenstein to express (but, I think, ultimately to reject) the temptation towards transcendental idealism that his logical atomism confronts.[7]

---

[6] Sullivan (1996) discusses in detail the phases in the development of Wittgenstein's treatment of solipsism in the *Tractatus*.

[7] For a presentation of Wittgenstein's solipsism in the spirit of the resolute reading of the *Tractatus*, see Floyd (1998).

When viewed on their own terms, though, rather than as a contribution to Wittgenstein's critique of transcendental idealism, the added remarks seem to me to add little that is helpful to the earlier version of the passage. Wittgenstein offers the notion of the metaphysical subject which, he says, is at the limit of the world. He does not explain how, if at all, the metaphysical subject differs from the thinking subject, but he gives the impression that the metaphysical subject may have some kind of ethical, and not merely semantic, significance. Wittgenstein claims that there is a sense in which in philosophy we may speak of the self, but he goes into no detail on what he means by this. Presumably speaking in philosophy is not to be equated with ordinary speaking. He still holds, that is to say, that the self is unsayable. What is unclear is whether he held that in philosophy we can do much more to speak about the I than he has just done in the 5.6s.

The most useful contribution the additional remarks make to Wittgenstein's account of solipsism is contrastive. Wittgenstein now makes it clear that the self that is in question in solipsism is not 'the human soul of which psychology treats' (5.641). He thus allows us to place his earlier denial of the thinking subject in context. He is not attempting to deny that there is a routine way of using the word 'I' to refer to myself, i.e. to the person I see in the mirror. What he is denying is that there is a distinct use of the word 'I' to refer to a necessarily existent entity such as the Cartesian ego has been taken to be. Nonetheless, it has to be conceded that even in its final version, the *Tractatus* is sketchy in explaining the distinction between the two supposed uses of 'I'. He evidently conceived of the empirical subject in something like a Humean fashion, but his lack of interest in the details of how this could be made to work is manifest.

6.7 Solipsism in the Blue Book

What I have sketched here is a route to solipsism and its unsayability that depends both on the atomism of the *Tractatus* and on its conception of logical form as the single most general form of representation. When Wittgenstein returned to philosophy in 1929, he did not abandon his previous work wholesale. His lectures in the early 1930s frequently endorsed positions he had argued for in the *Tractatus*. However, he did very soon question both of the claims – atomism and uniqueness – that underpinned his solipsism.

The first threat to Wittgenstein's atomism arose from the difficulty of analysing incompatible propositions such as those ascribing colours to points in visual space. At first, in his 1929 article 'Some Remarks on

Logical Form' (Wittgenstein 1929), Wittgenstein used this difficulty as a reason to abandon the logical independence of elementary propositions. Soon, though, he came to think that the very notion of an elementary proposition was problematic.

There were several reasons, too, for Wittgenstein's abandonment of the notion that there is a single language with which we confront the world. One notable influence was Ramsey, with whom Wittgenstein had extensive interactions in 1929. In his paper 'The Foundations of Mathematics' (Ramsey 1926), Ramsey argued that Wittgenstein's single absolute sense of unsayability should be replaced with a hierarchy of meanings of 'meaning', so that what is unsayable in one language might become sayable in the next. (Russell had sketched a similar idea in his Introduction to the *Tractatus*.) Ramsey also influenced Wittgenstein in coming to think that the Tractarian conception could offer no plausible account of scientific laws. And the particular case that we considered earlier as relevant to solipsism, namely the inexpressibility in Tractarian language of the sentence $\forall x(x = a_1 \vee x = a_2 \vee \ldots \vee x = a_n)$, came under threat. Wittgenstein now thought that it was implausible to dismiss this as unsayable and that instead the account of quantification he had offered in the *Tractatus* would have to be revised.

Given that Wittgenstein now no longer endorsed the assumptions on which his previous treatment of solipsism had depended, we might predict that he would no longer either endorse solipsism or hold that solipsism is unsayable. And that is indeed the position we find him adopting in the 1930s. In his influential discussion of Wittgenstein's middle period, Hacker (1986: 81) asserts that in this period Wittgenstein produced a 'detailed refutation' of solipsism. This seems to me to overstate the distance between the *Tractatus* and the middle period. Hacker is not entirely clear about where the 'detailed refutation' of solipsism is to be found, but I take it that he supposes the private language argument to be at least a central component of it. If so, then that seems to me to be a misunderstanding. The private language argument certainly attacks the distinction between private and public, but it is possible to abandon that distinction and still maintain a solipsistic conception. Indeed, the *Tractatus* itself is, as we have seen, an example of a work that advances solipsism while nowhere endorsing the private/public distinction. For this reason, it is a mistake, it seems to me, to present the private language argument as a refutation of Tractarian atomism. It certainly has Russellian sense data as one of its intended targets, but Tractarian simple objects need not be supposed to be private in the sense that is identified as problematic in the *Investigations*.

Wittgenstein's most extensive treatment of solipsism is in the *Blue Book* (dictated to his students in 1933–4). Here he does not attempt to refute solipsism but rather to defuse it by showing that any attempt to adopt the view will end up seeming disappointingly empty. This is because the conception that is available to the solipsist of the self that claims ownership of the world is too insubstantial to give the view any real traction. It is, in Wittgenstein's arresting image (Wittgenstein 1969a: 71), like someone sitting in a car who pushes the dashboard in an attempt to make it go faster.

The point at which Wittgenstein's *Blue Book* discussion most helpfully illuminates the *Tractatus* is the distinction he draws between uses of the word 'I' according to whether the possibility of error through misidentification is intelligible. Uses in which error is intelligible ('self as object') can be thought of in Tractarian terms as aiming to refer to the empirical subject. Uses in which error is unintelligible ('self as subject') have a surface grammar, which purports to make 'I' a referring term that refers to the thinking subject or Cartesian ego, but it is central to Wittgenstein's argument in the *Blue Book*, as in the *Tractatus*, that this surface grammar is radically misleading.

6.8 Conclusion

As we have seen, interpretative controversy has not been limited to whether Wittgenstein intended to endorse or to reject a solipsistic outlook. Even those who agree on this have differed on his reasons. I want, in conclusion, to offer some observations on this state of affairs. One of the most obvious (and, at times, frustrating) features of Wittgenstein's philosophical writing is his reluctance to offer arguments for his claims of the sort that are familiar in the writings of other philosophers. Why did he write in this singular fashion? One reason, no doubt, was aesthetic. As Russell reported,

> I told him he ought not simply to state what he thinks true, but to give arguments for it, but he said arguments spoil its beauty, and that he would feel as if he was dirtying a flower with muddy hands. (Russell to Ottoline Morrell, 27 May 1912, in Griffin 1992)

Another reason, though, was the manner in which Wittgenstein went about composing his work. By writing his thoughts in journals and only later assembling them into longer works, he prioritized the individual sentence over the continuous narrative. Although there are tantalizing gaps, we can to a large extent track how the *Tractatus* was assembled. This complicates the task of interpretation. Remarks that first emerge in one context sometimes appear in a quite different context in the finished work. It is sometimes controversial to what extent the new context was deliberate and to what extent an unintended by-product. Moreover, it is clear that Wittgenstein's views carried on developing after he had begun to compile the book. So, it is controversial to what extent we can rely, in interpreting a sentence in the final work, on what he said in the remarks which originally surrounded it in the notebooks. We should not assume that the latter are an unfailingly reliable guide to the interpretation of the former.

The survival of *Bodleianus* (Wittgenstein 2000: MS 104), the notebook in which Wittgenstein compiled the *Tractatus* by transcribing remarks from his notebooks, allows us to trace some of the process by which his thinking developed. The passage on solipsism and the self, in particular, changed its flavour considerably between the first draft and the final version.

When interpreting his work, however, it is also worth bearing in mind a further (though related) reason for the way Wittgenstein presented his ideas. This is that the way he thought very often did not proceed by means of arguments but by moments of insight. It is important not to overstate this. Although his method sometimes comes across as mystical, he was also highly methodical. Even when he himself did not consciously articulate arguments for his views, arguments can be offered on his behalf. Yet understanding his methods does, I believe, impose an interpretative constraint on our attempts to supply the arguments he omitted. Wittgenstein was not, it seems to me, an *elaborate* thinker. He proceeded largely by building up a sequence of insights for which he provided no arguments because, once obtained, they seemed to him to be sufficiently obvious hardly to require any.

I leave it to the reader to judge whether the account of Wittgenstein's Tractarian solipsism that I have sketched here obeys the interpretative principles just articulated.[8]

---

[8] Potter (2020) argues for the account in somewhat more detail.

CHAPTER 7

The Tractatus *and the First Person*

Maria van der Schaar

7.1 Introduction[1]

When reading Wittgenstein's 1913 'Notes on Logic' and the 1914 'Notes Dictated to Moore', one can see that many of his ideas came early to him. There are, though, some important differences between these notes and the *Tractatus*; the most striking one is that there is no mention of the philosophical I in these early writings. Wittgenstein introduces the idea in the *Notebooks*, in a note dated 23 May 2015: '*The limits of my language* mean the limits of my world' (Wittgenstein 1979: 49). Why does Wittgenstein introduce here the first-person indexical? And is this really the first occurrence in his writings that is philosophically relevant? Is there perhaps a relation with a letter to Russell from the day before? When Russell had written that he could not understand Moore's notes, Wittgenstein answers:

> And now I'm afraid that what I've written recently will be still more incomprehensible, and if I do not live to see the end of this war I must be prepared for all my work to go for nothing. ... The problems are becoming more and more lapidary and general and the method has changed drastically (die Methode hat sich durchgreifend geändert). (Letter from 22.5.1915, McGuinness and von Wright 1995: 101–2)

In what sense has Wittgenstein's method changed thoroughly since the notes from 1913 and 1914? It seems that the *Notebooks* note dated 23 May 1915 gives a glimpse of the new method, namely when Wittgenstein imagines having written a book *The World as I Found It*. As I will explain in this chapter, Wittgenstein's new method is throughout

---

[1] I thank Colin Johnston for comments on a first version of this chapter, and Oskari Kuusela for a stimulating discussion after the presentation of this material at the *Heytingday 2022* in Amsterdam, Dutch Royal Academy of Sciences (KNAW).

first-personal and thereby departs from his early often more Russellian approach to philosophical questions.

If the first person plays a fundamental role in Wittgenstein's approach to philosophical issues, there seems to be a danger of psychologism. As Wittgenstein writes in the *Tractatus*: 'Does not my study of sign-language correspond to the study of thought processes which philosophers held to be so essential to the philosophy of logic? Only they got entangled for the most part in unessential psychological investigations, and there is an analogous danger for my method' (4.1121).[2] How are we to prevent a psychologistic reading when we take a first-person methodology to be crucial to the *Tractatus*? When Wittgenstein turns to his *Notebooks* again in 1916, the transcendental reflections start soon. This might be seen as an answer to the threat of psychologism. Such reflections do play a role in the *Tractatus*, but precisely regarding the transcendental ego and the correlated *a priori*, there are crucial differences between Kant and Wittgenstein. These differences, in combination with a first-person method, may lead to solipsism. How is Wittgenstein to overcome psychologism, on the one hand, and transcendental idealism and solipsism, on the other?

In the next section, Wittgenstein's development towards the *Tractatus* will be described as a development towards a first-person methodology. Questions concerning language, logic, and ethics have to be addressed as a first person, from the inside. This first-person method demands something of the reader, too: one should be involved as a first person; one should *do* something as a philosopher when reading the *Tractatus*. In the third section, the question is raised, what the role of the first-person indexical is in remarks such as 'We make ourselves pictures of facts' (2.1); 'we use the sensibly perceptible sign ... of the *Satz* as a projection of the possible state of affairs' (3.11); 'we cannot think anything illogical' (3.03); and 'The *Satz* is a model of reality as we think it is' (4.01). Are these remarks compatible with Wittgenstein's idea that no judging subject is needed in logic, and that logic is to take care of itself? Is the use of the first-person indexical in these passages accidental, or is there an essential role for the first person in logic and language? Do these passages not bring in mental acts as empirical phenomena and an empirical subject, and would this not imply a form of psychologism? In the fourth section, the question is raised of how we are to understand the first person, indicated in such passages. Can we identify it with the transcendental ego, or with the subject of

---

[2] I use the Ogden and Ramsey translation (Wittgenstein 1922), making small changes where appropriate.

solipsism? And how do Wittgenstein's remarks on the philosophical I in the 5.6s relate to the general first-person methodology? Finally, in the concluding section, I will note how the idea of a first-person methodology also may help us in understanding Wittgenstein's remarks on ethics and internal relations.

7.2 The Beginnings of a First-Person Methodology

In the 1913 'Notes on Logic', Wittgenstein directly engages with issues raised by the work of Russell, his tutor at the time. Writing in English, Wittgenstein uses the term 'proposition' for a linguistic entity, to be called the *Satz* in the *Tractatus*. He thus departs from Russell, for whom a proposition is a non-linguistic abstract meaning. In order to make it possible to connect the topic to the *Tractatus*, and to prevent confusion with propositions in the modern, Russellian sense, I will use the term 'sentence' instead of 'proposition'.[3] Sentences, for Wittgenstein, are not names of truth-values, as Frege thought, nor are they names of complexes, as Russell sometimes suggests. Sentences are essentially different from names, for they are themselves facts; they are structured. Sentences in the strict sense have two poles: they can be true, and they can be false (Potter 2009b: B23); they are bipolar, having thus a different relation to the world than names. In logic, assertion is irrelevant: 'There are only unasserted propositions. Assertion is merely psychological' (Potter 2009b: C40; cf. C45). This means that 'The assertion-sign is logically quite without significance' (Potter 2009b: B32).[4] By excluding the assertion sign from logic, Wittgenstein defends a more radical form of anti-psychologism than we find in Russell or Frege.

Influenced by Frege, Russell had introduced the assertion sign in the logic of *Principia Mathematica* (1910) to indicate that the authors assert something (Whitehead and Russell 1910: 8–9). Being a science, logic makes assertions about the world, thereby expressing the most universal laws holding of objects, properties and relations in the world. On this conception of logic, shared by Frege and Russell, logic has content, and as

---

[3] Alas, 'sentence' is weaker than the German 'Satz', think of 'Grundsatz' and 'Lehrsatz', where 'Satz' cannot be translated as 'sentence'. As the sentence here is to be true or false, it is the sentence together with its meaning; not the mere sentence as sign.

[4] I follow Michael Potter's convenient numbering system of his edition of the 'Notes on Logic'. The B notes are probably a translation by Russell of notes dictated in Birmingham. The C notes, the Cambridge notes, can be read as a reformulation of or a comment on the B notes by Wittgenstein; apparently, Wittgenstein dictated them directly in English. See Potter (2009b: Appendix A).

Frege acknowledges in his mature writings, it has a special subject-matter, the logical functions referred to by the logical constants, such as negation and implication, and it has its own concepts, such as subsumption and subordination of concepts (Frege 1906: 428).

Already in the 1913 Notes, Wittgenstein realised that logic 'cannot treat [of] a special set of things' (Potter 2009b: C9; cf. C15). As he writes to Russell (Letter 22.6.1912, McGuinness and von Wright 1995: 15), 'Logic must turn out to be of a *totally* different kind than any other science.' And this likewise holds for philosophy: 'The word "philosophy" ought always to designate something over or under, but not beside, the natural sciences' (Potter 2009b: B67). 'Philosophy consists of logic and metaphysics: logic is its basis' (Potter 2009b: B61); 'Philosophy can neither confirm nor confute scientific investigation' (Potter 2009b: B60). In a certain sense, these passages could still be read as expressing a Fregean understanding of logic and philosophy. For Frege, logic is a foundational science on which all other sciences, including metaphysics and psychology, are founded (Frege 1893: xix).[5] The fact that Wittgenstein realises that logic has no special subject-matter and that assertions are irrelevant to logic will mean, though, that his method must also be very different from Frege's. Although it is true that a first-person engagement is essential to Frege's Begriffsschrift – this is precisely what the judgement stroke indicates (van der Schaar 2018), the *Tractatus* asks for a deeper engagement. Whereas a first-person engagement in Frege's Begriffsschrift is conditional on our aiming to know the laws of logic, the *Tractatus* demands an unconditional engagement of its reader as thinking agent.

In this section, I do not aim to make a comparison between Frege and Wittgenstein. It is the relation with Russell that is more apparent in the 1913 Notes. Although the influence is strong, Wittgenstein is already critical of Russell's conception of logic in 1912, and his conception of philosophy in 1913. In 1915 he criticises Russell's general method in philosophy more explicitly: 'Russell's method in his 'Scientific method in philosophy' is simply a retrogression from the method of physics.'[6] In 1914, Russell aims for a scientific method in philosophy, providing logical constructions of matter and the physical world. He combines a logical with an empirical approach to philosophical questions, where both are understood to be part of a scientific method.

---

[5] English translation: Frege (2013).
[6] (Wittgenstein 1979: 44). Perhaps Wittgenstein is referring to *Our Knowledge of the External World as a Field for Scientific Method in Philosophy*, where Russell advocates a 'logical-analytic method of scientific philosophy' (Russell 1914: 72), or to 'On Scientific Method in Philosophy,' Herbert Spencer lecture delivered at Oxford, 18 November 1914 and published by the Clarendon Press as a pamphlet the same year, later to be published in *Mysticism and Logic* (Russell 1918a).

This approach is used by Russell in his multiple relation theory of judgement that Wittgenstein was at least familiar with through *The Problems of Philosophy* (Russell 1912). During the time that Wittgenstein was preparing his thoughts for the 1913 Notes, Russell was working on a new variant of the multiple relation theory of judgement. Probably, Russell discussed this version with Wittgenstein. Essential to all variants of the multiple relation theory of judgement is that it is a non-propositional account of judgement and that the question of judgement is approached by means of an analysis of judgement- or belief-attribution: how is one to analyse 'Othello judges that Desdemona loves Cassio'? In 1913, Russell gives the following analysis of judgement: $J(S, F, x_1, x_2, \ldots x_n)$ (Russell 1984: 144), where J is a predicate standing for the relation of judging, S has to be substituted by a name for the judging subject, and F has to be substituted by a name for the logical form of what is judged. For Othello's judgement we get: $J(o, R(x,y), d, l, c)$, where $R(x,y)$ represents the logical form of what is judged by Othello, o, d, and c stand for, respectively, Othello, Desdemona, and Cassio, and l stands for loving as non-relating relation. The reasons why Russell has given this analysis are well-known.[7] Let me therefore directly focus on Russell's method, the way the question of judgement is addressed. Russell approaches the question from the outside; he addresses the question of what it is for *someone else* to make a judgement or to have a belief. He sees judgement as an empirical phenomenon in the world, preferring the term 'belief' to 'judgement', as the former denotes more clearly a 'particular dated event which may be studied empirically by psychology' (Russell 1984: 136).

For Russell, judging, like acquaintance, is an empirical relation in the world to be denoted by a predicate, J, while the judging subject is to be one of the related terms. The judging subject is thus an empirical object among others that can be given a name. Strictly speaking, we have to be acquainted with all the terms (objects, terms of a relation) of the analysed judgement, and this means that the name for Othello has to be changed to a definite description. For Russell, the only logically proper name that we could use here is the first-person indexical as standing for one's own mind. This does not change any of the methodological points, though, for one's own mind is likewise considered as a term of the empirical relation of judging. Russell's outsider's approach to the question of judgement holds as much for the analysis of Othello's judgement as for the analysis of one's own judgement. The problem with Russell's analysis of judgement is that

---

[7] A more extensive treatment of Russell's theories of judgement I give in (Van der Schaar, forthcoming).

it takes belief-attribution as starting point, while neglecting what it is for a first person to make a judgement by means of an utterance of the declarative 'Desdemona loves Cassio'.

For Wittgenstein's 1913 Notes, Russell's propositional account of judgement in 1904 is also relevant. Around 1904, Russell understands judgement and belief as attitudes towards propositions (Russell 1904: 523). What is common to the early and later analyses of judgement is that on both accounts judgement is understood as an empirical relation between a judging subject and a complex object, or several objects. In both cases, judgement can be represented by a predicate, and the judging subject is among the objects in the world to which a name can be given.

For Russell, judgement and acquaintance are external relations. Russell follows G.E. Moore's (logical) realism, in which the object of knowledge and thought is taken to be independent of the act of judging and thinking. As Peter Hylton puts it in his presentation of the views of the early Moore: 'An internal relation is one that is in some way essential to, or constitutive of, the identity of the objects related' (Hylton 1990: 121). For both Moore and Russell, the object of thinking, judging, or being acquainted is independent of being thought or judged by a subject. This thesis opposes the Bradleian idea that subject and object of thought can be understood only as part of a unified whole and that we cannot get hold on the object in abstraction from its relation to thought. Wittgenstein's thesis in the *Notebooks* of the logical identity of sign and signified relates to this issue (note dated 4.9.14). Later, he will refer to this as there being an internal relation between name and object named.

In the 1913 Notes, Wittgenstein makes, like Russell, a distinction between propositional attitudes, such as judgement, question, and command, and the 'unasserted proposition': 'Judgment, question and command are all on the same level. What interests logic in them is only the unasserted proposition' (Potter 2009b: C45; cf. B68). It thus seems that for Wittgenstein, too, judging is an empirical, external relation between a subject and an object; the proposition is independent of whether it is judged or not. For Wittgenstein, though, judgement is not a two-term relation between a subject and a sentence ('proposition'), but a four-term relation between a subject, a sentence, and its two poles, as we can see in the picture taken from Potter (2009b: B55):

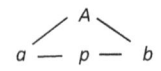

$$\begin{array}{c} A \\ \diagup \diagdown \\ a - p - b \end{array}$$

In the picture, the bipolarity, called *a* and *b*, that is, the proposition's being true or false, is not internal to the proposition; the picture suggests that we can think of a proposition p without its bipolarity. The analysis in the picture further shows that the judging subject can be given a name, '*A*', and that judgement is understood as an external relation. For the terms of the relation are given independently of the relation of judging. Like Russell, Wittgenstein thus gives an analysis of judgement from an outsider's point of view without asking what it is for a first person to make a judgement, what judgement is for oneself.

It is to be doubted, though, whether a picture can give an accurate presentation of 'A judges *p*' on the account presented in the Notes. The judging relation between *A* and the sentence seems to be unique, for the sentence has sense; it has direction. In the Cambridge Notes, Wittgenstein implies that judging is *analogous* to a relation (Potter 2009b: C15). The subject *A* is related to both poles of the sentence, but this 'is obviously not a relation in the ordinary sense' (Potter 2009b: C41). If the sentence is one of the terms of the relation of judging, it seems nothing but a name, but this does not fit in with Wittgenstein's stress on the distinction between names and sentences. 'When we say "A believes *p*," this sounds, it is true, as if here we could substitute a proper name for "*p*"' (Potter 2009b: B55), but this cannot be right. The *p* has to be a place-holder, not for that-clauses but for complete sentences including the verb. We have to mention a whole sentence judged by *A* (Potter 2009b: C29), *with* its declarative form, like 'this rose is red'.

There is one moment in the 1913 Notes when Wittgenstein seems to realise that the question of judgement is not to be addressed the Russellian way:

> Every right theory of judgment must make it impossible for me to judge that this table penholders the book. Russell's theory does not satisfy this requirement. (Potter 2009b: B33)

If one gives an analysis of 'A judges that *p*', the *p* has to be a sentence *for me* who is attributing the belief. Without this step, no full account of judgement can be given, and the nonsense objection cannot be warded off. Wittgenstein starts to realise that the question of judgement has to be addressed, not as a question regarding belief-attribution but as a question that has to be formulated in terms of the first-person indexical: what is it for me, as a first person, to make a judgement by means of an occurrence of the declarative sentence *p*? The judging agent as a first person cannot be referred to, because it is not a part of the empirical world; a first person's judgement is not a state of affairs with objects that can be named and stand in external relations to other objects. The first person is not external but internal to the act of judging and thinking; the act of judging is not an external relation between a subject and an object that have an identity independent of judgement and thought. In Norway, 1914, Wittgenstein explicitly uses the first-person indexical:

> The relation of 'I believe p' to 'p' can be compared to the relation of '"p" says (besagt) p' to p: it is just as impossible that *I* should be a simple as that 'p' should be. (Wittgenstein 1979: 119)

Any suggestions that 'I' could be used as a referring term have disappeared in the analysis. Wittgenstein now realises that no name is needed for the judging subject. The 'p' in the analysis indicates that it is *direct* rather than indirect speech that we have to turn to in the first place.

By 22 May 1915, when he writes to Russell that his method has changed thoroughly, Wittgenstein may have come to realise that we need a first-person approach not only regarding the question of judgement but in all philosophical questions that concern logic, language, and metaphysics. In the *Notebooks* note from 23 May 1915, we see that the philosophical question concerning the limits of language has become a question that concerns 'my language' and 'my world'. In the same note, Wittgenstein introduces an important aspect of his new method in the *Notebooks*:

> In the book 'The World [as] I found [it]' I should also have to report on my body and say which members are subject to my will, etc. For this is a method of isolating the subject, or rather of shewing that in an important sense there is no such thing as the subject; for it would be the one thing that could *not* come into this book.[8]

One imagines oneself to be writing down this book, and this first-person method makes any talk about the subject meaningless. Of course, Wittgenstein has to make use of the term 'subject', but this does not imply that the term has a meaning: '[Because] a way of speaking is nonsensical, it is still possible to go on using it'.[9]

---

[8] (Wittgenstein 1979: 50, emphasis in the original). The original translation uses 'a way of' instead of 'a method'. I prefer the latter, because the German has: 'eine Methode'.

[9] (Wittgenstein 1979: 50). The translation gives 'a bit of language' instead of 'a way of speaking', which is less apt, because this 'bit of language' cannot be a part of language. The German has 'Deswegen, weil eine Redeweise unsinnig ist, kann man sie noch immer gebrauchen'. Wittgenstein writes this just above the passage on the imagined book and the subject.

On 29 May, the same year, Wittgenstein asks: 'But is *language* ("die *Sprache*") the *only* language?' (Wittgenstein 1979: 52). 'Why should there not be a mode of expression through which I can talk *about* language? ... I myself only write *sentences* down here. And why? *How* is language unique?' There is only one language, the language that one uses and understands, the language one cannot go beyond, 'my language', the language of the first person (cf. 5.62). There is no other language in which one could formulate philosophical questions; there is no other language in which one could talk about one's language; there is just the language that one uses and understands. Philosophical questions concerning language and thought and its limit have to be asked from the inside (cf. 4.114), by a first person, who is already using the language. The limits of *my* language are the limits of *language*.

Instead of a spectator's point of view, we need an agent's point of view when we are involved in philosophical issues, as Peter Winch put it in relation to Wittgenstein's ethics (Winch 1972: 211). These are not two different points of view on an equal level, though, that one can change at liberty; one cannot step out of the agent's 'point of view', as it is not a point of view but an engagement of oneself as a first person, the agent, when addressing philosophical problems. A spectator describes empirical facts, but in philosophy we do not describe anything; there are no philosophical facts, as though they could be studied from the outside.

7.3 The *Tractatus*: The First-Person Method and the Problem of Psychologism

As we have seen earlier, the analysis of judgement plays an important role in the development towards a first-person method. What is Wittgenstein's criticism of Russell's account of judgement in the *Tractatus*? When Russell addresses the problem of judgement in the writings that Wittgenstein was familiar with, we see that the idea of a judging subject plays an essential role. In his early account of judgement, Russell understands judgement as an external relation between a subject and an objective proposition consisting of elements of the world. In this sense, judgement is a relation in the world on a par with other relations. The subject and the proposition are independent of the relation of judging. Furthermore, for Russell, judgement is an empirical relation, and this means that the judging subject is an empirical subject in the world. It is this theory that Wittgenstein criticises in 5.541: 'Here it appears superficially as if the proposition *p* stood to the object A in a kind of relation.' A similar criticism applies to

Russell's multiple relation theory of judgement, mentioned in 5.5422. As we have seen, this theory gives an analysis of judgement by taking belief-attribution to be paradigmatic. On this account, judging is likewise understood as an external, empirical relation, though in this case a multiple relation between the judging subject, Othello, in the example, and the objects Desdemona, Cassio, loving as term and the logical form. Judgement is an external relation in the empirical world, relating an empirical subject to such objects.

In 5.541–5.5422 Wittgenstein is not giving his own account of judgement but rather aims to show what is wrong with the analysis of judgement, as proposed by Russell. He also gives his own analysis of belief-attribution, in concise terms, as I do not think belief-attribution is a central issue for him. The point from the 'Notes on Logic' is repeated: the p that stands on the right side of 'judges' in 'A judges p' is a sentence, not a name. This means that what is on the left side of 'judges' cannot be a name either; 'A' as a name has to disappear in the analysis, for what is on the left side needs to have the same complexity as p. What is logically relevant in 'A believes that p', 'A thinks that p', and 'A says p' is nothing but '"p" says p'. The idea of an empirical subject disappears from the analysis, and what is expressed is a correlation of a picture-fact and the fact that p through a correlation of their elements. In the Othello case, the first 'p' describes a picture-fact in Othello, and this picture-fact is said to be projected on a fact, in this case a negative fact, the non-being of the state of affairs that Desdemona loves Cassio (cf. 2.06; see also Russell's introduction to the *Tractatus* (Wittgenstein 1922: 20)). The latter fact is described by the second p, while all p's in the sentence '"p" says p' are in the *attributor*'s language.

The language used in the proposed analysis is thus the language of the agent who is attributing a belief to A. In the analysis, 'Desdemona loves Cassio' on the right side of 'says' has to be a sentence for the one who attributes the belief, and nonsense is thereby excluded. The analysis of 'A judges p' may thus bring the reader of the *Tractatus* from a focus on A to which belief is attributed, to the one who does the attributing, who is *using* the language, the first person. Together with one's understanding that the idea of an empirical subject is irrelevant to a philosophical analysis of judgement, the passage can thus be understood not only as providing insight into Wittgenstein's first-person method but also as a preparation for the 5.6s on the philosophical I.

Why does the insight that the sentence p has to be a sentence for the attributor guarantee that nonsense judgements are excluded? To answer this question, we have to turn to the 3.0s on the thought ('der Gedanke'), for sentences are a special kind of thought, a thought 'expressed perceptibly through the senses' (3.1). After *the thought* has been introduced as the logical picture of the facts in TLP 3, we can find what James Griffin has called 'Wittgenstein's own theory of judgement' (Griffin 1964: 112). And this *is* a central issue in the *Tractatus*. Before one can give an account of belief-attribution, as in the 5.54s, one first has to understand what it is for oneself, as a first person, to judge and think. We have to understand that '[w]e cannot think anything illogical, for otherwise we should have to think illogically' (3.03). Judging nonsense is excluded, because it is not in our capacity to think that way. There is no way to construct a sentence illogically (3.031, 3.032), for the names in the sentence come with their possibility of being combined with other names in sentences; there is thus no way to combine them the wrong way. As the names are internally related to the objects as their *Bedeutung*, these objects come with the same possibilities of combination, as will be explained more fully later in the chapter. In this way, the sentence as a connection of names is a picture of a possible state of affairs. A judgement or thought, being not essentially different from a sentence, thus 'contains the possibility of the situation which it thinks. What is thinkable is also possible' (3.02).

How is the 'we' to be understood as it occurs in 3.03, as well as in other passages where the first-person indexical seems to be philosophically relevant? An early passage in the *Notebooks* gives: '*By* my correlating the components of the picture with objects, it comes to represent a situation and to be right or wrong' (26 November 1914, Wittgenstein 1979: 33–34, emphasis in the original). If my correlating would be understood as a mental act, a psychic fact in the empirical world, it could be investigated by psychology, but it would have no philosophical relevance. The remark is not repeated in the *Tractatus*. We have to be careful when using remarks from the *Notebooks* to understand the *Tractatus*, especially if they have an early date. The way this remark is formulated makes one think that names and objects are given independently of each other, which would then have to be related by an external, empirical act of the mind. The objects in the *Tractatus*, though, are the result of analysis, not starting points. Its equivalent in the *Tractatus*, 2.1513–2.1515, shows that we can only speak of a picturing relation as correlation of elements and the things they stand for *within* a picture. Mental acts, as external relations in the world, would never be able to make such a connection. If we abstract from conventional differences and consider a name purely as a name of this object, there is an internal relation between name and object; we cannot understand what a name is without bringing in the object to which it is correlated (3.34-3.3411). It is not that we first start with correlating names with objects, for these names have only a role in the sentences as we use them. Given that we use a certain sentence, that the sentence is significant, the names are already correlated with objects. It is the significant use within a sentence that gives the sign a meaning. The significant sentence, the thought, is thus an applied sentence, a sentence in use (3.5, 4). When Wittgenstein writes in the 4s that a sentence *says* something, he is speaking of the significant sentence, the sentence in use (4.022, 4.21). This means that the object named is the name's contribution to the sentence, not to be understood as a complex name but as expressing a certain truth-condition, as having bipolarity. When we see that a name is essentially a name as part of a sentence and that a sentence is essentially a sentence in use, we understand that the first person is internal to the sentence, just as it is internal to judging and thinking.

According to the context principle, the meaning of names can only be understood insofar as they have a role in a sentence (3.3). This explains that names and objects come with the same possibilities to enter certain structures, respectively, in sentences and in the corresponding possible situations. The accidental features of names can be explained in terms of conventions, that is, in psychological terms, and we can now see that these are irrelevant to the philosophical question of how names can stand for something. As in Frege's *Foundations of Arithmetic* (Frege 1980a), there is in the *Tractatus* a relation between the principle that the psychological is to be sharply separated from the logical, and the context principle: 'If the second principle [the context principle] is not observed, one is almost forced to take as the meanings of words mental pictures or acts of the individual mind, and so to offend against the first principle as well' (Frege 1980a: x). On Wittgenstein's account, if the context principle is not observed, one understands names and objects named to be given independently of each other. Name and object would then have to be related psychologically in order for the name to be the name of this object.

We can go back now to occurrences of 'we', as in 3.03 and 2.1: 'We make ourselves pictures of facts.'[10] The 'we' is to indicate any thinking agent, any user of language. First-person *plural*, for at this point

---

[10] The *Prototractatus* has less emphasis on the first-person plural: 'Die Tatsachen begreifen wir in Bildern' (Wittgenstein 1971: 2.1). The order in the *Tractatus* is the same order as in Herz's corresponding sentence: 'Wir machen uns innere Scheinbilder oder Symbole der äusseren Gegenstände' (Hertz 1894: 1).

Wittgenstein has not introduced yet the distinction between arbitrary, conventional aspects, and essential aspects of signs. If we then come to the 5.6s, we know that the philosopher can abstract from conventional differences, that part of language that relates to a community. Only the language used by the first-person singular, one's own language, is relevant to the philosopher. If one understands one's language, one understands language, the essence of language, and thereby one understands the limits of thought. The idea of the first person was there right from the beginning. It is most clearly put forward in 2.1, but it is already there in 2.0121, in the remark that we cannot think of an object without its possibilities to connect with others.

There is thus no need to mention mental acts or judging subjects in the analysis of a first person's judgement, or in the analysis of what we can say, think, and judge. Russell addresses the question of judgement, and philosophical questions in general as a spectator, as an outsider, as though he is dealing with an empirical question, but there is no such position for the philosopher, on Wittgenstein's account. We now see that philosophy is very different from the sciences, because of its first-person methodology. This still leaves us with the question of how to understand the first person in the *Tractatus*.

7.4 The First Person in the *Tractatus*: Solipsism and the Transcendental

The first person is finally thematised in the 5.6s, which start with the remark that the limits of my language mean the limits of my world that is crucial to understanding Wittgenstein's struggle with solipsism, as we will see later. By using the first-person method of imagining a book *The World as I Found It* (5.631), it becomes clear that the I cannot be found in this world. Neither is it anything besides the world (5.6331), perhaps as a kind of world-soul, in which different subjects could participate, as was suggested by Brian McGuinness (McGuinness 2002a: 138), for there is nothing beyond the world. It is true that 'die Weltseele' is mentioned in the *Notebooks* (23.5.15 (Wittgenstein 1979: 49)), but in the *Tractatus* this does not come back. The idea of a first person excludes the idea of different subjects, subjects that one would be able to count. We have seen that the attribution of thoughts to others, to humans, lions, and trees, is nothing but the acknowledgement of picture-facts in the world. The idea of a world-soul may have been a temptation for Wittgenstein when writing in his notebooks, but there is no place for it in the *Tractatus*. As the I is essentially first-personal, it is not the case that the world can be identified with 'the neutral, intersubjective states of affairs', as Marie McGinn (2006: 276–77) has proposed, in line with McGuinness. This is not to say that states of affairs are subjective, for the idea of a first person does not bring in a point of view, nor any specific characteristics that would allow us to make a distinction between different subjects. The first person in its purified form, the moment it reaches full understanding, is impersonal. There is simply no difference to make here. One's path towards this, the path of the reader, engaged in freeing oneself of philosophical demons, is unique, though, depending on the demons one has to struggle with.

Transcendental idealism seems to be one of the demons in the *Tractatus*. There is no doubt that there is a Kantian and Neo-Kantian background to Wittgenstein's thoughts, given the cultural background in the German-speaking world at the time, and elements of (Neo-) Kantianism in Frege's writings. Kant's anti-psychologism and his thesis of the priority of judgement over concepts were important strands of Neo-Kantianism. In some respects, Neo-Kantianism seems to be the stronger influence on the *Tractatus*. Wittgenstein's view on Newtonian mechanics is typically Neo-Kantian (6.34–6.341), and there is in the *Tractatus* no distinction between appearances and things in themselves; we cannot imagine anything beyond logical space. There are, though, important differences between Wittgenstein and the Neo-Kantians. In the first place, we have to realise that the question of validity of knowledge that has been central to Neo-Kantianism is absent from the *Tractatus*. The Neo-Kantian ideas of truth and knowledge as a value that Wittgenstein must have known through Frege's writings, are absent from the *Tractatus*. The more Kantian idea that subject and world form a unity that Wittgenstein was familiar with through Schopenhauer's writings, plays an important role in the *Tractatus*, but the importance of language gives a modification to it. In the *Tractatus*, language and world are internally related; language and world are a unity. The question thus arises: what is left of the subject, the I, for whom this is a unity? Not that much, as we will see.

Turning now to the more strictly Kantian views, there is no doubt that a transcendental question plays a role in the *Tractatus*. Given that there is language through which something is said about the world, what are its necessary conditions? Identity of logical form in the picture and what is pictured seem to play a central role in the answer. The problem, though, is that there is no way in which we could say something about logical form, given that it is a necessary condition for any language. There are thus no truths with content that we could determine as *a priori* conditions for the possibility of language. This means that the Kantian idea of philosophy as critique pointing out the limits of knowledge cannot be straightforwardly applied to a question of the limits of what we can say or think. All we can do is understand each sentence as the result of an *a priori* construction from elementary sentences; each construction we thus can foresee by means of the formal operations that we can apply to the elementary sentences (5.556). And we thus understand that there is no way in which this could go wrong. Equally, each elementary sentence already says something, as it consists of names that already come with their possibilities of combination. These two ways of constructing sentences determine the limit of what we can think from the inside. No judgemental form of unity is needed to bring any elements into a certain order to allow for judgement; formal logic already provides for that. All judgements, all sentences, have the same judgemental form that comes in when the names are connected in a chain: *Es verhält sich so und so*; so and so is the case (4.5; Wittgenstein 1973: 30). Given that names already contain their possibility of combination in sentences, there is no way in which names could be combined the wrong way, as we have seen in the previous section. And, as these names are internally related to the objects they name, and these objects thus come with corresponding possibilities of combination in states of affairs, what can be expressed in language coincides with the realm of logical space. The result of this transcendental approach to the question of language is that logic essentially applies to the world and that the Kantian distinction between formal and transcendental logic collapses (KrV: A57).[11] For Wittgenstein, formal logic *is* transcendental.

The *a priori* structure of the world is thus a purely formal one. There is no possibility of knowing this *a priori* structure, for it has no content. There is thus no possibility of synthetic *a priori* judgements; there is no extension of knowledge regarding the *a priori*. As Peter Sullivan has noted, this idea of a purely formal *a priori* has consequences for the way the ego is to be understood, for it means that the I has no substantial role to play: 'emptiness and formality go together' (Sullivan 1996: 211). Because logic is purely formal, and transcendental logic coincides with formal logic, the ego is empty. There is thus no question of how subjective conditions of thought could have objective validity (KrV: A90), and no transcendental deduction is thus needed.[12]

---

[11] I use KrV to refer to Kant's *Kritik der reinen Vernunft* (Kant 1998).
[12] The third section of Hao Tang's 2011 paper is illuminating on this point (Tang 2011).

This leaves us with the final question of whether the first person, the I in the *Tractatus* can be identified with the transcendental subject, the I in Kant's *Critique of Pure Reason*. For Kant, the *I think* is a transcendental notion (KrV: A341). This notion, or judgement, the *I think*, accompanies all our judgements. As Kant makes clear, nothing can be said about the I, about the transcendental subject, for as soon as we make a judgement about it, we would already make use of the ego (KrV: A346). The I in the *Critique of Pure Reason* thus seems to be as empty as the I in the *Tractatus*. I do think, though, that there is an important difference here between Kant and Wittgenstein. Wittgenstein is not in need of the same *I think* that accompanies all one's thinking and judging; there is for him no question of the unity of self-consciousness, from which the unity of thought arises. As we have seen, my language is the language, and this identification can also be read from right to left: the language is my language. There is no way in which thoughts as significant sentences could not be mine; no story is needed to account for 'the unity of the contents of one's thoughts, and *thereby* of oneself as the agent of that unity'.[13] For those less familiar with Kant's writings, a similar contrast can be made between Wittgenstein and Frege. The judgement stroke in front of the different sentences in a Begriffsschrift is without content, and so far there is an agreement between the three philosophers. But when we take the Fregean *Begriffsschriftsätze*, including the judgement stroke, together, we may see that the presence of the judgement stroke in these cases points to a unity of the judgements made that is not needed in the *Tractatus*. It is thus possible for Frege to give different variants of a Begriffsschrift with somewhat different axioms as concept-script assertions, as we can see when we compare the Begriffsschrift from 1879 with the one presented in the *Grundgesetze*, a distinction that does not get hold on the *Tractatus*.

If, then, the ego is just me, this may bring in a form of metaphysical solipsism, probably the strongest temptation for Wittgenstein in the *Tractatus* (5.62, 5.63): 'I am my world' and 'the world is my world' (5.641). Because the limit of my language is the limit of language, the limit of my world is the limit of the world. Thus, I am the world. As David Bell has pointed out, the identity 'I am the world' can be read in two ways. From right to left, it means that the world reduces to the I. This is metaphysical solipsism: the world is nothing but what appears to me; the world thus reduces to the metaphysical subject. In the *Tractatus*, one has to read it, though, from left to right: 'it is the I who disappears' (Bell 1996:

---

[13] (Longuenesse 2017: 81); I substituted 'one's' for 'her', and 'oneself' for 'herself' for stylistic reasons.

161); cf. Sullivan (2013: 265). Wittgenstein's is a 'self-effacing solipsism'. It is thus that 'solipsism strictly carried out coincides with pure realism' (5.64; 5.631–5.64).

The 'I' we use when speaking of the first person cannot be used as a referring expression, for there is no such object in the world that could be named. Together with the thesis that the 'I' has no substantial content, this seems to leave us empty-handed. This is true, but it also means that we have to look for the first person elsewhere. Overcoming the division of I and world, and the submission of oneself to the world has important consequences for the question of how to live. One way of understanding this is to relate the *Tractatus* to the author, to Wittgenstein himself. As Gottfried Gabriel puts it, solipsism is 'the *Leitmotif* in Wittgenstein's life and philosophy' (Gabriel 2017: title). Gabriel is right that Wittgenstein's struggle with solipsism is visible on the pages of the *Tractatus*. Diamond's thesis that the reader is to understand not the propositions but the author of the *Tractatus* (Diamond 2000b: 155) has a strong focus on the author, too. When we read the 'I' as the author, though, we also miss something. As Amos Oz writes, it is not the distance between what is written and the author that needs to be ploughed but the distance between what is written and you. You, reader, have to imagine to be in Raskolnikov's place (Oz 2003: Ch. 5).[14] The I is both the author and the reader.[15] The idea that philosophy demands a first-person methodology shows itself in the identification of the first person with you as a reader.

7.5 Conclusion: The First-Person Method in the *Tractatus*

We have seen that a first-person methodology is essential in order to understand judgement, thought, and the question of the limit of what we can think. To what extent can the method be noted elsewhere in the *Tractatus*? As we have seen earlier, internal relations play a role in the account of names and sentences and their meaning: there is an internal

---

[14] The chapter is deleted from the English edition (Oz 2017).
[15] Cora Diamond and James Conant have also drawn attention to the role of the reader with respect to the *Tractatus*, see for example Diamond (2000b: 164, 165) and Conant (2011: 628). Compare also the work of Kremer (2004). The students at the seminar *Thought and the Limits of Language*, Leiden 2022, have pointed to a problem with Diamond's understanding of the role of the reader. As the reader has to approach the sentences of the *Tractatus* in a make-believe way (Diamond 2000b: 169), it seems that the reader's method is a psychological one. In the end, though, I think that Diamond acknowledges the reader as a first person, as she takes the aim of the *Tractatus* to be a reader's self-understanding (Diamond 2000b: 161).

relation between name and object, and between a picture and the possible state of affairs it pictures, abstracting from conventional differences between languages. They also play a crucial role in logic. A standard account of internal relations does not seem to involve the idea of a first person. In 5.131, Wittgenstein understands the relation of logical consequence (*folgen*) as internal. As he explains, these relations 'exist as soon as, and by the very fact that, the sentences exist'. This explanation conforms to the one that may have come to him through Moore, the one we noted in Section 7.2: an internal relation is constitutive of the identity of the objects related. When Wittgenstein gives an account of internal relations for the first time, he puts it, though, in a different way: 'A property is internal if it is unthinkable that its object does not possess it.' And, if two objects stand in an internal relation, '[i]t is unthinkable that *these* two objects should not stand in this relation' (4.123). This already shows that the notion cannot be understood without bringing in the thinking or judging agent, the first person. How are we to reconcile this account with the explanation given in 5.131, and with the thesis that logic is to take care of itself? The point is that (non-elementary) sentences are ordered in a formal series, a series which is ordered through internal relations (4.1252). Every sentence is thus the result of successive applications of an operation upon elementary sentences (6.001). The language-using agent is internal to the sentence – there is no sentence without a first person using the sentence. This means that the logical relations between the non-elementary sentences can be recognised by us, because we ourselves are able to construct the non-elementary sentences from elementary sentences through the successive applications of the operation. It is thus possible for us to recognise these internal relations between sentences if they are formulated in a logically perspicuous language. We can then recognise them just by the look of these sentences, by our understanding of how they can be constructed.[16] If the logician has made such a logically perspicuous language, no inference rules are needed, and logic can take care of itself. The mere inspection of the sentences that function as premises and conclusion makes one see that the inference is valid.[17] This means that the truth of logical sentences, the tautologies, can be recognised from the symbol alone.[18] For we can see how the elementary sentences are internally

---

[16] 'da wir ja in einer entsprechenden Notation die formalen Eigenschaften der Sätze durch das blosse Ansehen dieser Sätze erkennen können' (6.122).
[17] 'so wird der innere Zusammenhang offenbar' (5.1311).
[18] 'dass man am Symbol allein erkennen kann, dass sie wahr sind' (6.113).

related to each other within such a logical sentence. This recognising or seeing we do on the basis of our logical capacity, but it does not result in propositional knowledge, for internal relations cannot be expressed in sentences the way we can express external relations (4.124).[19] One can recognise these internal, logical relations only insofar as the sentences are part of one's own language, the language of the first person. The 'seeing' is a first-person understanding of these logical relations, captured by our ability – 'how to go on' (cf. Kremer 2004: 62).

It also seems that the idea of the first person is not to be neglected with respect to the question of the value of life. Ethics, at least, ethics as it is understood in the *Tractatus*, concerns 'a man's understanding and assessment of his own life', as Peter Winch put it (Winch 1972: 2). On the one hand, Wittgenstein writes that the meaning of life cannot be found in the world (6.41, 6.432): all sentences are of equal value, and this means that no state of affairs is of more value than any other. On the other hand, the world of the happy (*der Glückliche*) is different from the world of the unhappy (6.43). It makes a difference to the world, to my world, whether I am happy or not. This must mean that the happy and the unhappy view the world in different ways; in this way the value of one's life may penetrate everything in the world, and may change the world, my world, without changing any state of affairs as part of it. The question is thus how I see the world, a question for me as a first person. Seeing the value of the world and of life is not something I can learn from others by teaching, for we cannot talk about it in terms of true or false sentences. As Wittgenstein is to put it later in his discussion with Schlick on ethics: 'The ethical cannot be taught.'[20] In the same discussion, Wittgenstein refers to his 'Lecture on Ethics' from 1929 or 1930: 'I have in my talk on ethics talked in the first person. I believe that this is something essential. Here one can say nothing factual, I can only step out as personality, and speak in the first person' (Waismann 1965: 14). Here a new element of the first-person methodology is introduced, a personal element, because people may differ in the way they see value in the world and their life. As Wittgenstein puts it

---

[19] Here my paper connects to Kuusela (2023): Kuusela makes it clear that logical knowledge is non-propositional.

[20] 'Das Ethische kann man nicht lehren' (Waismann 1965: 14). As Miles Burnyeat put it in relation to Augustine's *De Magistro*: 'no man ever does or can teach another anything' (Burnyeat 1987: 1). As Burnyeat explains, this relates to Augustine's conception of knowledge as understanding. Of course, I can tell you about a fact that happened, and you may thereby have learned something that has the form of propositional knowledge. What cannot be taught is something that demands understanding, something that relates to the connection of true propositions. Understanding is something that one can only do for oneself.

in the lecture, '[T]his is an entirely personal matter' (Wittgenstein 1965: 8), because it concerns a personal experience, such as *I wonder at the existence of the world*. Whereas the logical connections between sentences that penetrate the whole of language are the same for any user of language, there may be a huge difference in the way people see the world as a whole. Such a personal element was absent when questions of language and logic were addressed. As in the *Tractatus*, in the lecture on ethics Wittgenstein takes the verbal expression of such an experience to be nonsense: 'I am misusing language' (Wittgenstein 1965: 8). '[I]t is nonsense to say that I wonder at the existence of the world, because I cannot imagine it not existing' (Wittgenstein 1965: 9). The fact that it is nonsense says something about the essence of our experience. Most personal experiences can be described as an empirical phenomenon in the world; one's wonder at the existence of Mount Everest is a state of affairs among others that may be studied by psychology. Ethical experiences that relate to the meaning of life cannot be described that way; they are first-personal in a deeper sense. For such questions relate to you, the reader, the first person: you see the meaning of your own life, when you know how to live your life, when you know how to go on.

CHAPTER 8

Arithmetic in the Tractatus Logico-Philosophicus

Mathieu Marion and Mitsuhiro Okada

Wittgenstein's remarks on mathematics occur within two stretches of the *Tractatus Logico-Philosophicus*, 6.02–6.031 and 6.2–6.241. They contain a definition of natural numbers (6.02) in terms of repeated applications of an operation (6.021) and a definition of multiplication (6.241), which both presuppose in turn an account of 'operations' briefly outlined in 5.2–5.254. Apparently, Wittgenstein wrongly assumed not only that these would form a sufficient basis for an account but also that the latter could be seamlessly extended from arithmetic to other parts of pure mathematics, without any need to show how this could be achieved. Russell had independently expressed a similar opinion two years earlier, in *Introduction to Mathematical Philosophy*:

> All traditional pure mathematics, including analytical geometry, may be regarded as consisting wholly of propositions about the natural numbers.[1] That is to say, the terms which occur can be defined by means of the natural numbers, and the propositions can be deduced from the properties of the natural numbers – with the addition, in each case, of the ideas and propositions of pure logic. (Russell 1919a: 4)

For both Russell and Wittgenstein, the key was, therefore, to give an account of 'propositions about the natural numbers' or, as Russell put it, of the following 'five primitive propositions which Peano assumes':[2]

(1) 0 is a number.

(2) The successor of any number is a number.

---

[1] Strictly speaking, analytical geometry requires that the logicist account be extended to real numbers.
[2] These 'primitive propositions' correspond to what are usually known today as the 'Peano Axioms' (an expression also used by Russell), since they were first presented in 1889 by Giuseppe Peano in his *Arithmetices principia* (Peano 1967: 94). Although these issues cannot be discussed here, one should note that proposition (5) is a translation of Peano's version of the principle of mathematical induction, of which logicists (Frege and Russell), originally proposed (impredicative) second-order versions, and that it was unclear at the time if it should be considered as an axiom or as a theorem needing to be proved.

(3) No two numbers have the same successor.

(4) 0 is not the successor of any number.

(5) Any property which belongs to 0, and also belongs to the successor of every number which has the property, belongs to all numbers. (Russell 1919a: 5–6)

As we shall see shortly, however, Wittgenstein's viewpoint does not coincide with Russell's at all. At all events, since Wittgenstein did not explain how to extend his account of arithmetic, we will consciously limit our discussion to natural numbers and arithmetical operations.

The aforementioned limitations notwithstanding, Wittgenstein's account of arithmetic and his philosophical discussion contain valuable insights, and the objective of this chapter will be to try and bring them to the fore in a pedagogical manner. It will be divided into four parts. To understand what Wittgenstein was trying to achieve, we need first to give in the next section a brief account of his criticisms of the 'logicist' programme. One cannot get into great details because this would require us to discuss other parts of the book, a task that would take up too much space. In Section 8.2, we will present Wittgenstein's account of natural numbers and arithmetical calculations. This will be followed in Section 8.3 by a discussion of the associated philosophical remarks and, in the conclusion, with a brief look ahead at later developments within Wittgenstein's 'middle period', only insofar as they shed further light on his aims in 6.02–6.031 and 6.2–6.241.[3]

8.1 Rejecting Logicism

To understand 'logicism', it helps to think of logic as the theory of concepts and of classes that are formed by objects that 'fall under the concepts', to use Frege's turn of phrase. Logicism was the attempt by Frege in his *Grundgesetze der Arithmetik* (Frege 2013) and Russell and Whitehead in their *Principia Mathematica* (Whitehead and Russell 1910) at deriving mathematics from logic or, paraphrasing Carnap, at deriving

---

[3] There is no space to discuss problems of interpretation or to give a full account of Wittgenstein's philosophy of arithmetic. With the exception of a brief discussion of Hancock and Martin-Löf (1975), there is no critical discussion of the secondary literature. Readers interested in more advanced and more exhaustive presentations are referred to the writings of Lello Frascolla (Frascolla 1994: ch. 1, 1997, 2007: 182–198, 2016) and of Michael Potter (Potter 2000: ch. 6, 2009a, 2020: 384–387), and more pointedly on the general form of operation and problems with Wittgenstein's notation to (Sundholm 1992).

the basic or 'primitive' concepts of arithmetic – 'o', 'successor', and 'number' in the 'primitive propositions' (1)–(5) discussed earlier – from logical ones through 'explicit definitions' and deriving the theorems of arithmetic from logical axioms 'through purely logical deductions' (Carnap 1983: 41). Although Wittgenstein knew both works and their authors, we will focus here on Russell's attempt at deriving arithmetic from logic, the more proximate target of his critiques.[4]

When he began writing out this derivation, Russell discovered a paradox – one of a number of paradoxes that were discovered at the time, see Russell (1908: 222–224) – involving Cantor's proof that there is no greatest cardinal number and the notion of a universal class containing all objects. It was about the 'class of all classes that are not members of themselves': if this class is a member of itself, then it is not a member of itself and if it is not a member of itself, then it is a member of itself. Wittgenstein suggested a solution to Russell's paradox at 3.333, which is usually considered to be an unsuccessful attempt at bypassing it, but he simply saw the derivation of paradoxes as a reason to do away with the theory of classes altogether, in accordance here with Heinrich Hertz's requirement that if one is presented with two competing 'images' that picture as many as possible of an object's 'essential relations', one should choose the one containing the 'smaller number of superfluous entities and relations' (Hertz 1899: 2). Hertz's own idea had been to motivate doing away with the contradictions involved, in mechanics, with the concept of 'force' by doing away with it (Hertz 1899: 7–8).

Russell provided his own diagnosis for these paradoxes, based on an analysis of their common structure, under the form of a rule, known as 'the vicious circle principle': 'Whatever involves *all* of a collection must not be one of a collection' (Russell 1908: 225). It is easy to see that this prohibition would block the derivation of his paradox. Russell had already introduced 'types' in Appendix B to *The Principles of Mathematics* (Russell 1903: 523–528), in order to capture the idea that every propositional function $\Phi(x)$ must have a range within which x lies, that is, a 'range of significance' for it to be a proposition.[5] In the hierarchy of types, the lowest type 0 would be that of objects or 'individuals', type 1 would be that

---

[4] Russell's *Introduction to Mathematical Philosophy* (Russell 1919a) remains an excellent informal introduction, and so is Carnap's 1931 paper (Carnap 1983). See also Shapiro (2000: 115–124) for a short pedagogical introduction and Urquhart (2003) for a more advanced presentation.
[5] A 'propositional function' is an expression that contains a variable x and 'expresses a *proposition* as soon as a value is assigned to x' (Whitehead and Russell 1925: 38).

of 'classes of individuals', type 2 that of 'classes of classes of individuals', etc.

The vicious circle principle forced him to update this theory with the introduction of 'orders': a class of type 1 is of order 0 or 'predicative', if it could be defined without reference to classes; a class of type 1 is of first order if it is not predicative but can be defined only in terms of predicative classes; a class of type 1 would be of second order if it is not predicative but can be defined only in terms of classes of type 1 of first order, etc. This is known as the 'ramified theory of types', and Wittgenstein's criticisms are aimed at Russell's attempt at deriving the basic concepts of arithmetic within it.

Adapting an idea of Frege, Russell defined the number of a class as the class of all classes that are in a 'one–one' relation or equinumerous to it.[6] So the number of horses of a quadriga is the class of all four-membered classes (or quadruples of individuals), this being a type 2 class in the aforementioned hierarchy. Thus, 0 is defined as the class of all type 1 classes that have no members, so as a class of type 2 with only one member, the empty class, and the successor of the number of a class C as the number of the class consisting of C and another individual x which is not in C (Russell 1919a: 23). Finally, 'x is a natural number' if it belongs to every class that contains 0 and a successor for each of its members. We can see that Russell has offered here a logical derivation of Peano's three primitive notions, but we should notice immediately that this definition is 'impredicative', since the class of natural numbers is of type 3 and defined in terms of every class of that very type.[7]

There are two major difficulties with this construction of natural numbers in terms of classes. First, the existence of natural numbers depends on the existence of an appropriate number of individuals: in a world with only three individuals, it would not be possible even to define the number 4 as above, that is, as the class of all four-membered classes. Russell thus introduced an 'axiom of infinity' that states that there are infinitely many (distinguishable) individuals (of type 0), and whenever it was needed to prove a theorem T, he simply introduced it, in effect stating as a theorem of logic: if there are infinitely many individuals, then T. This axiom has nothing 'logical' to it, it is just an empirical matter, as Chwistek in 1921 and Ramsey in 1925 were to point out.[8] Wittgenstein had already voiced this objection in a letter to Russell in 1913: 'it is for *physics* to say

---

[6] See Russell (1919a: 15,18) for the notion of 'one–one' relation.
[7] See Shapiro (2000: 119). There is an echo of this in Wittgenstein's criticism of the 'ancestral relation' in 4.1273 as involving a circularity. See Marion (1998: 42–44) and Frascolla (2007: 197).
[8] See, respectively, Chwistek (1967: 338) and Ramsey (1926: 382).

Arithmetic in the Tractatus Logico-Philosophicus 149

whether any thing exists. The same holds for the axiom of infinity: whether there exist $\aleph_0$ things is a matter for experience to determine' (McGuinness 2008: 58). In the *Tractatus*, he provided another argument, namely that the axiom of infinity is a 'pseudo-proposition' or, briefly put, that it unsuccessfully tries to express what can only be shown:

> 5.535 – This also disposes of all the problems that were connected with such pseudo-propositions.
>
> The solution of all the problems that Russell's 'axiom of infinity' brings with it can be given at this point.
>
> What the axiom of infinity is intended to say would express itself in language through the existence of infinitely many names with different meanings.

The second major difficulty has to do with ramification into 'orders', which was forced by the vicious circle principle. In the previous definition of 'natural number' in terms of 'every class that contains 0 and a successor of each of its members', one would need to restrict the definition of 'every class' to a certain 'order' in the hierarchy of type 2 classes. This meant that n is a type 2 first-order natural number if it belongs to every predicative class that contains 0 and a successor of each of its members; n is a type 2, second-order natural number if it belongs to every first-order class that contains 0 and a successor of each of its members, etc. When trying to define 'x is a natural number', one would have to quantify over every class of type 3, as mentioned earlier but, in order to avoid impredicativity, only over classes of a certain order. This causes problems with respect to mathematical induction, that is (5), according to which 'any property which belongs to 0, and also belongs to the successor of every number which has the property, belongs to all numbers'.[9] Suppose one has proven, with 'S' standing for the successor function, that F(0) and F(a) → F(Sa), and that one would like to infer that the property 'belongs to all numbers'. For any order k, if F is a property of that order, then this is justified by the definition and it is also automatically the case for properties of order below k (as can be gathered from the earlier presentation), but there is no way to infer that a natural number x has all properties of order higher than k.[10] So Russell introduced the 'axiom of reducibility',[11] which states that for

---

[9] There are also problems arising when one tries to derive the axioms for the calculus. These are briefly explained using the example of the least upper bound in Urquhart (2003: 298–299).
[10] See Myhill (1974: 20).
[11] See 12*1 in *Principia Mathematica* (Whitehead and Russell 1925: 167).

each type, there is for every class a coextensive 'predicative' class of order 0. This allowed him to ignore the hierarchy of orders and to use induction on properties of all orders.

In the same letter from 1913 quoted earlier, Wittgenstein argued that this axiom is not 'logical':

> Imagine we lived in a world in which nothing existed except $\aleph_0$ *things* and, over and above them, ONLY a *single* relation holding between infinitely many of the things and in such a way that it did not hold between each and every other thing and further never held between a finite number of things. It is clear that the axiom of reducibility would certainly *not* hold good in such a world. But it is also clear to me that whether or not the world in which we live is really of this kind is not a matter for logic to decide. (McGuinness 2008: 58)

This claim is reprised in the *Tractatus*:

> 6.1232 – It is possible to imagine a world in which the axiom of reducibility is not valid. It is clear, however, that logic has nothing to do with the question whether our world really is like that or not.

Russell was convinced, as he came to see the introduction of the axiom of reducibility in a system of logic as a defect (Russell 1919a: 193). In the second edition of *Principia Mathematica*, he was to write: 'This axiom has a purely pragmatic justification: it leads to the desired results, and to no others. But clearly it is not the sort of axiom with which we can rest content' (Whitehead and Russell 1925: xiv). He also attempted to derive Peano's 'primitive propositions' (1)–(5) discussed earlier without the axiom of reducibility in Appendix B of the second edition (Whitehead and Russell 1925: 650–658), but this proof was incorrect.[12]

At the time Wittgenstein wrote and published his *Tractatus*, these difficulties with Russell's program were not seen to be insurmountable. For example, Ramsey, who agreed with Wittgenstein's critique, found a way to avoid the need for the axiom of reducibility and to reintroduce a simple theory of types and by widening classes of individuals to include impredicatively defined ones such as 'the tallest person in this room'. He thus assumed a greater dose of ontological realism than Wittgenstein or even Russell were prepared to assume. He did keep, however, the axiom of infinity but under a different form than Russell's (Ramsey 1926: 382–384).[13] But Wittgenstein

---

[12] This was shown in Myhill (1974).
[13] The difference with Russell is linked to Ramsey's agreement with Wittgenstein's elimination of the identity sign in 5.53–5.533. This made it impossible to express Russell's version of the identity of

wanted instead to jettison the theory of classes altogether. He wrote in the *Tractatus* that the theory of classes is 'completely superfluous in mathematics' (6.031), and when Ramsey, who had just translated the *Tractatus*, visited Wittgenstein in Lower Austria in 1923, he wrote back home that Wittgenstein is 'a little annoyed that Russell is doing a new edit[ion] of Principia [Mathematica] because he thought he had shown R[ussell] that it was so wrong that a new edition would be futile' (Wittgenstein 1973: 78).

So, Wittgenstein was prepared to make a fresh start, thus to provide an account of 'propositions about the natural numbers' on a different basis. He held that the fundamental building blocks of mathematics, so to speak, are equations and that these are not 'propositions about the natural numbers' but 'pseudo-propositions' (*Scheinsätze*) (6.241 and 6.2) – this point will be discussed in Section 8.3. This implies that the propositional calculus does *not* apply. He also had a striking insight, namely that, with equations, one proceeds by *substitution*:

> 6.2341 – It is the essential characteristic of mathematical method that it employs equations. . . .
>
> 6.24 – The method by which mathematics arrives at its equations is the method of substitution.
>
> For equations express the substitutability of two expressions and, starting from a number of equations, we advance to new equations by substituting different expression in accordance with the equations.

What Wittgenstein meant by the 'method of substitution' will be explained in Section 8.2, when discussing his 'proof' of '2 × 2 = 4' at 6.241.

Wittgenstein's idea was thus to propose a 'logic-free' equation calculus as an alternative basis. This is again in line with the influence of Hertz noted earlier: if the *Tractatus* is meant to be a work of 'clarification', then the rejection of the attempt at defining numbers in terms of classes in favour of an approach in terms of equation and substitution, being in line with Hertz's own clarificatory work on 'force' in mechanics mentioned earlier, could be called a form of 'clarification by replacement'.[14] This is in line with Quine's views on 'explication' in *Word and Object*:

> *[E]xplication is elimination.* We have, to begin with, an expression or form of expression that is somehow troublesome. It . . . puts kinks in a theory or

---

indiscernibles, that forced his axiom of infinity to rely on the existence of an infinity of discernible individuals.

[14] This apt expression is taken from Preston (2008: 63), whom we also follow here in quoting from Quine.

encourages one or another confusion. But it also serves certain purposes that are not to be abandoned. Then find a way of accomplishing those same purposes through other channels, using other and less troublesome form of expression. The old perplexities are resolved. (Quine 1960: 260)

Taking here the concept of 'class' as the 'troublesome' expression to be replaced results in an essentially adequate description of Wittgenstein's remarks on arithmetic. In this section reasons for replacement were adduced; the next one will investigate further what replacement Wittgenstein had in mind.

8.2 Defining Natural Numbers and Multiplication

To understand how Wittgenstein defines numbers at 6.02 in terms of 'repeated applications of any operation', we have first to go back to his brief outline of 'operations' at 5.2–5.254.[15] In his notation, 'Ω' designates any operation and, if one takes 'a' as a base, that is, as not being the result of the prior application of any operation, then '$\Omega'a$' represents 'the result of an application of the operation 'Ω' to 'a'. Wittgenstein's use of the elevated comma to express 'the result of. . .' is related to Russell's '$\imath$', in chapter *14 of *Principia Mathematica*, where it forms singular-term expressions that serve as formal counterparts to definite descriptions. However, Wittgenstein's elevated comma is not equivalent to Russell's '$\imath$'. Its role here is rather that of an application operator.

Since an operation 'can take one of its own results as its base' (5.251), one can obtain by iteration a 'series of forms' (*Formenreihe*):

$$a, \Omega'a, \Omega'\Omega'a, \Omega'\Omega'\Omega'a, \ldots$$

where '$\Omega'\Omega'\Omega'a$' is the result of three successive applications of the operation '$\Omega'a$' to 'a' (5.2521). At 5.2522, Wittgenstein introduces a 'general term' for these series of forms:

$$[a, x, \Omega'x]$$

where 'a' is the basis, 'x' any arbitrary term in the series, and '$\Omega'x$' the term immediately following it in the series of forms.

---

[15] This is in line with Wittgenstein's own marginal note to Ramsey's copy of the *Tractatus* as reported by Lewy: 'The fundamental idea of math. is the idea of calculus represented here by the idea of operation' (Lewy 1967: 421). In this respect, Wittgenstein remains close to (Frege and) Russell. But his definition is in terms of 'operations', not in terms of classes. This is the reason why one finds characterizations of the *Tractatus* on natural numbers as 'no-classes logicism' (Frascolla 1997: 354) or 'logicism without classes' (Marion 1998: chap. 2).

Arithmetic in the Tractatus Logico-Philosophicus

With 'Ω' as the variable for *any* operation, Wittgenstein defines at 6.02 natural numbers as indices or 'exponents' (6.021) of the repeated applications of any operation: '0' is defined as no application of 'Ω' and '+1' defined as one additional application of the operation 'Ω', so we have:

$$x =_{def.} \Omega^{0'}x$$
$$\Omega'(\Omega^{n'}x) =_{def.} \Omega^{n+1'}x$$

One should note immediately that Wittgenstein defined here '0' and '+1' as 'constructors' in terms of applications of an operation, thus that he neither took them as primitive as one would in a primitive recursion scheme, nor defined them in the manner of the logicists. In accordance with the 'general term' at 5.2522, he offers an iteration scheme at 6.02:

$$[\Omega^{0'}x, \Omega^{n'}x, \Omega^{n+1'}x]$$

for repeated applications of an operation:

$$x =_{def.} \Omega^0 x$$
$$\Omega'x =_{def.} \Omega^{0+1}x$$
$$\Omega'\Omega'x =_{def.} \Omega^{0+1+1}x$$
$$\Omega'\Omega'\Omega'x =_{def.} \Omega^{0+1+1+1}x$$
$$\ldots$$

From which he defines the natural numbers at the exponent level:

$$0 + 1 =_{def.} 1$$
$$0 + 1 + 1 =_{def.} 2$$
$$0 + 1 + 1 + 1 =_{def.} 3$$

And so on

This definition of natural numbers as 'exponents of an operation' (6.021) is reminiscent of the 'Church numerals' in the λ-calculus, as will be explained later. At 6.03, Wittgenstein writes their 'general form' thus:

$$[0, \xi, \xi + 1]$$

and he also sketches a 'proof' of '2 × 2 = 4' at 6.241, in essentially the same way as in the λ-calculus, providing a definition of multiplication as *calculation* on these numbers:

$$(\Omega^n)^m x =_{def.} \Omega^{m \times n} x$$

How this proof works will be explained shortly, but one should first notice the absence of a definition of addition in Wittgenstein's text, as he did not need it to define multiplication.[16] To understand why, one should recall the ideas of the definition of a function by recursion and of primitive recursion. A function f is said to be defined by recursion from previously given functions, say, g and h if the initial value $f(0)$ is defined using g and for every n, $f(n + 1)$ is defined using h, so that if one knows how to compute g and h one can also compute f. Thus, a 'primitive recursive function' could be defined as follows:

$$f(\bar{x}, 0) = g(\bar{x})$$
$$f(\bar{x}, n+1) = h(f(\bar{x}, n), \bar{x}, n)$$

with $\bar{x} = x_1, \ldots, x_k$ for some k and g and h are already defined recursive functions.[17] With '0' and '+ 1', that is, the successor function 'S', taken as 'primitive' in systems of primitive recursive arithmetic, one first defines addition in terms of '0' and 'S' and secondly multiplication in terms of addition:

$$x + 0 = x$$
$$x + S(y) = S(x+y)$$
$$x \times 0 = 0$$
$$x \times S(y) = (x \times y) + x$$

Now Wittgenstein does nothing of the sort. As pointed out, he did not take the constructor '+1' as 'primitive', but defined it as a single application of an operation and his definition of multiplication does not presuppose that of addition, as in this primitive recursive format which was unknown to him at the time. It is very likely that it was Ramsey who introduced it to Wittgenstein in 1929, showing him Skolem's 1923 paper where he introduced primitive recursive arithmetic, 'The Foundations of Elementary Arithmetic Established by Means of the Recursive Mode of Thought, without Use of Apparent Variables Ranging over Infinite Domains' (Skolem 1967).[18]

In a little-known research paper, Hancock and Martin-Löf suggested a reading of Wittgenstein as defining natural numbers in terms of the principal argument of functions defined by recursion (Hancock and

---

[16] Potter provided the missing definition for addition:
$$\Omega^m(\Omega^n x) =_{\text{def}} \Omega^{m+n} x$$
(Potter 2000: 184). We stress instead the fact that Wittgenstein did not define addition, as one would have expected, had he followed a primitive recursion scheme. But Potter had already aptly noted that Wittgenstein did not provide recursive definitions of arithmetic functions (Potter 2009a: 298), a point which is at the centre of our own interpretation.

[17] This definition should normally be completed with the definition of the class of primitive recursive functions, which includes constant functions, the successor function, the projection function such as $f(x, y, z) = y$, and compositions such as $f(x) = g(h(x), k(x))$ where g, h, k are primitive recursive functions.

[18] See McGuinness (2006: 25).

Martin-Löf 1975: 9). Since their paper is hard to find, we should briefly present their interpretation. For

$$f(x_1, \ldots, x_k, x) = y$$

where $x_1, \ldots, x_k$ are the subordinate arguments and y the value of f for these arguments, they give the following iteration scheme, with 'S' standing for the successor function:

$$f^0(x) = 0 \qquad \frac{f^n(x) = y \quad f(y) = z}{f^{S(n)}(x) = z}$$

where the exponent 'n' is thus the 'principal argument' and 'x' the subordinate argument of the function '$f^n(x)$'. Since the iteration scheme is obviously a special form of the recursion scheme, they obtained their formulation from Wittgenstein's by considering it in its general form. Given that Wittgenstein did not provide any such general scheme (for defining primitive recursive functions), because he did not think, for reasons just given, in terms of primitive recursion, this interesting interpretation introduces elements foreign to Wittgenstein's thinking at the time of writing the *Tractatus*.

As was already mentioned, the earlier insight that in arithmetical equations one proceeds by substitution and the definition of natural numbers as exponents bear some analogy with the λ-calculus, introduced by Church 11 years after the *Tractatus*.[19] The λ-calculus has only one transformation rule, called 'β-reduction', which is variable substitution. Given that Wittgenstein defined numbers in terms of 'repeated application of any operation', it is tempting to draw instead parallels with 'Church numerals'.[20] For any function f, these are indeed defined in analogous manner: 0 is not applying the function, 1 is applying once, 2 is applying it twice, etc. So, we have:

$$\lambda f.\lambda x.x =_{\text{def.}} 0$$
$$\lambda f.\lambda x.fx =_{\text{def.}} 1$$
$$\lambda f.\lambda x.f(fx) =_{\text{def.}} 2$$
$$\lambda f.\lambda x.f(f(fx)) =_{\text{def.}} 3$$
$$\ldots$$

The reader can easily see the parallels between these definitions in terms of a function f and Wittgenstein's, earlier, in terms of the operation Ω. Now, since Wittgenstein did not introduce a variable-binding device equivalent to

---

[19] See Church (1932).
[20] See, for example, Frascolla (1997: 357) and Marion (1998: 11). For the Church numerals, see Church (1941: ch. 2).

Church's 'λ', the match is far from perfect.[21] Still, it is possible to read him as using *implicitly* lambda abstraction. His use of the elevated comma as an application operator allows us to see parallels between the two definitions.

As far as 'substitutions' in Wittgenstein's sense are concerned, they need further clarification. He illustrates at 6.241 the method of substitution, that is, 'from a number of equations to new equations, replacing expressions by others in accordance with the equations', by a concrete example, the proof of the pseudo-proposition '$2 \times 2 = 4$':

6.241 – Thus the proof of the proposition $2 \times 2 = 4$ runs as follows:

$$(\Omega^\nu)^{\mu\text{'}}x = \Omega^{\nu \times \mu\text{'}}x \quad \text{Def.,}$$

$$\Omega^{2 \times 2\text{'}}x = (\Omega^2)^{2\text{'}}x = (\Omega^2)^{1+1\text{'}}x$$

$$= \Omega^{2\text{'}}\Omega^{2\text{'}}x = \Omega^{1+1\text{'}}\Omega^{1+1\text{'}}x = (\Omega\text{'}\Omega)\text{'}(\Omega\text{'}\Omega)\text{'}x$$

$$= \Omega\text{'}\Omega\text{'}\Omega\text{'}\Omega\text{'}x = \Omega^{1+1+1+1\text{'}}x = \Omega^{4\text{'}}x$$

All replacements except one are in accordance with various definitional equalities expressed here by the '$=_{\text{def.}}$' symbol. For example, the first replacement

$$\Omega^{2 \times 2\text{'}}x = (\Omega^2)^{2\text{'}}x$$

is just a concrete use of the definitional equality

$$(\Omega^\nu)^{\mu\text{'}}x =_{\text{def.}} \Omega^{\nu \times \mu\text{'}}x$$

Such replacements make use of a rule of transitivity.[22] It is important to notice that Wittgenstein also uses another completely different sort of 'substitution' here, which is essential for his 'proof'. It is the move located at the penultimate step, namely:

$$(\Omega\text{'}\Omega)\text{'}(\Omega\text{'}\Omega)\text{'}x = \Omega\text{'}\Omega\text{'}\Omega\text{'}\Omega\text{'}x$$

---

[21] The absence of a variable-binding device also limits the expressive capacity when defining functions. The Church-Turing Thesis asserts that the class of λ-definable functions is equivalent to the class of computable functions on natural numbers. Wittgenstein failed, however, to capitalize on his own insight, since he did not introduce any variable binding device. His equation calculus is thus weaker in expressive power than Church's and one cannot claim for it the full scope of the Church-Turing Thesis.

[22] In an equation calculus, the rule of substitution could be expressed thus:

$$\frac{t[u/x] = s[u/x] \quad u = w}{t[w/x] = s[w/x]}$$

The rule of transitivity implicit here would thus be a special case of it:

$$\frac{t = u \quad u = w}{t = w}$$

Arithmetic in the Tractatus Logico-Philosophicus

This is the use of the application with the elevated comma, which reads:

$$(\Omega'\Omega)'(\Omega'\Omega)'x = (\Omega'\Omega)'(\Omega'\Omega'x) = \Omega'\Omega'\Omega'\Omega'x$$

Although Wittgenstein does not have a variable-binding device such as Church's 'λ', as explained earlier, it is obvious this 'proof' follows essentially the same procedure, where this application is important to conclude it, leading to the 'Church numeral' value or 'Ω^4' in the previous example. The execution of 'applications' – another sort of 'substitution' – is a necessary part of Wittgenstein's 'proof', which is expressed in the form of β-reduction in the λ-calculus. In other words, Wittgenstein does not use only replacement in accordance with definitional equalities, he also uses the previous 'application', but he indistinctly calls both 'substitution'.

The similarity between his treatment of numbers and arithmetic functional definitions and their calculations in the *Tractatus* and the λ-calculus should now be more clearly visible. But the previously mentioned discovery of Skolem's 1923 paper, in 1929, led Wittgenstein to think in terms of primitive recursion and thus quietly to drop this approach in the 'middle period', as will be discussed in Section 8.4.

8.3 Philosophical Remarks

Wittgenstein rounded off his account with philosophical claims about equations and the method of substitution. His starting point is the simple claims that:

> 6.2323 An equation merely marks the point of view from which I consider the two expressions: it marks their equivalence of meaning [*Bedeutungsgleichheit*].

And that in an equation the sign of equality merely means that its two sides can be substituted for one another:

> 6.23 If two expressions are combined by means of the sign of equality, that means that they can be substituted for one another. But it must be manifest in the two expressions themselves [*an den beiden Ausdrücken selbst zeigen*] whether this is the case or not.

Wittgenstein develops these points into a critique of Frege, who would claim that in an equation such as '2 × 2 = 4', the two sides of the equality sign have the same 'reference' (*Bedeutung*), while they express different 'senses' (*Sinn*). In other words, the two sides of an equality are two different ways to refer to the same abstract object. Wittgenstein insisted against this view that in the method of substitution, one can *see* the 'equality of meaning' (*Bedeutungsgleichheit*):

> 6.232 Frege says that the two expressions have the same meaning [*Bedeutung*] but different senses [*Sinn*].
>
> But the essential point about an equation is that it is not necessary in order to show that the two expressions connected by the sign of equality have the same meaning, since this can be seen [*ersehen*] from the two expressions themselves.
>
> 6.2321 – And the possibility of proving the propositions of mathematics means simply that their correctness can be perceived [*einzusehen*] without its being necessary that what they express should itself be compared with the facts in order to determine its correctness.

Thus, Wittgenstein gets around Frege's *Sinn-Bedeutung* distinction by pointing out that the correctness of an equation can be seen. This implies that there are no 'abstract objects' for which arithmetical terms go proxy, and for this reason no equation could express a 'thought' (6.21). This is why they are 'pseudo-propositions' (6.2): they do not assert anything. Expressions such as '2 × 2 = 4' or 'two times two equals four' may be what one could call 'records of calculations'[23] in ordinary language, but the correctness of the steps in the 'proof' at 6.241 and its result are seen and what is seen is not asserted. Again, that arithmetical equations are 'pseudo-propositions' means that logical calculi – the 'method of tautologies' – do not apply to them. Wittgenstein's account is meant to be 'logic-free'.

Now, for something to be seen (*ersehen*) it must be 'manifest' or 'show' (*zeigen*) itself, and Wittgenstein also insisted that the 'equivalence of meaning' between the expressions on the two sides of an equation is not assertible:

> 6.2322 It is impossible to *assert* the identity of two expressions. For in order to be able to assert anything about their meaning, I must know their meaning, and I cannot know their meaning without knowing whether what they mean is the same or different.

One will have noted that this makes the 'saying-showing' distinction (4.1212) central to Wittgenstein's philosophy of arithmetic in the *Tractatus*. The point here is that, although one could express in ordinary language that '2 × 2 = 4', this is not in reference to abstract objects, but a

---

[23] This expression is taken from Kremer (2002: 294).

record of the above 'proof', the correctness of whose steps is merely seen and never asserted as such.

This point touches on a central problem of exegesis. One must recall here the so-called 'austere' or 'resolute' readings of the *Tractatus*, that reject the idea that there might be some features of the world that show themselves but could only be expressed in propositions that are 'nonsense' (*Unsinn*), thus that there is a special sort of 'nonsense' that points at them. This is the view developed by Diamond, against the more traditional reading, represented by Anscombe:

> I believe that the *Tractatus* takes what you might call an austere view of nonsense. Nonsense is nonsense; there is no division of nonsense ... then there are no propositions through which we are able to gesture, however ineptly, at unspeakable truths. (Diamond 2000b: 153)

> ... there are no nonsense-sentences that are as it were closer to being true than others. I am rejecting an idea that was put very clearly by Elizabeth Anscombe: that there are some sentences which are nonsense but which would say something true if what they are an attempt to say could be said. (Diamond 2000b: 158)

It is not as if there would be two categories: first, 'plain nonsense' and, secondly, some special sort of nonsense that nevertheless manages 'to gesture towards those things that cannot be put into plain words' (Diamond 2000b: 150). Diamond's argument is about features of reality or ontology, whose 'unspeakable truths' come out as simply 'plain nonsense' under her reading, and the case of arithmetic is never truly dealt with. Still, the 'saying-showing' distinction is the first victim of this approach, since it is with help of it that this second sort of nonsense can be articulated:

> What exactly is supposed to be left ... after we have thrown away the ladder? Are we going to keep the idea that there is something or other in reality that we gesture at, so that *it, what* we are gesturing at, is there but cannot be expressed in words?

> *That* is what I want to call chickening out. What counts as not chickening out is then this, roughly: to throw the ladder away is, among other things, to throw away in the end the attempt to take seriously the language of 'features of reality'. To read Wittgenstein himself as not chickening out is to say that it is not, not really, his view that there are features of reality that cannot be put into words but show themselves. What *is* his view is that that way of talking may be useful or even for a time essential, but it is in the end to be let go of and honestly taken to be real nonsense, plain nonsense, which we are not in the end to think of as corresponding to an ineffable-truth. (Diamond 1991b: 181)

To paraphrase Diamond, her reading would amount to the claim that it is Wittgenstein's view that arithmetical equations would possess no features that show themselves and can thus be seen but without the possibility of being put into words and asserted. This is clearly not Wittgenstein's view of the matter in the stretches 6.02–6.031 and 6.2–6.241 (as well as his critiques of *Principia Mathematica* presented in Section 8.1), and the risk here is to simply declare that the remarks of which they are composed are, along with the rest of the book (but with the exception of its 'frame'), 'plain nonsense'. To put it bluntly, this would amount to saying that Wittgenstein undermined his own criticism of Russell by decreeing it in the end to be 'plain nonsense'. Now, this issue can only be raised here in the hope of eliciting further discussion, thus without claiming to have resolved it. Our only argument here will be that the 'austere' reading, as understood here, cannot be the final word – at least about arithmetic, since Wittgenstein, contrary to the implications of this reading, continued to think about these issues in the 'middle period', with the 'saying-showing' distinction still at work, as will be shown in Section 8.4.

Wittgenstein also wrote somewhat cryptically that 'mathematics is a logical method' (6.2, repeated at 6.234). To see what he could have meant, one should bear in mind the link between the earlier definition of numbers and the 'general form of propositions' at 6:

$$[\bar{p}, \bar{\xi}, N(\bar{\xi})]$$

When introducing the notion of 'operation' earlier in the book, Wittgenstein had already linked this concept to 'propositions':

> 5.22 An operation is the expression of a relation between the structures of result and of its basis.
>
> 5.23 The operation is what has to be done to the one proposition in order to make the other out of it.

This is the reason why Wittgenstein speaks of 'truth operations' rather than 'truth functions'. With '$\bar{\xi}$' being the result of collecting all values of the propositional variable 'ξ', he introduced the operation 'N', defining '$N(\bar{\xi})$' as the joint negation of all of these values (5.502). (This is analogous to the 'Sheffer stroke'.) Thus, all truth operations are expressible in terms of this operation 'N', and the general form of the proposition at 6, modelled on the general term at 5.2522, takes as its basis the set of all elementary propositions '$\bar{p}$', and shows how to go from any arbitrary step in the series of forms '$\bar{\xi}$' to the next one '$N(\bar{\xi})$', by an application of the operator 'N'. Now, if there are no other 'operations' than the truth operations on propositions – and Wittgenstein does not indicate that there might be any – then the previous definition of numbers is intimately linked to the repeated applications of 'N'. This is presumably why Wittgenstein could write that 'mathematics is a logical method' or that:

> 6.22 The logic of the world, which is shown in tautologies by the propositions of logic, is shown in equations by mathematics.

It is well-known that soon after his return to philosophy in 1929, Wittgenstein realized that his thesis of the independence of the elementary propositions had to go, and that with it the whole edifice of the *Tractatus* collapsed, including the general form of propositions at 6. This puts his whole approach to arithmetic in jeopardy, and it is sometimes assumed it also collapsed with the whole edifice. It is not clear at first glance, however, why abandoning the general form of propositions would necessarily involve jettisoning the view of 'operations' as generating a series of forms upon which the definition of natural numbers and multiplication are based. This is not an issue to be settled here, but one should note that the reasons for the abandonment of the general form of propositions are independent of his account of arithmetic, given that the whole point of it is that equations are 'pseudo-propositions', therefore that the 'method of tautologies' does not apply. At all events, we shall see in the next section that Wittgenstein gave a very different reason for giving up his approach in terms of the 'general term of series of forms' at 5.2522.

8.4 Looking Ahead

A brief look at further developments after Wittgenstein returned to philosophy in 1929 might help clarify further some of the issues raised so far. First, one should finally notice the elephant in the room: the conspicuous absence in the *Tractatus* of any form of mathematical induction, that is, Peano's proposition (5) discussed earlier. Lacking it, Wittgenstein could not *prove* anything over all natural numbers. For that reason, Ramsey rightly called Wittgenstein's standpoint an 'obviously a ridiculously narrow view of mathematics' (Ramsey 1926: 350). Wittgenstein returned to Cambridge in 1929 to discuss with Ramsey, and their discussions clearly had an effect on his views, as he began thinking in terms of proofs, not mere calculations. It is also likely, as mentioned earlier, that it was Ramsey who introduced him to the 1923 paper, where Skolem introduced primitive recursive arithmetic.

This is not the place for a detailed discussion of the evolution of Wittgenstein's thoughts within his 'middle period', but two points ought to be made in relation to the issues raised earlier. First, Wittgenstein abandoned his previous approach in terms of applications of an operation, resembling 'Church numerals', within a year of coming back to Cambridge. There is an explicit repudiation in *Philosophical Remarks* § 109:[24]

> One always has an aversion to giving arithmetic a foundation by saying something about its application. It appears firmly enough grounded in itself. And that of course derives from the fact that arithmetic is its own application.
>
> ...
>
> Every mathematical calculation is an application of itself and only as such does it have a sense. That is why it is not necessary to speak about the general form of *logical* operation here.
>
> ...
>
> On the one hand it seems to me that you can develop arithmetic completely autonomously and its application takes care of itself since wherever it's applicable we may also apply it. On the other hand a nebulous introduction of the concept of number by means of the general form of operation – such as I gave – cannot be what's needed. (Wittgenstein 1975: 130–131)[25]

It is fitting to note that the reason given for this repudiation has nothing to do with the consequences of having abandoned the general form of propositions at 6: it is about the application of arithmetic, and here Wittgenstein's target was most probably Russell's claim in *Introduction to Mathematical Philosophy* that, as an interpretation, *Principia Mathematica* provides arithmetical concepts with a definite meaning, which allows in turn for applications of arithmetic. As he quipped: 'We want "0" and "number" and "successor" to have meanings which will give us the right allowance of fingers and eyes and nose' (Russell 1919a: 9).[26] Still, Wittgenstein's reason for calling his introduction of numbers *via* the general form of operation 'nebulous' might very well be that he had

---

[24] We thank Mauro Engelmann for help regarding this passage. It is composed from different passages in the manuscripts. In the three extracts cited here, the first and third paragraphs are taken from MS 108, pp. 115–116 written on 21 March 1930 and the middle one from MS 107, p. 180, dated 2 November 1929.

[25] Wittgenstein appears nevertheless to have been hesitant about this conclusion: Evidence shows that Wittgenstein supervised later on Waismann (with discussions in June 1930 reported in Waismann (1979: 102–107)), as the latter was to lecture at Königsberg in September 1930, on 'The Nature of Mathematics: Wittgenstein's Standpoint' (Waismann 1986), and in his lecture, Waismann used the notion of 'operation' at a crucial juncture, to distinguish between 'system' and 'totality' (Waismann 1986: 64–66), this being related to the distinction at 5.501 between, respectively, 'operation' (or 'formal law') and 'propositional function'.

[26] See Marion (2011: 144–145).

realized that he tied his notion of 'operations' too tightly to the *logical* 'truth operations' on propositions.

Second, having thus abandoned his previous approach, Wittgenstein also began to shift from calculations to proofs, as mentioned, as he also quietly began to think instead in terms of primitive recursion with '0' and '+1' taken as primitive. This would eventually lead him to the discovery, in May 1932, of a suitable counterpart to mathematical induction in the form of a rule for the uniqueness of a function introduced by recursion.[27] In his paper, Skolem simply assumed, without stating it, a quantifier-free induction rule stated here in natural deduction form (for arbitrary terms $u(x)$ and $v(x)$, omitting parameters):[28]

$$u(x) = v(x)$$
$$\vdots$$
$$\frac{u(0) = v(0) \qquad u(x+1) = v(x+1)}{u(x) = v(x)}$$

With arbitrary terms '$u(x)$', '$v(x)$', '$w(x, y)$', and 'S' the successor function, Wittgenstein's uniqueness rule could be written:

$$\frac{u(0) = v(0) \qquad u(S(x)) = w(x, u(x)) \qquad v(S(x)) = w(x, v(x))}{u(x) = v(x)}$$

Goodstein, who happened to be in the room when Wittgenstein lectured about it, proved that for primitive recursive arithmetic, the rule of uniqueness implies mathematical induction.[29]

These developments confirm that Wittgenstein had moved away from the setting of the *Tractatus* into a primitive recursive one. But he still had qualms and did not simply adopt Skolem's primitive recursive arithmetic. We can see here that his own inclinations at the time of writing the *Tractatus* are still at work. Given that he was as explained earlier in favour of a 'logic-free' account of arithmetic, he certainly would have appreciated Skolem's primitive recursive arithmetic, given that it is quantifier-free. But Wittgenstein wanted to go further in getting rid of logic: he introduced the uniqueness rule to get rid of the (nested) implication symbolized by the full stops on the right above the horizontal bar in Skolem's quantifier-free induction rule. Wittgenstein also had qualms about the rule because it seems natural to read the inference to '$u(x) = v(x)$' as involving an implicit universal quantifier 'for all . . .'. We can see here – as well as in other places that cannot

---

[27] See Marion and Okada (2018) for a detailed discussion. [28] See Okada (2007: 123).
[29] Again, see Marion and Okada (2018).

be discussed here – the 'saying-showing' still at work. We can illustrate this with his own version of the rule of uniqueness discussed earlier:[30]

$$\left.\begin{array}{l}\alpha\cdots\varphi(1)=\psi(1)\\ \beta\cdots\varphi(c+1)=F(\varphi(c))\\ \gamma\cdots\psi(c+1)=F(\psi(c))\end{array}\right\} \quad \begin{array}{c}\Delta\\ \varphi(c)=\psi(c)\end{array}$$

Here, the brace should be taken to mean that 'Δ follows from α, β, γ', and one could rewrite the rule as:

$$\frac{\varphi(1)=\psi(1) \quad \varphi(x+1)=F(\varphi(x)) \quad \psi(x+1)=F(\psi(x))}{\varphi(x)=\psi(x)}$$

Still, Wittgenstein had qualms about the way one should read the rule:

> If three equations of the form α, β, γ are proved, we say 'the equation Δ is proved for all cardinal numbers'. This is a definition of this latter form of expression in terms of the first. It shows that we aren't using the word 'prove' in the second case in the same way as in the first. In any case, it is misleading to say that we have proved the equation Δ or A. Perhaps it is better to say that we have proved its generality, though that too is misleading in other respects. (Wittgenstein 1974a: 397, 2005: 446)

He is not denying here that 'Δ follows from α, β, γ'. He is pointing out instead that if one says that 'the equation Δ is proved for all cardinal numbers', one goes further than what has been achieved, and he is at the same time pointing out that quantifiers are still implicit or 'hidden' here as well as in Skolem's quantifier-free induction rule. One could summarize Wittgenstein as saying that while one may *assert* that 'the equation Δ is proved for all cardinal numbers', one is then going beyond what the proof *shows*: it can at best be said to *show* its generality. This distinction is rooted in both the distinction between 'saying' and 'showing' and the distinction in 5.521 between generality and the quantifiers.[31]

There are numerous passages supporting this interpretation. Here are two examples:

---

[30] See Wittgenstein (1974a: 397, 2005: 446). One should note that '+1' is now taken as primitive, following Skolem: this is an indication that Wittgenstein has changed settings from his own in the *Tractatus* to primitive recursion.

[31] Recall that in 5.521 Wittgenstein listed three (equivalent) ways of describing the values of a variable: direct enumeration, giving a propositional function, and 'giving a formal law that governs the construction of the propositions, in which case the bracketed expression has as its members all the terms of a series of forms'. We can see here that, although he has given up his idea of a 'formal law', Wittgenstein still associates the quantifiers with the provision of propositional functions in attempts – illicit as it turns out – at asserting the generality shown in the proof.

> An algebraic proposition always gains only arithmetical significance if you replace the letters in it by numerals, and then always only *particular* arithmetical significance.
>
> Its generality does not lie in itself, but in the possibility of its correct application. And for that it has to keep on having recourse to the induction.
>
> That is it does not assert its generality, it does not express it; the generality is, rather, shown in the formal relation to the substitution, which proves to be a term of the inductive series. (Wittgenstein 1975: §168)
>
> But here we must not believe perchance that this sign should really be "$(\xi) \mid 1, \xi, \xi + 1 \mid$"![32]
>
> The point of our formulation is of course that the concept 'all numbers' has been given only by a structure like '$\mid 1, \xi, \xi + 1 \mid$'. The generality has been *represented* by this structure in the symbolism and cannot be *described* by an $(x) . fx$. (Wittgenstein 1974a: 431–432, 2005: 469)

Such uses of the 'saying–showing' distinction confirm the above reading of 6.02–6.031 and 6.2–6.241. They also imply that Wittgenstein could not have thought in the first place that this distinction is 'plain nonsense', and this is also part and parcel of his view that arithmetic should be 'logic-free', which is probably the central motive behind his own account of it in the *Tractatus*. This has been shown here both through his critique of *Principia Mathematica* and through his own definitions of natural numbers and multiplication.

---

[32] The use of parentheses, as in '(ξ)' and the notation '$(x).fx$', was a common device at the time for representing universal quantification.

CHAPTER 9

'Normal Connections' and the Law of Causality

Joshua Eisenthal

9.1 Introduction

The 6.3s occupy a special place in the *Tractatus*. Proposition 6 itself is the culmination of much of the earlier discussion of the book: the formal introduction of the general propositional form, encapsulating the idea that every proposition with sense is a truth-function of elementary propositions. The ensuing subsections of the 6s concern various domains of discourse – logic (6.1s), mathematics (6.2s), natural science (6.3s), and ethics (6.4s) – leading up to Wittgenstein's remarks about the method of philosophy itself in the 6.5s. The propositions of logic and mathematics are tautologies and equations, respectively, neither of which are propositions with sense (6.11, 6.21). Propositions of ethics, for their part, are impossible, for ethics 'cannot be put into words' (6.42). The discussion of natural science in the 6.3s is a distinctive section, then, for it is here that we are considering the phenomenon of senseful discourse. Indeed, in the penultimate remarks of the *Tractatus*, we are told that the correct method in philosophy 'would really be the following: to say nothing except what can be said, i.e. propositions of natural science' (6.53).

In this chapter, I want to orient the discussion around a single, obscure remark in the 6.3s, a remark that has been almost entirely neglected in the literature.[1] The remark in question is 6.361, and for reasons that will shortly become apparent it will be useful to start with the German:

6.361 In der Ausdrucksweise Hertz's könnte man sagen: Nur *gesetzmäßige* Zusammenhänge sind *denkbar*.[2]

---

[1] Hyder (2002: §6.2.3) is the only existing commentary that I am aware of.
[2] The emphasis is Wittgenstein's. For the German text, see Wittgenstein (1989). In this chapter, I use the translation by Pears and McGuinness (Wittgenstein 1974b) unless otherwise noted, and I use the standard convention for referencing remarks in the *Tractatus* by citing the line number. I also introduce a similar convention for referencing passages from Hertz's *Principles of Mechanics* by citing the section number.

'Normal Connections' and the Law of Causality

When Ogden and Ramsey first translated this into English, they rendered it as follows: 'In the terminology of Hertz we might say: Only *uniform* connections are *thinkable*'.[3] However, when commenting on the draft of this translation, Wittgenstein wrote:

> 'Only uniform connexions are thinkable'. 'uniform', I think, is wrong. To get the right expression, please look up the English translation of Hertz's 'Principles of Mechanics'. In the German text it is '*gesetzmäßige Zusammenhänge*'. (Wittgenstein 1973: 35)

Turning to *Principles of Mechanics* (Hertz 1894) then (and beginning once more with the German), we find that '*gesetzmäßige Zusammenhänge*' are defined at §119: 'Ein Zusammenhang eines Systems heißt ein gesetzmäßiger, wenn er unabhängig von der Zeit besteht'. The English translation of *Principles* (Hertz 1899) renders this: 'A connection of a system is said to be normal (*gesetzmäßiger*) when it exists independently of the time'. Thus, following Wittgenstein's suggestion (as Ogden evidently failed to do), 6.361 can be translated as follows:

> 6.361 In the terminology of Hertz one might say: Only *normal* connections are *thinkable*.

It is perhaps unsurprising that translators of the *Tractatus* were not keen to rely on the translation of *Principles*. Indeed, D. H. Jones, the translator of Hertz's text, was evidently aware of the peculiarity of his choice when he included the German term in parentheses immediately after 'normal'.[4] Although no translation is perfect, one of my concrete goals in this chapter will be to argue that Wittgenstein had good reason to appeal to the English translation of *Principles*. In particular, the use of 'normal' immediately prompts the reader to ask what role this kind of connection plays in the context of Hertz's mechanics, and makes it obvious that that question must be answered first if we are to come to understand why Wittgenstein would claim that only these types of connection are thinkable (thereby implying that *abnormal* connections are *unthinkable*).

With this in mind, our first task (in Section 9.2) will be to survey the relevant aspects of Hertz's text. *Principles* begins with a long philosophical

---

[3] In the translation by Pears and McGuinness, we find instead: 'One might say, using Hertz's terminology, that only connections that are *subject to law* are *thinkable*'. 'Subject to law' is a more literal way to translate '*gesetzmäßig*' into English.

[4] The word 'normal' often occurs in mathematical physics. In vector calculus, for instance, normal vectors and normalized vectors are orthogonal to a given surface and have unit magnitude, respectively. Neither of these uses correspond to Hertz's 'normal connection' however.

introduction, the most well-known feature of which is Hertz's austere 'image theory' of representation. Hertz uses this image theory to compare and evaluate three different formulations of mechanics: the traditional formulation, an energetics formulation, and Hertz's own formulation. The main body of *Principles* then takes up the task of spelling out the Hertzian formulation in full detail. There are two aspects of Hertz's work that are especially salient to Wittgenstein's remarks in the 6.3s. First, there is the notion of 'distinctness' that Hertz describes as one of the main advantages of both the energetics and Hertzian formulations over the traditional formulation. And second, there is the role played by normal connections, beginning with their role in Hertz's 'fundamental law' – the only basic empirical proposition that his formulation requires.

With this in hand, we will return (in Section 9.3) to the 6.3s in the *Tractatus*, beginning with Wittgenstein's lengthy remarks about mechanics at 6.341. Here, Wittgenstein presents a somewhat elaborate analogy involving three different nets (square, triangular, and hexagonal) that are used to describe a picture formed by black spots on a white surface. The analogy is supposed to illustrate a number of ideas: that mechanics 'imposes a unified form of description on the world' and that the mere possibility of describing the world using mechanics is uninformative (what is informative, by contrast, is the 'precise *way* it is possible to describe it by these means' (6.342)). Wittgenstein also writes that we are told something about the world 'by the fact that it can be described more simply with one system of mechanics than with another' (6.342). I will argue that a satisfactory interpretation of these remarks is only possible with reference to Hertz's discussion of the different formulations of mechanics, and in particular those different formulations' relative distinctness. Turning at last to the reference to 'normal connections' at 6.361, I will argue that this is closely connected to Wittgenstein's nearby remarks about the 'law of causality' (6.32, 6.321, 6.36, and 6.362). On Wittgenstein's view, a (fundamental) abnormal connection would lie outside the realm of 'causal descriptions', indeed outside the realm of descriptions *simpliciter*. This is the key to understanding Wittgenstein's remark that only normal connections are thinkable.

Before proceeding, it is worth keeping in mind that Hertz's influence extended throughout Wittgenstein's career. Besides being one of only a handful of figures to be explicitly cited in the *Tractatus*, Wittgenstein also referred to Hertz both times he gave a public address at Cambridge[5] and came close to using a passage from *Principles* as the motto for the

---

[5] See McGuinness (2002a: ix).

Philosophical Investigations.[6] It would, of course, be unsurprising if Hertz's influence was especially evident in Wittgenstein's remarks about natural science (not to mention mechanics in particular). And indeed, in lengthy remarks discussing mechanics in his *Notebooks* entry of 6 December 1914, Wittgenstein mentions Hertz twice.[7] This notebook entry went on to form the basis of 6.341–6.343 in the *Tractatus*, passages that take up more than a third of the entire 6.3 sequence. Hence a close scrutiny of Hertz's mechanics – a substantive task in its own right – may well allow for a substantialy improved understanding of many of Wittgenstein's remarks about the propositions of natural science.

9.2 Hertz's Mechanics

9.2.1 An Image Theory of Representation

Hertz begins the introduction to *Principles* as follows:

> The most direct, and in a sense the most important, problem which our conscious knowledge of nature should enable us to solve is the anticipation of future events, so that we may arrange our present affairs in accordance with such anticipation. . . . In endeavoring thus to draw inferences as to the future from the past, we always adopt the following process. We form for ourselves inner simulacra [*Scheinbilder*] or symbols of external objects; and the form which we give them is such that the necessary consequents of the images in thought are always the images of the necessary consequents of the things pictured. (Hertz 1899: 1)

Here, concisely stated, is Hertz's image theory. The theory is notably austere – the only fundamental requirement on an image is that its necessary consequences in thought are images of the necessary consequences in nature of the thing pictured. This can be glossed as the requirement that an image provides successful predictions of the behavior of the pictured objects. In this way, we are 'enabled to be in advance of the facts, and to decide as to present affairs in accordance with the insight so obtained' (Hertz 1899: 1). According to Hertz, this matching of necessity in thought and necessity in nature ('*denknotwendig*' and '*naturnotwendig*', respectively) is the only correspondence we can hope for between our conceptions of things, on the one hand, and the things themselves, on the other.

In order to compare and evaluate different images, Hertz specifies three criteria: permissibility (*Zulässigkeit*), correctness (*Richtigkeit*), and

---

[6] See Kjærgaard (2002: 126) and Janik (2000: 149).   [7] See Wittgenstein (1979: 35–36).

appropriateness (*Zweckmässigkeit*). In brief, we can immediately rule out as impermissible – specifically logically impermissible (*logisch unzulässig*) – any images that 'contradict the laws of our thought'. If we have two or more permissible images of a given object available, we can then rule out as incorrect (*unrichtig*) those whose 'essential relations contradict the relations of external things', those images that are not in conformity with the fundamental requirement. But in general this may still be insufficient to settle on the best image. Hertz thus spells out the criterion of appropriateness as a further means by which to choose between multiple permissible and correct images:

> Of two images of the same object that is the more appropriate which pictures more of the essential relations of the object, – the one which we may call the more distinct. Of two images of equal distinctness the more appropriate is the one which contains, in addition to the essential characteristics, the smaller number of superfluous or empty relations, – the simpler of the two. (Hertz 1899: 2)

Here it is evident that the requirement of appropriateness splits into two sub-requirements, distinctness (*Deutlichkeit*) and simplicity (*Einfachkeit*). A perfectly distinct image would capture *all* the essential relations (*wesentliche Beziehungen*) in nature, and a perfectly simple image would capture *only* those relations. To sum up, then, the most appropriate image is the one that comes the closest to capturing all and only the essential relations among the pictured objects.

Hertz employs the image theory to compare three different formulations of mechanics. The first is the 'customary representation of mechanics', the formulation 'varying in detail but identical in essence, contained in almost all the text-books which deal with the whole of mechanics' (Hertz 1899: 4). This presentation of the theory is not dissimilar to how the subject is still taught today. It begins with four primitive notions – space, time, mass, and force – and is anchored around Newton's three laws of motion. According to Hertz, although Newton's laws 'contain the seed of future developments', they do not 'furnish any general expression for the influence of rigid spatial connections' (Hertz 1899: 5). In order to accommodate all possible influences of such connections, we need to make use of d'Alembert's principle.[8] With this in hand, we have closed 'the series of independent fundamental statements which cannot be deduced from each

---

[8] A statement of d'Alembert's principle (or the d'Alembert-Lagrange principle) is that the total virtual work performed by all the impressed forces acting on a system, added to the total virtual work performed by all the 'forces of inertia', sums to zero (here I follow Lanczos (1962: §4)). For a discussion of d'Alembert's original formulation of the principle, see Fraser (1985).

'Normal Connections' and the Law of Causality

other'; hence, we have 'a first system of principles of mechanics, and at the same time the first general image of the natural motions of material bodies' (Hertz 1899: 5).

The second formulation of mechanics, 'of much more recent origin than the first' (Hertz 1899: 14), is the *energetics* formulation. This formulation 'likes to treat the phenomena which occur in its domain as transformations of energy into new forms, and to regard as its ultimate aim the tracing back of the phenomena to the laws of the transformation of energy' (Hertz 1899: 14). Unlike the first formulation, this second formulation has not been fully worked out. Indeed, Hertz notes that perhaps there has never been a textbook 'which from the start teaches the subject from the standpoint of energy and introduces the idea of energy before the idea of force' (Hertz 1899: 15). Nevertheless, Hertz has little doubt that such a formulation is possible, and he proceeds to sketch 'the general plan according to which such a representation of mechanics must be arranged' (Hertz 1899: 15). Where the customary formulation begins with space, time, mass, and force, the energetics formulation begins with space, time, mass, and *energy*. Energy itself occurs in two generic forms: kinetic energy, associated with bodies' velocities, and potential energy, associated with their relative positions. Instead of appealing to Newton's laws of motion and d'Alembert's principle, the energetics formulation appeals to 'one of the integral principles of ordinary mechanics which involve in their statement the idea of energy' (Hertz 1899: 16). Hertz chooses Hamilton's principle for this purpose,[9] and from this point, again, everything is deductive inference: 'All that we can further add are only mathematical deductions and certain simplifications of notation' (Hertz 1899: 16). Thus, we have a second general image of the natural motions of material bodies.

The third formulation of mechanics is Hertz's own formulation, spelled out in detail in the body of *Principles*. Hertz treats only space, time, and mass as primitive, thus deriving notions of force and energy from connections (spatial relations) among masses. In order to be able to do this, Hertz assumes that 'it is possible to conjoin with the visible masses of the universe other masses obeying the same laws' (Hertz 1899: 25–26). This is Hertz's hypothesis of 'hidden masses'.[10] With its aid, Hertz can treat the effects of both energy transformations and impressed forces as due to

---

[9] A statement of Hamilton's principle is that, for a given initial and final state, the integral of a system's Lagrangian is stationary under arbitrary variations of the system's configuration. See Lanczos (1962: 113).

[10] For a discussion of the role played by Hertz's hidden masses and the interpretive controversy surrounding them, see Eisenthal (2018).

connections between visible and hidden masses. As with the energetics formulation, only a single principle is needed within Hertz's formulation. Here, Hertz introduces his own 'fundamental law', asserting that 'if the connections of the system could be momentarily destroyed, its masses would become dispersed, moving in straight lines with uniform velocity; but that as this is impossible, they tend as nearly as possible to such a motion' (Hertz 1899: 28). From this point, 'we can derive all the rest of mechanics by purely deductive reasoning' (Hertz 1899: 28). This completes the third general image of the natural motions of material bodies.

9.2.2 The Most Distinct Image

As already noted, Hertz applies his three criteria of permissibility, correctness, and appropriateness to evaluate the three different formulations and compare them with one another. For present purposes, it is Hertz's evaluation of each representation's appropriateness that is of particular interest, especially the first sub-requirement of distinctness.[11] Beginning, then, with the traditional formulation of mechanics, Hertz asks:

> Is this image perfectly distinct? Does it contain all the characteristics which our present knowledge enables us to distinguish in natural motions? (Hertz 1899: 10)

Hertz's answer is a definitive 'No'. In particular, Hertz argues that the domain of acceptable forces is routinely restricted beyond what is required by Newton's laws themselves. For instance, it is standard to rule out the existence of any fundamental forces whose actions would violate conservation of energy, and to assume that 'only such forces exist as can be represented as a sum of mutual actions between infinitely small elements of matter' (Hertz 1899: 10). Other properties of forces may be more controversial:

> Whether the elementary forces can only consist of attractions and repulsions along the lines connecting the acting masses; whether their magnitude is determined only by the distance or whether it is also affected by the absolute or relative velocity; whether the latter alone comes into consideration, or the acceleration or still higher differential coefficients as well – all these properties have been sometimes presumed, at other times questioned. (Hertz 1899: 10–11)

---

[11] For different reasons Hertz's evaluation of each representation's *simplicity* is also important, though I postpone a discussion of this matter for another time.

Though the specifics are disputed, there is general agreement that Newton's laws, on their own, do not sufficiently fix the phenomena. Similar considerations apply to the kinds of connections accommodated by d'Alembert's principle:

> It is mathematically possible to write down any finite or differential equation between coordinates and to require that it shall be satisfied; but it is not always possible to specify a natural, physical connection corresponding to such an equation: we often feel, indeed sometimes are convinced, that such a connection is by the nature of things excluded. And yet, how are we to restrict the permissible equations of condition? (Hertz 1899: 11).

In sum, straightforward appeals to Newton's laws of motion and d'Alembert's principle fail to sufficiently hone in on the phenomena insofar as we typically need to impose further constraints. In this way, the customary formulation of mechanics fails to be perfectly distinct.

When considering the advantages of the energetics formulation, Hertz turns immediately to the question of its appropriateness, 'since it is in this respect that the improvement is most obvious' (Hertz 1899: 17). In order to derive Hamilton's principle from Newton's laws of motion within the traditional formulation, one must explicitly restrict attention to *conservative* systems – systems in which the potential energy depends only on the system's instantaneous configuration. In contrast, by treating Hamilton's principle as axiomatic within the energetics formulation, the fact that all systems are conservative becomes a conclusion rather than a premise. As a consequence of this, the forces that one derives within the energetics formulation (in particular, the forces that are derived from a potential function) come equipped with a number of properties that have to be put in by hand in the traditional formulation: These forces never violate conservation of energy, can always be represented as a sum of mutual actions between infinitesimal 'elements of matter', and only depend on relative distances rather than velocities or higher order differentials. In one fell swoop, then, the energetics formulation hones in on the phenomena in a much more satisfying way. Thus, Hertz declares, 'our second image of natural motions is decidedly more distinct: it shows more of their peculiarities than the first does' (Hertz 1899: 17).

When Hertz turns to his own formulation, he declares that, in respect of distinctness and simplicity, 'we may assign to it about the same position as to the second image; and the merits to which we drew attention in the latter are also present here' (Hertz 1899: 39). Nevertheless, Hertz argues that the third image does have slight advantages. Regarding distinctness in particular, Hertz's own formulation can accommodate a larger class of rigid connections than the energetics formulation because it can accommodate *nonholonomic* constraints (constraints that depend on the differentials of the coordinates of the system).[12] Such constraints do seem to occur in nature, such as a sphere constrained to roll without slipping on a surface.[13] In this particular respect, then, Hertz's formulation is more distinct than the energetics formulation: It captures more of the essential relations in nature.[14]

Having surveyed Hertz's discussion of the three different formulations' relative distinctness, our remaining task before returning to the *Tractatus* is to delve briefly into the main body of *Principles* and consider the notion of normal (and abnormal) connections that are introduced there.

9.2.3 Normal Connections

As already noted, Hertz captures the effects of impressed forces and energy transformations by appealing to connections between visible and hidden masses. In essence, his mechanics is a mechanics of rigidly constrained systems (think of a clockwork mechanism, for example).[15] At its most general, the existence of a connection between the points composing a system simply means that knowledge of some of the components of the displacements of the points implies something about the remaining components (§109). Hertz limits his attention to *continuous* connections (§115) calling a system with only continuous connections a 'material system' (§121). Hertz also defines *internal* (§117) and *normal* connections (§119). An internal connection is one that only affects the system's configuration (the relative positions of its constitutive points), hence does not affect its absolute position. A normal connection – of particular interest in this chapter – is one that is independent of time. With these definitions in hand, Hertz can then define a *free* system as 'a material system which is subject to no other than internal and normal connections' (§122). A free system, in other words, is one whose connections are continuous, independent of absolute position, and independent of time.

---

[12] For a discussion of holonomous and nonholonomous constraints in Hertz's mechanics, see Lützen (2005: 192–197). For a more general discussion, see Butterfield (2004: 40).

[13] For Hertz's discussion of this case, see Hertz (1899: 20–21).

[14] At any rate, this is what Hertz claimed on behalf of his formulation. For a detailed discussion, see Lützen (2005: §§15.3, 20.3, and 22).

[15] This should not be taken too literally; Hertz's treatment of mechanical systems is, in fact, highly abstract – see Eisenthal (2018, 2022: §3).

'Normal Connections' and the Law of Causality

Hertz's fundamental law is stated formally as follows:

> **Fundamental Law.** Every free system persists in its state of rest or of uniform motion in a straightest path. (§309)

Hertz's remarkable claim is that this single law, a kind of generalized principle of inertia, is sufficient to describe all the phenomena of classical mechanics.[16] In some cases, the application of the law is relatively simple, such as with certain idealized systems which can be treated as isolated.[17] The more difficult cases, however, are systems that cannot be treated as isolated; indeed, from the perspective of Hertz's framework, one way or another those systems will not appear to be free systems. How, then, can their motions be described by the fundamental law?

Hertz's strategy here is to treat any apparently unfree system as a part of a larger free system: 'Every unfree system we conceive to be a portion of a more extended free system; from our point of view there are no unfree systems for which this assumption does not obtain' (§429).[18] Hertz divides such unfree systems into two groups – *guided systems* and *systems acted on by forces*. For present purposes, it is the guided systems that are of particular interest.[19] These are defined as follows:

> A guided motion of an unfree system is any motion which the system performs while the other masses of the complete system perform a determinate and prescribed motion. A system whose motion is guided is called a guided system. (§431)

In saying that the remaining masses (of the complete system) 'perform a determinate and prescribed motion', Hertz is saying that their coordinates can be given as functions of time. This means that the connections of a guided system will in general depend on time, hence will be 'inconsistent with the requirements of normality' (§436). The appeal to guided systems now becomes a general strategy for accommodating systems which depend on time: 'we now consider every system whose equations of condition in the ordinary language of mechanics contain the time explicitly, and which in our mode of expressions is apparently abnormal, as a guided system, i.e.

---

[16] For a more detailed explanation of the fundamental law, see Eisenthal (2022: 286–289).
[17] Hertz gives as examples 'rigid bodies moving in free space or perfect fluids moving in closed vessels' (§316).
[18] Regarding all unfree systems as parts of larger free systems in this way may seem surprisingly speculative. To see things otherwise requires appreciating the abstract nature of Hertz's approach. For some discussion, see Eisenthal (2022: §3).
[19] For a discussion of systems acted on by forces, see Eisenthal (2021).

as a system which with other unknown masses satisfies the conditions of normality' (§436). This is how Hertz aims to show that systems that appear to depend on time (hence appear to have abnormal connections) fall under the fundamental law: the complete systems of which they are a part are, in fact, free systems with normal connections.

Although it may be a cogent strategy to treat guided systems as parts of larger free systems, this fact is not immediately helpful in determining their motions. The connections of a guided system still contain the time explicitly, and hence the fundamental law 'is not directly applicable' (§437). However, Hertz notes that a number of principles that can be derived from the fundamental law do govern the motion of guided systems. For example, the principle of least acceleration and Hamilton's principle (§§438–440) still apply when a system's connections depend on time.

We are now ready to return to the *Tractatus* and to Wittgenstein's explicit reference to normal connections at 6.361. Before turning to that particular remark, however, we should begin with a consideration of the discussion of mechanics that takes place earlier in the 6.3s.

9.3 Mechanics in the *Tractatus*

9.3.1 The Net Analogy

Wittgenstein's most explicit discussion of mechanics is also the single longest remark in the *Tractatus*. In full, 6.341 reads as follows:

> 6.341 Newtonian mechanics, for example, imposes a unified form on the description of the world. Let us imagine a white surface with irregular black spots on it. We then say that whatever kind of picture these make, I can always approximate as closely as I wish to the description of it by covering the surface with a sufficiently fine square mesh, and then saying of every square whether it is black or white. In this way I shall have imposed a unified form on the description of the surface. The form is optional, since I could have achieved the same result by using a net with a triangular or hexagonal mesh. Possibly the use of a triangular mesh would have made the description simpler: that is to say, it might be that we could describe the surface more accurately with a coarse triangular mesh than with a fine square mesh (or conversely), and so on. The different nets correspond to different systems for describing the world. Mechanics determines one form of description of the world by saying that all propositions used in the description of the world must be obtained in a given way from a given set of propositions – the axioms of mechanics. It thus supplies the bricks for

building the edifice of science, and it says, 'Any building that you want to erect, whatever it may be, must somehow be constructed with these bricks, and with these alone'. (Just as with the number-system we must be able to write down any number we wish, so with the system of mechanics we must be able to write down any proposition of physics that we wish.)

The analogy itself is straightforward enough. If we wanted to describe a picture formed by black spots on a white surface, we could give our description a 'unified form' by laying a square net over the surface and saying which holes are black and which are white. As we could have used a triangular or hexagonal net instead of a square one, the form (the shape of mesh) is 'optional'. However, one of these forms might prove to be simpler than another; 'it might be that we could describe the surface more accurately with a coarse triangular mesh than with a fine square mesh, and so on'. Wittgenstein is evidently employing this analogy to suggest that an (axiomatized) formulation of mechanics can be thought of as corresponding to a choice of one such net, and that, in this kind of way, mechanics imposes a unified form of description on the world: 'all propositions used in the description of the world must be obtained in a given way from a given set of propositions – the axioms of mechanics'.

Some of the implications of this analogy are spelled out at 6.342:[20]

> The possibility of describing a picture like the ones mentioned above with a net with a given form tells us nothing about the picture. (For that is true of all such pictures.) But what *does* characterize the picture is that it can be described *completely* by a particular net with a *particular* size of mesh.
>
> Similarly the possibility of describing the world by means of Newtonian mechanics tells us nothing about the world: but what does tell us something about it is the precise *way* in which it is possible to describe it by these means. We are also told something about the world by the fact that it can be described more simply with one system of mechanics than with another.

These remarks are again straightforward enough when considering the analogy itself. Whatever the picture formed by the black spots on the white surface, we can describe it by using a sufficiently fine square, triangular, or hexagonal net. Hence, the mere possibility of being able to

---

[20] 6.342 begins: 'And now we can see the relative position of logic and mechanics. (The net might also consist of more than one kind of mesh: e.g. we could use both triangles and hexagons.)' The relative position of logic and mechanics is something which I discuss only very briefly in this chapter (see Section 4), but it is obviously of crucial importance for connecting Wittgenstein's remarks in the 6.3s with broader themes in the *Tractatus*.

do this does not reveal anything informative about a particular picture. In contrast, it would be informative to know that a particular picture can be 'described *completely* by a particular net with a *particular* size of mesh'. This is informative precisely because the vast majority of possible pictures would *not* be completely (i.e., perfectly) described by that same net with that same size of mesh. So far so good. Applying this back to mechanics, then, Wittgenstein is claiming that the mere possibility of giving a mechanical description of the world is uninformative. What is informative, by contrast, is 'the precise *way* in which it is possible to describe it by these means'. Furthermore, we are told something about the world 'by the fact that it can be described more simply with one system of mechanics than with another'.

Only a handful of commentators have attempted to interpret Wittgenstein's net analogy.[21] Among those, most have suggested that the different nets should be thought of as different coordinate systems. But if this is the correct approach to understanding Wittgenstein's remarks, the analogy would seem to be a very limited one. A central component of the analogy is that a coarser net might nevertheless provide a more accurate description of the picture on the surface. In the case of coordinate systems, however, any one of them can be used to any arbitrary degree of accuracy. Hence, the point of the analogy seems to have been lost entirely.[22] More would need to be said to properly evaluate the existing interpretations of the net analogy, but for present purposes the point of most relevance is that these interpretations do not draw out the connection with Hertz.[23]

With Hertz's comparison of the different formulations of mechanics in mind, the following approach to interpreting 6.341 suggests itself: the three different nets – square, triangular, and hexagonal – can be thought of in comparison with the three different formulations – traditional, energetics, and Hertzian. Indeed, this approach is immediately prompted by Wittgenstein's remark that we are 'told something about the world by the fact that it can be described more simply with one system of mechanics than with another' (6.342). Furthermore, when Wittgenstein says that the use of one of the nets might be simpler than the use of another, this can be

---

[21] I am aware of interpretations by Black (1964), Griffin (1964), Barker (1979), Hyder (2002), and Tejedor (2015).

[22] Barker (1979) incorporates this point in a sustained criticism of Black's and Griffin's interpretations. It is noteworthy that Barker's article has been very much neglected in more recent literature.

[23] Barker (1979) and Hyder (2002) are the two commentators who take Hertz's influence most seriously.

thought of in comparison to Hertz's notion of one formulation of mechanics being more *distinct* than another.[24] Recall Hertz's account of one of the main advantages of the energetics formulation over the traditional formulation. Instead of *stipulating* that forces are conservative – something that is not strictly required by Newton's laws themselves – the forces that are derived within the energetics formulation, starting from Hamilton's principle, are *automatically* conservative. Insofar as mechanical forces are, in fact, conservative (they obey conservation of energy, only depend on relative distances, and so on), the energetics formulation is therefore more distinct than the traditional formulation. Returning to the net analogy, the need to introduce additional stipulations when using a particular formulation of mechanics would correspond to the need to employ a finer mesh when using a particular net. This would then be a clear example of the kind of thing Wittgenstein had in mind when writing 'it might be that we could describe the surface more accurately with a coarse triangular mesh than with a fine square mesh'.

A more challenging interpretive task awaits us with Wittgenstein's claim that the mere possibility of describing the world with mechanics is uninformative. Mechanics is typically regarded as a substantive theory with substantive content, so that the possibility (or impossibility) of describing the world with it would certainly be informative. On this point, we can begin with the following observation about theory choice quite generally. It is now commonplace that scientific theories are never straightforwardly falsified and that individual scientists are never logically compelled to accept one theory over another.[25] Rather, a new theory is adopted when a large enough portion of the relevant scientific community becomes persuaded by the elegance of the new theory against the clumsiness of the old. If we acknowledge that a certain number of stipulations, not to mention *ad hoc* assumptions, are involved in any theory, then we have a relatively straightforward way to begin to interpret Wittgenstein's remarks at 6.342. For if the introduction of stipulations is unrestricted, it may well be uninformative to be told that a theory *can* be made to fit the facts. (Perhaps *any* theory can be made to fit the facts if massaged enough.) What is informative, by contrast, is the *way* a theory fits the facts. Mechanics, for

---

[24] The different formulations' relative simplicity (in Hertz's sense) may also be relevant here, but it would obscure the issue to delve into the details on this point. For Hertz, an image is simpler if it contains fewer unnecessary elements, and it is not immediately clear how this would be captured in Wittgenstein's net analogy.
[25] Such a view has become widespread at least since Thomas Kuhn's *Structure of Scientific Revolutions* (Kuhn 2012), first published in 1962, with roots in the work of Quine and Duhem.

instance, is a truly impressive theory (on any formulation) because it can accommodate so many phenomena on the basis of so few fundamental propositions.

Note, however, that there is nothing specific to mechanics in the account of theory choice just outlined – the same considerations would apply to any theory in any of the sciences. But mechanics is not like any scientific theory: It is 'an attempt to construct according to a single plan' all the propositions needed 'for a description of the world' (6.343). In other words, mechanics is (or purports to be) a *fundamental* theory. At its root, mechanics is a theory of matter and motion, a completely general theory of the behavior of objects in space and time. Mechanics can thus be seen to underlie every other kind of scientific theory; theories that concern some more specific behavior of objects in space and time. As Wittgenstein notes, however, mechanics itself is only one 'attempt' (*Versuch*) to construct a fundamental theory (6.343), an attempt that was supplanted, in an important sense, by the theory of relativity. As Wittgenstein is seeing things, all such attempts – all candidate fundamental theories – impose a unified form on the description of the world; they all 'supply the bricks for building the edifice of science' (6.341).

On this point, it is instructive to think of Newton's discussion of the notions of space and time in *De Gravitatione* and later in *Principia*.[26] Here it emerges that the core motivation feeding into Newton's definitions of 'absolute' space and time stems from the need to articulate coherent definitions of the basic kinematical notions: determinate positions, trajectories, velocities, and so on. Although Newton overstepped insofar as his notion of absolute rest is not actually required for mechanics,[27] Newton's first law of motion is now typically understood as a claim about the inertial structure of spacetime: the first law implies that there is a family of inertial frames of reference from the perspective of which there is agreement concerning which bodies in the universe are moving with a constant velocity. Importantly, specifying an inertial structure in this way is fundamental for any further physics. If we are not in a position to identify definite locations or velocities, we cannot make sense of any particular force laws (such as the law of gravitational attraction). In fact, any scientific description of phenomena whatsoever relies, at least implicitly, on some

---

[26] For English translations, see Newton (2004: §II and §III).
[27] Using contemporary mathematical resources, we distinguish between 'Newtonian' spacetime, with a full commitment to the preferred frame of reference that absolute space implies, and 'Galilean' spacetime, which commits only to a family of inertial frames. When contemporary philosophers speak of the spacetime of classical mechanics, they typically mean Galilean spacetime.

sort of spatio-temporal framework. In this way, mechanics, as a fundamental theory, is a theory *within which* other empirical propositions can be articulated.[28]

This points to a way of interpreting 6.342 that does involve specific features of mechanics, in particular, an interpretation that involves the conception of mechanics as a fundamental theory. When Wittgenstein says 'the possibility of describing the world by means of Newtonian mechanics tells us nothing about the world', we can interpret this as claiming that it is always possible (in a fairly weak sense) to describe phenomena using the resources of classical physics, including, in particular, the classical notions of space and time. Of course, in the face of what we now regard as relativistic phenomena (not to mention quantum phenomena), it is no longer appealing to do so. But this is a fact that Wittgenstein's account can readily accommodate: We are told something about the world by the *way* it is possible to describe it by using a classical or nonclassical framework; we are told something by the fact that we achieve, or fail to achieve, an elegant uniformity in our descriptions of nature.

Let us now turn, finally, to Wittgenstein's explicit reference to Hertz at 6.361.

9.3.2 Only Normal Connections Are Thinkable

At a first pass, Wittgenstein's claim that only normal connections are thinkable is very puzzling. Merely by defining normal connections as independent of time and abnormal connections as dependent on time, both kinds of connections appear to be at least *thinkable* already. Furthermore, we have a whole class of systems – guided systems – that have abnormal connections. This is why Hertz shows that, even though the fundamental law cannot be applied directly to a system with abnormal connections, a number of other principles (such as the principle of least acceleration) can. Far from being unthinkable, then, we appear to be able to work successfully with abnormal connections within Hertz' mechanics.

However, as we have seen, the abnormal connections of guided systems are in an important sense only apparent. In the final analysis, a guided system is a partial system, and the complete system of which it is a part has

---

[28] The same can be said of the theories of both special and general relativity, each of which articulates more sophisticated spatio-temporal frameworks. For some relevant discussion in this direction, see Friedman (2001: 79–81) and DiSalle (1995).

only normal connections. Indeed, Hertz writes that 'if, owing to any particular form of the equations of condition, this assumption is not permissible, then these equations of condition already involve a contradiction to the fundamental law or its assumptions, and no questions asked concerning the system would be mechanical problems' (§436). In other words, if we had before us a *fundamental* abnormal connection, then we would have left the realm of mechanics altogether.

Let us grant, then, that it is this kind of connection – a connection that depends on time fundamentally – which is unthinkable according to 6.361. Even in these kinds of cases, however, at least Hertz himself does not seem to regard such systems as inconceivable. Hertz is circumspect regarding the potential universal validity of mechanics and takes care to note that the theory certainly does not seem to apply to biological systems. (On Hertz's view, to claim that living creatures are governed by mechanics has the character of a *permissible* but *improbable* hypothesis; see §§319–320.) For Hertz, then, the fundamental law can serve as a demarcation between mechanical and nonmechanical phenomena: Systems that violate the fundamental law are simply systems that are not described by mechanics. Although such a view may strike us as a perfectly reasonable one, it is evidently not Wittgenstein's view. For Wittgenstein, the occurrence of a fundamental abnormal connection would not indicate that we are dealing with a nonmechanical phenomenon; such a connection is *unthinkable*. Now, why would Wittgenstein claim that?

Let us begin to attempt to answer this question by turning to the immediate comment on 6.361:

> 6.3611 We cannot compare a process with the 'passage of time' – there is no such thing – but only with another process (such as the working of a chronometer).
>
> Hence we can describe the lapse of time only by relying on some other process. Something exactly analogous applies to space: e.g. when people say that neither of two events (which exclude one another) can occur, because there is *nothing to cause* the one rather than the other, it is really a matter of being unable to describe *one* of the two events unless there is some sort of asymmetry to be found. And *if* such an asymmetry *is* to be found, we can regard it as the *cause* of the occurrence of the one and the non-occurrence of the other.

The opening sentences of 6.3611 suggest what might appear to be a way to make sense of 6.361. Perhaps a system with abnormal connections is unthinkable because we would seem to be comparing such a system with the passage of time itself, and that would be impossible if there is no such thing as the passage of time. However, there is an immediate problem with this line of interpretation. We would not need to compare an abnormal system to the passage of time (which, of course, we never do); we would only need to compare it to other (normal) systems. In particular, we would only need to compare it to the kinds of systems that we use as clocks.

To take a different tack, we can note that Wittgenstein's main topic in 6.3611, evident from what he goes on to say in his remarks about space, is the role of certain kinds of asymmetries in our descriptions. A description of a difference between two objects relies, of course, on there being a difference to describe.[29] This applies equally well to a difference across time (e.g., one object accelerating in comparison to another moving at a constant velocity) as well as across space (e.g., one object being larger than another). An eternally homogeneous universe would be a perfect void – there would be no discernible objects to be described at all.[30] In this way, the remarks about temporal and spatial asymmetries in 6.3611 can be recognized as concerned with the possibility of any kind of description at all.

Now, why does Wittgenstein pivot in the final paragraph of 6.3611 to a discussion of causality? Indeed, it is evident that causality takes center stage in the nearby framing remarks. 6.361 is itself the first comment on 6.36:

> 6.36 If there were a law of causality, it might be put the following way: There are laws of nature.
>
> But of course that cannot be said: it makes itself manifest.

Then, following the 6.361s, 6.362 states, 'What can be described can happen too: and what the law of causality is meant to exclude cannot even be described'. Our immediate task is thus to bring this connection between temporal and spatial asymmetries, on the one hand, and the notion of causality, on the other, into focus.

The notion of causality is discussed earlier, at 6.32 and 6.321:[31]

> 6.32 The law of causality is not a law but the form of a law.

---

[29] Put another way: The possibility of a description relies on the possibility of distinguishing the object in question, otherwise there is nothing to describe. Compare 2.02331, 'if there is nothing to distinguish a thing, I cannot distinguish it, since otherwise it would be distinguished after all'.

[30] Hyder (2002: §6.2.3) presents a detailed discussion of this idea, drawing a connection with Maxwell's characterization of natural laws 'as those independent of time and space' (Hyder 2002: 178).

[31] The first mention of causality in the *Tractatus* is at 5.136–5.1362, but I do not discuss those remarks in this chapter.

> 6.321 'Law of causality' – that is a general name. And just as in mechanics, for example, there are 'minimum-principles', such as the law of least action, so too in physics that are causal laws, laws of the causal form.

In mechanics there are indeed 'minimum-principles', principles that state that some quantity takes a minimum value.[32] Wittgenstein gives the example of the law of least action, and other examples that we have already encountered include the principle of least acceleration and Gauss' principle of least constraint. Indeed, Hertz's fundamental law is a further example: In following a 'straightest' path a free system will be following a path of minimum curvature. There is of course no single, overarching 'minimum-principle'; rather, there are various different principles that share a recognizable form. At 6.33 and 6.34, Wittgenstein mentions further 'forms in which the propositions of science can be cast', the most straightforward example of which is the form of a conservation law. Just as there are various minimum principles, so too there are various conservation principles – conservation of mass or momentum or energy, and so on. Here again we have a group of principles that share a recognizable form. Returning to the notion of causality: when Wittgenstein writes that the law of causality 'is not a law but the form of a law', he is claiming that, in an analogous way, although there are different *laws of the causal form*, there is no single, overarching, law of causality. Note, however, that the causal form is a special case because it operates at a higher degree of generality: 'If there were a law of causality, it might be put in the following form: There are laws of nature' (6.36). The suggestion here is that the so-called law of causality is best understood as an attempt to capture the common form of any and all natural laws. But what could that common form be?

Recall the discussion of temporal and spatial asymmetries at 6.3611:

> [W]hen people say that neither of two events (which exclude one another) can occur, because there is *nothing to cause* the one rather than the other, it is really a matter of being unable to describe *one* of the two events unless there is some sort of asymmetry to be found. And *if* such an asymmetry *is* to be found, we can regard it as the *cause* of the occurrence of the one and the non-occurrence of the other.

This provides a hint for the common form of natural laws: descriptions of events in terms of spatial and temporal asymmetries. One might then be

---

[32] So-called minimum principles are often better described as 'extremal' principles – the quantity in question is typically required to be a (local) minimum, maximum, or point of inflection.

tempted to call such descriptions 'causal', but we must note that they are really just descriptions *simpliciter*. The supposed contrast class of 'non-causal' descriptions would be made up of attempts to describe differences where there aren't any. If we did not employ any temporal or spatial asymmetries in our descriptions, we would not be describing anything. (If there were no temporal or spatial asymmetries in our world, then our world would be eternally homogeneous.) Thus, Wittgenstein's remark, 'What can be described can happen too: and what the law of causality is meant to exclude cannot even be described' (6.362).

We are now, finally, in a position to understand Wittgenstein's elliptical remark about the unthinkability of abnormal connections. According to 6.341, mechanics 'imposes a unified form of description on the world' such that 'all propositions used in the description of the world must be obtained in a given way from a given set of propositions – the axioms of mechanics'. This applies equally to any adequately axiomatized formulation of mechanics, but with reference to Hertz's formulation in particular, all propositions used in the description of the world would be obtained from just a single axiom: the fundamental law. On Wittgenstein's view, classical mechanics, as a fundamental theory, is an attempt to situate all true descriptions of nature within a single, overarching system. On that understanding, violations of the fundamental law would not simply indicate the limited scope of the theory. Unless and until the framework of mechanics is replaced by some alternative framework, to violate the fundamental law is to step outside the realm of ('causal') descriptions altogether. As we have seen, a fundamental abnormal connection would represent a violation of the fundamental law, hence a violation of the bounds of what can be described. It is in this sense, then, that only normal connections – only lawlike (*gesetzmäßig*) connections – are thinkable.

9.4 Conclusion

This chapter has been oriented around 6.361 and Wittgenstein's second and final reference to Hertz in the *Tractatus*.[33] We have seen that a satisfactory interpretation of this remark requires detailed attention to Hertz's reformulation of mechanics in *Principles*, for it is only with this in hand that we can understand why Wittgenstein would claim that only normal connections are thinkable. Furthermore, we have seen that attention to Hertz's work makes many of Wittgenstein's remarks in the

---

[33] For a discussion of Wittgenstein's first reference to Hertz at 4.04, see Eisenthal (2022).

6.3s significantly less obscure than they might otherwise appear, particularly where they concern mechanics. One concrete result of this discussion is an insight into why Wittgenstein links the notion of causality to the common form of all natural laws, and why 'what the law of causality is meant to exclude cannot even be described'.

Of the many closely connected issues that warrant further discussion, one of particular importance relates to the framing remarks of the whole 6.3 sequence, especially 6.3 itself:

> 6.3 The exploration of logic means the exploration of *everything that is subject to law* [*aller Gesetzmäßigkeit*]. And outside logic everything is accidental.

Here we have a nominalization of the very same word that occurs in 6.361 – *gesetzmäßig*, 'subject to law' – the word that has been at the center of much of the discussion of this chapter. But note that the notion of law that is operative at 6.3, in connection with logic, appears quite different to the notion of law that is operative within the 6.3 sequence, in connection with the natural sciences. I have suggested that the common form of all natural laws is the appeal to descriptions of events in terms of spatial and temporal asymmetries, but this, as we have seen, collapses down to descriptions of events *simpliciter*. The crucial point here is that a substantive notion of natural law – of lawlikeness in nature – seems to have dropped out of the picture. This connects with one of the leading ideas in the *Tractatus*: the claim that the modal notions of necessity and contingency *only* find their significance in logic.[34] As 6.37 puts it, 'There is no compulsion making one thing happen because another thing has happened. The only necessity that exists is *logical* necessity'. The thought here, in line with the thought at 6.3, is that natural laws do not have the kind of *causal significance* that we typically take them to have. A proper discussion of this point, however, will have to wait for another occasion.

---

[34] Compare 5.525: 'The certainty, possibility, or impossibility of a situation is not expressed by a proposition, but by an expression's being a tautology, a proposition with a sense, or a contradiction'.

CHAPTER 10

The Ethical Dimension of the Tractatus

Ilse Somavilla

Starting from Wittgenstein's remark "The meaning of the book is an Ethical one" in his letter to Ludwig von Ficker, I will discuss the aspects which reveal and testify the ethical dimension of the *Tractatus*. This means discussing the limits of language, viz. the difference between what can be *said* and what can only be *shown*, the *view sub specie aeternitatis*, the relation between ethics and aesthetics, the dimension of wonder, the significance of silence, and Wittgenstein's mystical approach towards the sphere outside the world of facts.

10.1 Wittgenstein's Ethical Approach to the Limits of Language: Saying versus Showing

Wittgenstein's ethical concern is revealed in his careful treatment of language, due to the awareness of its possibilities and its limits. This results in his distanced approach towards metaphysical questions, that is, in his determination not to treat these issues within a philosophical discourse.

As early as in his preface to the *Tractatus*, Wittgenstein emphasizes his intention to "draw a limit to thinking, or rather – not to thinking, but to the expression of thoughts," and that this limit can only be drawn in language. What lies on the other side of the limit would be simply nonsense. Thus, he carefully analyses sensical and nonsensical propositions, distinguishing between what can be *said* and what cannot be said but only *shown*. Whereas in the main part of the *Tractatus* he pursues his investigations by means of logic, a shift from a scientific approach to a kind of mystical one can be observed in the last few sections of the book. It is here that his ethical concern becomes most obvious; however, I contend that throughout the *Tractatus* Wittgenstein's treatment of language can be seen as an ethical one, as is his very use of language: His style of writing in its precise and careful use of words according to his high ethical standards – according to "simplex sigillum veri" – demonstrates his remark "Ethics and aesthetics are one" (6.421). His entire preoccupation with the philosophy of language confirms Weininger's words "Logic and ethics are fundamentally the same, they are no more than duty to oneself."[1]

The distinction between saying and showing, which determines Wittgenstein's philosophy in many respects, is relevant for both his analytical approach in a scientific sense and for his mystical approach towards the world outside language and science. His remark that we ought to put ourselves outside logic, that is, outside the world in order to be able to represent logical form, hints at the connection between the "two worlds" with respect to logic and to the aspect of saying versus showing. In his distinction between propositions that make sense and propositions that are nonsensical in philosophy, he states: "The proposition *shows* its sense. The proposition *shows* how things stand, *if* it is true. And it *says that* they do so stand" (4.022).

Insofar as the proposition is a picture of reality, it shows its sense and communicates to us a state of affairs. Therefore, it must be essentially connected with the state of affairs, while the connection lies in its logical picture. The proposition can represent the whole of reality, but it cannot represent what it must have in common with reality – that is, logical form (cf. 4.12). Logical form mirrors itself in the proposition and that which mirrors itself in language, language cannot represent. "That which expresses *itself* in language, *we* cannot express by language. The propositions *show* the logical form of reality. They exhibit it" (4.121). However, whereas in the so-called scientific part of the *Tractatus*, tautologies and antinomies are considered to be "senseless" (sinnlos), propositions concerning ethical and religious issues are considered to be "nonsensical" (unsinnig). I will come back to this later when discussing the non-scientific, mystical part.

It is the task of philosophy to show and to separate the difference between what can be said clearly and what cannot be expressed in words. Moreover, in showing the difference between, and thus the limits of language and science, a differentiation is made visible between what can and cannot be thought:

[Philosophy] should limit the thinkable and thereby the unthinkable.
It should limit the unthinkable from within through the thinkable. (4.114)

It will mean the unspeakable by clearly displaying the speakable. (4.115)

---

[1] Weininger (1906: 159). Cf. the German original: "Logik und Ethik sind im Grunde aber nur eines und dasselbe – Pflicht gegen sich selbst" (Weininger 1903: 207).

Wittgenstein is convinced that "[e]verything that can be thought at all can be thought clearly" and that "[e]verything that can be said can be said clearly" (4.116).

However, what about that which can neither be thought nor said clearly? Is this the realm where science and philosophy come to an end – where merely silence exists? Is this what Wittgenstein's last sentence in the *Tractatus* hints at, and is this to be understood as an appeal to silence in terms of a plea or rather a binding consequence in terms of a "must"?

It would seem so, yet what about the aspect of *showing* which Wittgenstein again and again mentions – as a kind of counterpart to saying, as a kind of alternative to and thus solution for an ultimate silence of resignation in view of the limits in language and philosophy? As we will see later, silence is tightly connected with a mystical approach.

Not only are logic and ethics fundamentally the same, as Weininger wrote, as mentioned before, but there is also a connection between logic, science, and mysticism despite its apparent contradiction.[2] With regard to Wittgenstein, one might speak of both rational and intuitive insights, similar to the view *sub specie aeternitatis* described by Spinoza. This view was very important for Wittgenstein, as can be observed in the *Notebooks*, in the *Tractatus* and even in later years.

10.2 The View Sub Specie Aeternitatis

In his *Ethics* (Spinoza 1992), Spinoza writes that it is in the nature of reason to regard things as necessary, not as contingent. As this necessity is the very necessity of God's eternal nature, it is in the nature of reason to regard things in the light of eternity – that is, under the view *sub specie aeternitatis*. This view is the highest form of perceiving things and differs from the inadequate perception of opinion and imagination and also from the adequate perception of reason. According to Paul Engelmann, Spinoza's concept *sub specie aeternitatis* was the only philosophical term Wittgenstein occasionally used – not only in his writings but also in his conversations.[3] Access to this concept he presumably found in Schopenhauer's aesthetics, where Schopenhauer explicitly refers to Spinoza. As early as in the *Notebooks* and later in the *Tractatus*, Wittgenstein makes use of the concept in his treatment of the connection between ethics and aesthetics.

---

[2] Cf. Russell in his essay "Mysticism and Logic", in Russell (1918).   [3] Cf. Somavilla (2006: 152).

> The work of art is the object seen *sub specie aeternitatis*; and the good life is the world seen *sub specie aeternitatis*. This is the connexion between art and ethics.
>
> The usual way of looking at things sees objects as it were from the midst of them, the view *sub specie aeternitatis* from outside.
>
> In such a way that they have the world as background.
>
> Is this it perhaps – in this view the object is seen *together with* space and time instead of *in* space and time?
>
> Each thing modifies the whole logical world, the whole of logical space, so to speak.
>
> (The thought forces itself upon one): The thing seen *sub specie aeternitatis* is the thing seen together with the whole logical space. (Wittgenstein 1979: 83, 7.10.16, emphasis in the English edition)

Immediately after this passage, Wittgenstein brings an example of the difference between contemplating an object, say, a stove, from the ordinary view, seeing it as a thing "among the many things in the world," as against contemplating the stove as one's world. Thus, a present image can be regarded both as a "worthless momentary picture in the whole temporal world, and as the true world among shadows" (Wittgenstein 1979: 83, 8.10.16).

The term *sub specie aeternitatis* denotes a view of the world that transcends the world of facts, a view quite different from a scientific one. Whereas the so-called ordinary view of things follows the principle of sufficient reason and is thus restricted by the forms of time and space, the view *sub specie aeternitatis* transcends time and space. In the *Tractatus* (5.61) Wittgenstein writes that logic fills the world, and this does not only mean that the limits of the world are also the limits of logic, but it also suggests that in the world nothing happens which would contradict the laws of logic, viz. the laws of God's eternal nature in Spinoza's sense. In a view *sub specie aeternitatis*, things are perceived in their necessary and logical connection. At the same time, one recognizes that the facts of the world are not the end of the matter, but that what is essential – the meaning of the world – lies outside the world, outside space and time.

> The contemplation of the world sub specie aeterni is its contemplation as a limited whole. The feeling of the world as a limited whole is the mystical feeling. (6.45)

The Ethical Dimension of the Tractatus

The man capable of viewing the world *sub specie aeternitatis* differs from the man looking at the world in the ordinary sense. Whereas the former can be called a happy man, the latter is considered an unhappy man. To strive after a happy life as "the purpose of existence," Wittgenstein, alluding to Dostoyevsky, considers the ultimate goal in one's life.[4] However, this does not mean to strive after worldly goods and pleasures but to lead an ethical way of life devoted to the spiritual, a life that can renounce the amenities of the world which to it are merely "so many graces of fate" (Wittgenstein 1979: 13.8.16). And even if all our wishes were fulfilled, "this would still only be, so to speak, a grace of fate, for what would guarantee it is not any logical connexion between will and world, and we could not in turn will the supposed physical connexion" (Wittgenstein 1979: 5.7.16).[5] However, in devoting his life to the spirit, the happy man is freed from the desires of the will, and in Schopenhauer's terms enabled to merely contemplate, as a "clear eye of the world." This is achieved by aesthetic contemplation. "Is it the essence of the artistic way of looking at things, that it looks at the world with a happy eye?" Wittgenstein asks on October 20, 1916. What in the *Tractatus* he defines as the mystical, in the *Lecture on Ethics* (Wittgenstein 1965) as "wonder at the existence of the world," is here described as aesthetic miracle: "Aesthetically, the miracle is that the world exists. That there is what there is" (Wittgenstein 1979: 20.10.16).

As can be seen in the later sections of the *Tractatus*, Wittgenstein became increasingly critical towards science and analytically orientated philosophy, and a preference for an intuitive approach can be observed, a kind of contemplative and mystical attitude in particular towards the realm outside the world of facts. Whereas Spinoza describes intuitive perception as the third kind of perception – in addition to the perception of imagination and reason – Wittgenstein tends to identify intuitive perception with aesthetic, ethical, and sometimes even philosophical perception, putting them all on the same level so to speak, in ascribing to them all the view *sub specie aeternitatis*.[6] While for Spinoza the view *sub specie aeternitatis* is to be understood as the contingent perception of reason that leads to a life of virtue, Wittgenstein claims that the view *sub specie aeternitatis* is directed towards any sphere of the human mind and culture, especially the fields of language, philosophy, and art. As a consequence, his

---

[4] Cf. Wittgenstein (1979: 6.7.16).   [5] Cf. also TLP 6.374.
[6] Cf. Wittgenstein's remark in his diary of the 1930s: "Style is the expression of a general human necessity. This holds for a writing style or a building style (and any other). Style is general necessity viewed sub specie aeterni" (Somavilla 1997: 28; 9.[5.30]).

efforts in writing and acting were orientated towards unreachably high ethical standards – ethical standards he implicitly also demanded of other men, in particular of authors and artists.

In the sphere of religion, the view *sub specie aeternitatis* enables us to recognize and accept the necessity of God's plans. As Spinoza emphasizes, "will" is not "the desire by which the spirit desires or rejects things" but the ability "to accept and renounce." The man of virtue who recognizes the nature of God will accept his plans in all its forms, even though it is in times of sufferings. It is in this recognition and ability to accept that his freedom lies – despite Spinoza's deterministic world-picture. Already in the *Notebooks*, Wittgenstein felt dependent on a higher power or an "alien will," a Godlike instance that needs no further explanation or justification, even for all forms of evil in the world. To live happily, therefore, means to live in "agreement with the world," and "in agreement with that alien will" on which one depends (cf. Wittgenstein 1979: 8.7.16). The harmonious relation to the world and to God, which is guaranteed by the perception of necessity of all happenings in the world, leads to an acceptance of this power (causing them) without further questions regarding its reasons. As this perception or view transcends time and space, it lacks any fears or hopes for the future. In other words, the happy man lives not in time but in the present. He leads a life devoted to the present, to the moment, not directed towards temporality, which in spite of eternity shows itself as mere appearance, as deception. Therefore, the man leading a happy life must not fear death. In moments of viewing the world *sub specie aeternitatis*, in aesthetic contemplation, or – in other words – in an attitude of oblivious wonder, Wittgenstein – similar to an artist – seems to have been liberated from what is transitory and profane, being totally absorbed in the object of philosophizing. Thus, the characteristic of a happy and harmonious life cannot be a physical one but only a metaphysical one (cf. Wittgenstein 1979: 30.7.16).

10.3 The Dimension of Wonder

Wittgenstein's approach to the world can in various ways be described as an attitude of silent wonder, even as a mystical approach to the world about which I will speak in the last section of the chapter. The dimension of wonder revealed in his philosophical writings can on the one hand be observed in a silent attitude towards the world, reminiscent of ancient Greek philosophers, and, on the other, in a dynamic attitude of puzzlement in view of the variety of the phenomenal world, as obvious in his later philosophical investigations. It is already in the last few pages of the

Tractatus that Wittgenstein's attitude of wonder is revealed in both aesthetic and ethical ways.

10.3.1 Wonder as Aesthetic Contemplation

As regards the aesthetic significance of wonder, we are reminded of the aesthetic contemplation described by Schopenhauer – a contemplation in which the "pure subject of knowledge" is absorbed by looking at an object, by being lost in it so that subject and object become one (Schopenhauer 2010). The subject is elevated beyond the world of suffering with its pain, and – on finding himself on a higher level – intuits the "Platonic idea" in the object of his contemplation. In these "rare happy moments," any analysing form of questioning and search for attempts at explanations would be out of place. In his apprehension of the eternal and universal idea inherent in the transitory, concrete, and present object of contemplation (be it a tree or other beautiful and admirable object in the world or be it an object of art), the aesthetic observer, viz. the "pure subject of knowledge," consists merely of intellect, deprived of all sensuality, of all forms of the principle of sufficient reason, that is, of space and time. There is a strong ethical component in Schopenhauer's description of the aesthetic contemplation – namely in so far as the observer's intellect rises beyond the sensual and thus beyond the burden of the body to an extent that he is spiritual being. The similarity to Schopenhauer's description of the ethical human being in his *Metaphysics of Ethics* is obvious.

As far as Wittgenstein is concerned, we can observe parallels to Schopenhauer as early as in the *Notebooks 1914–1916* and in the *Tractatus*. This applies above all to ethical and aesthetic considerations and to the aspect of wonder – especially as regards the passages where we can speak of the mystic-pantheistic tendencies in Wittgenstein's philosophy. The sentence "Not *how* the world is, is the mystical, but *that* it is" (6.44) suggests an approach of wonder to the world in the form of a silent and devout attitude towards the cosmos without the effort to explain. This sentence can be seen in line with the experience to "wonder at the existence of the world," which Wittgenstein mentions as his "experience par excellence" for his understanding of absolute value in his *Lecture on Ethics* held in November 1929 (Wittgenstein 1965). When Wittgenstein was then asked to give a lecture to the Heretics, he decided to speak about something he considered of the utmost importance but did not want to treat it as a topic of philosophical discussion: ethics. Instead, he presented the topic not in a scientific way but by means of referring to his personal experience. In this lecture, the ethical meaning of wonder in its deep and universal sense especially comes to light. Among the three examples given for his personal understanding of what ethics might be, Wittgenstein explicitly mentions "wonder at the existence of the world" as his first and foremost example.

10.3.2 The Ethical Aspect of Wonder

It is exactly this wonder at the world as something miraculous and not self-evident that reveals its ethical dimension – in contrast to the kind of wonder at something sensational that strikes us. Here, the difference between relative and absolute value is obvious, as is also the case with the other examples provided: the feeling of absolute safety and the feeling of guilt. Whereas the sentence "I feel safe in the house when it is raining outside" is understandable in everyday language and thus to be considered a meaningful sentence, the sentence "I feel safe whatever happens around me" would strike us as nonsense; however, it is an example of absolute value. All of the examples Wittgenstein gives are examples of ethical value and thus to be considered part of the world beyond time and space. As in the world there is no value (6.41), and as propositions fail in expressing "anything higher" (6.42), the phrase "to wonder at the existence of the world" reveals the nonsensicality of ethical expressions. Wittgenstein speaks of a "misuse" (*Mißbrauch*) of language, which he sees as characteristic of any ethical and religious expressions. Every attempt at saying something about absolute/ethical values therefore reveals the limits of language and would thus be a "running against the walls of our cage."

Apart from the *Lecture on Ethics*, the ethical aspect of wonder is particularly discernible towards the end of the *Tractatus*, where Wittgenstein holds what one could describe as a mystical attitude towards the world. Wonder at the "existence of the world," viz. "*that* it exists," incorporates an ethical dimension arising from an attitude of awe: awe in the sense of being conscious of a sphere that is mysterious and ineffable and which eludes rational and verbal explanation. This attitude of awe is carried by distance and awareness of one's own limits. From a religious-phenomenological viewpoint, an attitude of awe arises from tranquillity and wonder at the inexplicable and holy.[7] As Pascal in his *Pensées* writes about the position of man in nature, man would "shudder" at the sight of

---

[7] Cf. Munz (1995: 71).

the wonders surrounding him, and he would rather be prepared to contemplate in silence but striving to explore them.[8]

Wittgenstein's wonder at the existence of the world lies on the same level as his attitude of silence towards the sphere of the ineffable: in other words, the ethically grounded wonder leads to an ethically grounded silence. As he later remarked to members of the *Vienna Circle*: "Astonishment at the fact of the world. Every attempt to express it leads to nonsense" (Waismann 1979: 93). Wonder, therefore, is closely connected with "nonsense," which he saw in every attempt at verbalizing ethical and religious questions, for this would go beyond the limits of meaningful language and, at the same time, beyond the limits of the world.

Not only in his early writings but also later, in fact, throughout his life, Wittgenstein's philosophizing has a strong ethical component or flavour that can be perceived in his very language, his style of writing. In Wittgenstein's approach to the objects of his philosophizing, there is a kind of subtlety that finds expression in an extraordinary sensibility for the language he uses. His reflections result in an extremely deliberate choice of words and structuring of sentences in terms of which he tries to grasp the object of his philosophizing.[9] The more precious and higher the object of philosophizing appears to Wittgenstein, the more modest he becomes – being conscious of the limits of language and of science. This is the origin of his distinction between the sayable and the non-sayable (on a higher level), between what can be said clearly and what can only be "shown" – a distinction he drew in the *Tractatus*, yet which he basically kept throughout his writings. What can be "shown" – in ethical and aesthetic matters – can be experienced by the ability to wonder. The state of wonder or contemplation transcends the level of linguistic or scientific analysis and can at best be expressed aesthetically, for example, in poetry, painting, or music. Wittgenstein's frequent use of metaphors, similes, and fictitious examples in later years is a means to at least hint at what cannot be expressed by ordinary language.

In moments of wonder we realize beauty (in an aesthetic approach), but we may also experience a feeling of awe (in an ethical approach) while becoming aware of man's powerlessness when facing a higher sphere, something mighty, viz. an "alien will" upon which we are dependent.

---

[8] Cf. Pascal (1958: 17).
[9] Wittgenstein's attitude of wonder about the objects of his philosophizing can be observed as late as in 1946: "O, why do I feel as if I wrote a poem when writing philosophy? It is as if there was something small that has a wonderful meaning. Like a leaf, or a flower" (Wittgenstein 2000: MS 133).

Similarly to his reflections in the *Wartime Notebooks* on the necessity of being in agreement with the world and with that alien will, which means obeying the will or God, Wittgenstein later rejected Schlick's opinion that the more profound interpretation of the nature of the good in theological ethics is that God wants the good because it is good. Instead, Wittgenstein held the opinion that the deeper meaning of the good is that it is good because God wants it – without giving any further grounds: "If there is any proposition expressing precisely what I think, it is the proposition 'What God commands, that is good'" (Waismann 1979: 115).

In their pursuit of scientific explanations and approach towards metaphysical questions lies a decisive difference between Wittgenstein's way of thinking and that of the Vienna Circle: whereas most members of the Vienna Circle were striving for an explanation in their philosophical disputes and consequently considered everything that cannot be explained by science as meaningless, Wittgenstein was against *any* kind of explanation or establishment of reasons – in particular when it came to ethical and religious questions. When he refused to speak about these questions in the *Tractatus*, members of the Vienna Circle thought that Wittgenstein held a similar position to their own. However, he was misunderstood: whereas the majority of the Vienna Circle refused to speak about the metaphysical because they regarded it as non-existent, viz. from a positivist position, Wittgenstein refused to speak about metaphysics because of his high respect for what he esteemed the higher sphere. While being aware of the impossibility of grasping the ineffable by a scientific procedure, he nonetheless never gave up searching for a way to come closer to it. His respect for both the visible world and the world beyond is connected with his awareness and acknowledgement of the limits of scientific-rational explanations. In his foreword to the *Philosophical Remarks* (Wittgenstein 1975), he expresses his feeling of resentment about the "vast stream of European and American civilization," characterized by the pursuit of ever-growing progress and belief in science. While defining the purpose of philosophy as bringing clarity and perspicuity into propositions[10] and thus attaining truth, Wittgenstein sensed the contrary in the spirit of modern civilization to his spirit. The reason for his distanced attitude towards the typical Western scientist and his isolated position within the trend of his time with its purpose-oriented thought and methods, presumably lay in his fear of loss in clarity and truthfulness, thus a loss of respect and awe towards the cosmos. Similar to Wittgenstein, Edith Stein wrote that by

---

[10] Cf. TLP 4.112: "The object of philosophy is the logical clarification of thoughts. ... The result of philosophy is not a number of 'philosophical propositions', but to make propositions clear."

violent striving after breaking the limits instead of holding on in awe and submitting to the laws of the phenomenal world, the clarity of men's spirit will be clouded (Stein 1959). In order not to lose an attitude of awe towards the world, it is decisive to accept one's limits, which Wittgenstein hinted at as early as in 1915 with his well-known sentence: "*The limits of my language* mean the limits of my world" ((Wittgenstein 1979: 23 May 1915); TLP 5.6, emphasis in the original).

10.4 The Significance of Silence

Wittgenstein's concluding remark in *Tractatus* 7 hints at the importance he gave to the dimension of silence in philosophy – an importance he also expressed in his letter to Ludwig von Ficker when enquiring about publishing the *Tractatus* in the *Brenner*. As mentioned at the beginning of my chapter, he wrote that the meaning of his book was an "Ethical one" and that it actually consisted of two parts: the one he had written and the one he decided to keep silent about. And that it was this part which he considered to be the essential one.[11] Thus, the dimension of silence is not to be seen as something negative, something involved with resignation in philosophy but as a kind of path to further insight – insight into other important fields like ethics or art.

In his letter to Ficker, Wittgenstein clearly emphasized the ethical aspect of his way of writing philosophy – insofar as he chose to keep silent about ethical and religious matters in philosophy, thus distancing himself from those who would only "babble" [schwefeln] about these issues.[12] In doing so he would limit "the ethical from Within" – just as he would "limit the unthinkable from within by the thinkable," as quoted before. Consequently, he described his work as "strictly philosophical and at the

---

[11] Cf. Wittgenstein (1969b: 35).
[12] Cf. Wittgenstein (1969b: 35): "Zugleich mit diesem Brief geht das Manuskript an Sie ab. ... Und da ist es Ihnen vielleicht eine Hilfe, wenn ich Ihnen ein paar Worte über mein Buch schreibe: Von seiner Lektüre werden Sie nämlich – wie ich bestimmt glaube – nicht allzuviel haben. Denn Sie werden es nicht verstehen; der Stoff wird Ihnen ganz fremd erscheinen. In Wirklichkeit ist er Ihnen nicht fremd, denn der Sinn des Buches ist ein Ethischer. Ich wollte einmal in das Vorwort einen Satz geben, der nun tatsächlich nicht darin steht, den ich Ihnen aber jetzt schreibe, weil er Ihnen vielleicht ein Schlüssel sein wird: Ich wollte nämlich schreiben, mein Werk bestehe aus zwei Teilen: aus dem, der hier vorliegt, und aus alledem, was ich *nicht* geschrieben habe. Und gerade dieser zweite Teil ist der Wichtige. Es wird nämlich das Ethische durch mein Buch gleichsam von Innen her begrenzt; und ich bin überzeugt, daß es, *streng, nur* so zu begrenzen ist. Kurz, ich glaube: Alles das, was *viele* heute *schwefeln*, habe ich in meinem Buch festgelegt, indem ich darüber schweige. Und darum wird das Buch, wenn ich mich nicht sehr irre, vieles sagen, was Sie selbst sagen wollen, aber Sie werden vielleicht nicht sehen, daß es darin gesagt ist."

same time literary"[13], obviously meaning that the task of philosophy is to exclude metaphysical matters and restrict itself to what can be said clearly and explained scientifically, while the word "literary" hints at approaches other than scientific means – the means of *showing* literature (and in particular poetry) can convey.

As discussed earlier, Wittgenstein's ethical concern in the *Tractatus* is revealed in his distanced attitude towards metaphysical questions, precisely towards any attempt at establishing a theory of ethics. Ethics is transcendental and therefore excludes any verbal or scientific explanations; ethics belongs to the world outside the world of facts, thus beyond language and science. There can be no propositions about ethics, because propositions cannot express "anything higher," as mentioned before. This means to find other ways of approach – by either literature and art,[14] or by a kind of mystical approach in an attitude of silence.

Therefore, silence as the consequence of the limits of language does not only mean the philosophical consequence or résumé in an analytical sense in order to separate the thinkable from the unthinkable but is predominantly relevant for Wittgenstein's attitude towards the sphere of the ineffable – an attitude leading to his decision to remain silent about this sphere. Instead, he meets the world outside the one to be grasped by science, in an attitude of wonder and of awe, not unlike a mystic.

10.5 Wittgenstein's Mystical Approach to the World

The ineffable and thus inexpressible "*shows* itself; it is the mystical" (cf. TLP 6.522).

In her book *Mystik und Widerstand*, Dorothee Sölle describes three steps on the way to mysticism, defining wonder as the first step.[15] With regard to the *Tractatus*, Wittgenstein's silent attitude of wonder towards the world leads to a mystical approach. He thus clearly distances himself from discussing metaphysical questions, because "for an answer which cannot be expressed the question too cannot be expressed" (6.5). Consequently, one must not ask questions concerning the meaning of life and death, the existence of a God, etc., as one cannot expect any sufficient answer. The only approach to the ineffable is the mystical. This is why people endowed

---

[13] Wittgenstein (1969b: 33).
[14] In literature, Wittgenstein saw a means to describe ethical or religious issues without establishing a theory about them, and he highly appreciated novels written by Dostoyevsky and Tolstoy (cf. Drury 1981: 101).
[15] Cf. Sölle (1997: 124): "Der erste Schritt auf dem mystischen Weg ist das Staunen."

The Ethical Dimension of the Tractatus

with a mystical ability could not communicate in words their experience of becoming aware of the meaning of life.

Mysticism offers an insight quite different from a scientific view and rational knowledge. One might speak of an intuitive, not discursive access to the world and to philosophizing. As Wittgenstein maintains: "There is indeed the inexpressible. This *shows* itself" (6.522). And he continues to write in a cryptic way, revealing a mystical approach towards the world. According to Brian McGuinness, Wittgenstein's mysticism embraces four themes mentioned by Russell concerning mysticism: the powerlessness of the will, the nature of ethics, the immortality that timelessness confers, and the vanishing of the problem of life. Moreover, McGuinness ascribes Wittgenstein's "peculiar form of solipsism," observable in 5.62–5.63 to mysticism.[16]

Similarly to Russell, who wrote that there is some value in the feelings of the mystic, which may inspire not only the artist but even the scientist, Wittgenstein also sees mysticism – in the sense of a kind of solipsistic approach to the world – as the inspiration even for the scientist.[17] However, while for Russell philosophy is not as inexpressible as is mysticism, for Wittgenstein the logical properties cannot be expressed either, but only shown. There are several passages where Wittgenstein speaks in similar terms about logic, ethics, and the mystical (cf. McGuinness 1966: 310). Both logic and ethics are transcendental (6.421, 6.13). To understand logic, we need a certain experience of "not that such and such is the case but that something *is*" (5.552) – a statement very similar to 6.44, where he states: "Not *how* the world is, is the mystical, but *that* it is."

Whether Wittgenstein himself had mystical experiences remains an open question – even though the mystical experience of the protagonist in a play by Ludwig Anzengruber exerted a tremendous impact on Wittgenstein so that for the first time he became aware of the significance of religion.[18] Still, as I see it, Wittgenstein's mysticism must not be

---

[16] Cf. McGuinness (1966: 307).

[17] Cf. Wittgenstein (1979: 1.8.16): "Only from the consciousness of the *uniqueness of my life* arises religion – science – and art." Cf. also McGuinness (1966: 306).

[18] Cf. Norman Malcolm, to whom Wittgenstein reported that Anzengruber's play had caused a change in his attitude towards religion, as he was struck by the stoic thought of being independent of fate and circumstances caused by the mystical experience of the protagonist (Malcolm 1984: 58).

In the Third Act, First Scene of Anzengruber's play *Die Kreuzelschreiber*, the protagonist, called the Steinklopferhanns, tells the audience how lost and sick he was. Not willing to continue this life, he decides to go outside and die surrounded by nature. After a fair amount of time laying on the ground, in which he admired the mountains and the sky above him, he feels refreshed and suddenly totally safe in the feeling that nothing could happen to him, that he belongs to his surroundings and his surroundings belong to him (cf. Anzengruber 1872: 278ff). Years after Wittgenstein attended

understood in a religious sense, viz. a union with God, but rather in a pantheistic sense similar to Spinoza. In fact, Wittgenstein's identification of the I with the world and his soul with the world soul (as discussed in the *Notebooks*) might be compared not only to Schopenhauer's identification of the individual will with the world will, viz. the will in a metaphysical sense, but also to Spinoza's concept of *amor intellectualis dei* – *the* union of one's spirit with God's spirit – as the highest goal to achieve for a human being. Besides, Wittgenstein's pantheistic mysticism can be seen in view of the connection between God as the substance, viz. *natura naturans* with nature, viz. *natura naturata*, as described by Spinoza.

10.6 Conclusion

To summarize, I want to emphasize the significance of ethics underlying Wittgenstein's philosophizing in the *Tractatus*. Even though the majority of the *Tractatus* is written in a scientific way, Wittgenstein's awareness of the limits of language and science as well as his criticism of scientific procedures should not be overlooked. This is evident already in the Preface to his book, where he emphasizes that the value of his work "consists in the fact that it shows how little has been done" when the problems of philosophy treated in the text have in essentials been solved. Instead, he realized that all scientific means and methods are bound to fail when trying to solve the real problems of life or to explain ethics and religion, while in moments of a mystical approach of wonder at the world, we might apprehend what ethics means. Wittgenstein's use of words like "feel" or "wonder at" to express the intuitive, non-rational is characteristic of his drawing a boundary between the realm of science and the realm that eludes positive answers. As he put it:

> We feel that even if *all possible* scientific questions be answered, the problems of life have still not been touched at all. Of course there is then no question left, and just this is the answer. (6.52)

His remark that the strict philosophical method would be to say nothing but propositions of natural science, thus excluding any metaphysical questions, might be misleading. It seems to suggest a preference for a scientific method; however, it only reveals his deeper ethical concern – that is, his resolve to distance himself from any attempt at establishing a theory

---

the play, he referred to the experience of absolute safety as one of the three examples given for his personal understanding of ethics.

about metaphysical problems. In other words, Wittgenstein's understanding of philosophy entails the *separation* between what can be *said* and what can only be *shown*, thus a separation of the world of facts from the sphere beyond the world of facts, which is inaccessible by language and by science. According to Andreas Georgallides, it is the mystical which solves the paradox between Wittgenstein's scientific approach by sensical propositions, and his declaration of philosophical propositions as nonsense. As such, Georgallides offers a third interpretation of the *Tractatus* – an alternative to the "traditional view"[19] and the "resolute reading view."[20] According to Georgallides, "the *Tractatus* does not express truths but rather, a mystical tone which affords a possible resolution to the tractarian paradox."[21]

As to the dimension of ethics in Wittgenstein's thought, I see a connection to the mystical approach. Belonging to the so-called higher sphere, ethics cannot be explained by propositions without resulting in nonsense. It can only be approached by the kinds of personal experiences Wittgenstein refers to in his *Lecture on Ethics*. And the examples he provides for his personal understanding of ethics are determined by a mystical approach. This applies not only to the "experience of wonder at the existence of the world" and the "feeling of absolute safety" but also to the feeling of guilt, which reveals the connection between ethics and religion in face of an unknown god, viz. *deo abscondito*.[22]

As a consequence of the impossibility of grasping ethics, Wittgenstein refuses to discuss the topic in philosophy and to establish a theory of ethics. As he later emphasized in his conversations with the Vienna Circle: "Even if this theory were true, it would not interest me – it would not be the exact thing I am looking for" (Waismann 1979: 116). Similarly, he rejected any explanation of ethics – not because it might be false but for the very reason that it was an *explanation* (cf. Waismann 1979: 116).

Despite his refusal to provide a philosophical discussion, I contend that ethics plays an important role in the *Tractatus* and emphasizes the aspect of the non-verbal in Wittgenstein's philosophizing. Even though the treatment of language is clearly at the centre of his philosophical concern, the significance of silence in view of the limits of language determines his approach towards what cannot be said via sensical propositions.

---

[19] Cf. Anscombe (1971) and Hacker (1972).
[20] Cf. Diamond (1991b), Conant (2000, 2002), Ricketts (1996), Goldfarb (1997), Kremer (2001).
[21] Cf. Georgallides (2021).
[22] Cf. Wittgenstein's remark noted a few days before his *Lecture on Ethics*: "What is Good is Divine too. That, strangely enough, sums up my ethics" (Wittgenstein 1999: 5e, 2000: MS 107 192c).

As I have tried to show, the ethical dimension in the *Tractatus* can be discerned in various aspects of his work, for example, in a distanced attitude towards what can be said and explained by means of language and by science, resulting in accepting the limits of language. Instead of scientific intrusion, Wittgenstein urges us to meet the world in an attitude of reverence, awe, and wonder – seeing it *sub specie aeterniatis*. Instead of trying to discuss metaphysical questions within the realm of philosophy, he hints at a mystical approach to the ineffable.

In this regard, even the metaphor of the ladder, in which the reader is asked to discard the propositions of the *Tractatus* in order to see the world rightly, could be interpreted in terms of seeing the world *sub specie aeternitatis* and thus in the light of ethics, which lies outside the world of facts.

CHAPTER 11

"Obviously Wrong": The Tractatus *on Will and World*

Duncan Richter

In her *Introduction to Wittgenstein's Tractatus*, Elizabeth Anscombe writes that, according to Wittgenstein:

> The connection of will with the world is that "the facts" belong to the task one is set. If one has reached a solution, this is made to be a solution, not by any alteration of the facts that may have taken place – any such alteration, even if one intended it, is accidental and merely a "grace of fate" – but by an alteration "in the limits of the world" (6.43).
>
> It is this part of the *Tractatus* that seems to me most obviously wrong. (Anscombe 1971: 171)

My goal is to understand and assess this judgment. This will require an examination of what Wittgenstein says and why (in Part 11.1), which will involve reference to Schopenhauer (in Part 11.2), who is surely at least one of the philosophers Wittgenstein has in mind when he talks about the will. So I will look at some of what Schopenhauer says about the will, as far as this is relevant to understanding the *Tractatus*, at what Wittgenstein says about it in the *Tractatus* and elsewhere, and at what Anscombe says about it (in Part 11.3), and see who is most right (Part 11.4). Despite the wide scope of the chapter, my primary focus will be on the *Tractatus* itself and whether Wittgenstein is as wrong as Anscombe thinks. My conclusion will be that he is not.

11.1

In *Tractatus* 6.43, Wittgenstein writes:

> If good or evil willing alters the world, then it can only alter the limits of the world, not the facts; not that which can be expressed through language.
>
> In short, the world must then thereby become an altogether different one. It must, so to speak, wane or wax as a whole.
>
> The world of the happy is a different one from that of the unhappy.

There are several things one might note about this passage. One, which should perhaps not be noted too early to allow for other thoughts, is that there is a hint of nonsense here. If good or evil willing alter something that cannot be expressed through language, then it looks as though they alter something that we cannot speak or think about. And it is nonsense to talk about a something that one cannot talk about. Which suggests that the first paragraph is nonsense. The second paragraph, which looks like a summary of the first paragraph ("In short..."), would then also be nonsense – which leaves the final paragraph not much better off, since we have nothing now to use to make sense of the idea of different worlds. As readers of the *Tractatus*, however, we are not supposed to throw away the ladder until after we have used it, so I am getting ahead of myself, however important it might be to be alive to the possibility that all this is nonsense.

Other points to note are that Wittgenstein seems to identify good willing with the happy and evil willing with the unhappy, that he talks about willing changing the world (though not the facts), and that the change in question is referred to in connection with some kind of (presumably non-spatial) size. Even if we are ultimately meant to overcome such talk, it is reasonable to wonder where it might come from as well as to what it might amount. The search for a source leads to Wittgenstein's wartime notebooks and to Schopenhauer. I will return to these sources later.

In the *Tractatus*, we can distinguish between the ethical will, the phenomenal will, and the metaphysical will. Proposition 6.423 distinguishes between the ethical will, of which nothing can be said, and the phenomenal will, which is of interest only to psychology. The ethical will, according to 6.43, changes nothing that can be expressed through language, no facts. The metaphysical subject is discussed, for instance, in 5.633 and 5.641. It is not the human being but the limit of the world. Fairhurst (2019) and Kuusela (2017: 45) identify this metaphysical subject with the ethical will.

To understand what Wittgenstein says about the will, then, it might help to understand what he says about the subject. For this reason, we should recall 5.631:

> There is no thinking, representing subject.
>
> If I wrote a book *The World as I Found It* then I would also have to report on my body in it and say which parts are subject to my will and which not, etc., that is to say, this is a means to isolate the subject, or rather to show that in an important sense there is no subject: Of it alone, that is, could there *not* be talk in this book.

Here, Wittgenstein does not deny that I or my body or my will or the subject exist, but he does say that "in an important sense there is no subject." The subject that does not exist seems to be the subject for whom the world might be thought to be representation. It is the subject that finds the world but is not part of it. It is not body or will in any ordinary sense but perhaps rather what might be supposed to own body and will. However, Wittgenstein says, there is no such thing.

The search for the ethical will has so far led us to the metaphysical subject, which seems not to exist. It can in some sense be talked about (see 5.641), but it is not an object in the world. It can at most be talked about indirectly, through the fact that the "world is my world." Even then, the kind of solipsism that we have here is one that coincides with pure Realism. So this I "shrinks to an extensionless point" (5.64). If the ethical will is the metaphysical subject, then it does indeed look chimerical, as Anscombe says.

Perhaps, though, it would help to focus more on the ethical aspect of the will. In her essay on "Wittgenstein and Ethics," Anne-Marie Søndergaard Christensen argues:

> When Wittgenstein emphasizes that language is an activity, he calls our attention to the fact that it necessarily involves a *subject* (e.g. TLP 2.1). The subject is not an independent entity able to enter into relationships with other facts in the world; the subject "does not belong to the world: rather it is a limit of the world" (TLP 5.632). (Christensen 2011: 803)

Christensen rightly notes that even the early Wittgenstein sees language as involving things that we do (see 2.1, for instance). She goes on to say that representation requires a subject and that the idea of a subject involves the idea of will, understood as the possibility of action. Since an action is not a mere event but is, analytically, connected to a will, representation, which is something we do, requires a subject with a will, and hence, at least in a certain sense, ethics, understood as "a structure established by the way we act and the way we relate to these actions, ... not ... a particular normative view of right and wrong, but simply the possibility of having such a normative view" (Christensen 2011: 805).

The very idea of a rational subject, one who can represent the world in language, might not necessarily seem to involve will (the subject might be indifferent as to how the world is, one might think), but perhaps it does at least involve the *possibility* of will, as Christensen says. There is at least room, that is to say, for the possibility of non-indifference as to what happens in the world. Christensen says that "our understanding of a subject involves notions of thinking, willing, and action" and that these "are only possible against the background of some normative structure" (Christensen 2011: 805). Thinking requires sense, which involves rules of grammar, hence normativity. Willing, too, involves some (not necessarily ethical) sense of good and bad. So she seems right about this. Thinking is a kind of action, and most willing involves action too, so the idea of a subject seemingly cannot be separated from that of action.

Eli Friedlander approaches these issues from a different angle but comes to a similar conclusion: thinking and willing ought not to be thought of as really distinct either from each other or from ethics:

> There is no *distinct* sphere of representations that are attributable to a thinking subject that would have beliefs, thoughts or wants without thereby willing. One might also say that thinking, believing and wanting, as we would be tempted to conceive of them as states of a thinking subject that then wills actions, are not distinct kinds of experiences, but pertain ultimately to the activity of life that is concretizing meaning. (Friedlander 2017: 114, emphasis in the original)

Willing is not a distinct act, as if I first want to raise my arm, then will to raise it, and then find that it has, as a result, risen. Willing to raise my arm *is* raising it willingly, or at least trying to raise it. Wanting that falls short of willing is neither doing nor trying. And the I that thinks about raising my arm is not different from the I that raises it. The thinking subject is the willing subject. Because of this, if for no other reason, it is doubtful that not willing at all is even possible, as Friedlander points out (see Friedlander 2017: 115). Complete indifference to what goes on in the world might not be as conceivable as one might have thought, in other words.

Representing or seeing also seems to require will because without will it seems camera-like, a mere scanning without purpose or attention. As Modesto Gómez-Alonso puts it:

> Were our relation to the world merely conceived as a *cognitive* and *perceptual* relation, that is, as an *external* relation to objects that appear (and disappear) in the theatre of consciousness, filling its stage with contents, our world would be a ghostly succession of disconnected and impenetrable events, in such a way that it would seem something alien from us, something that has become in a manner cut off from us and to which we are merely related as alienated *observers*. (Gómez-Alonso 2016: 85, emphasis in the original)

Gómez-Alonso identifies two problems with the account of our relation to the world as external and cognitive. One is that it falsely describes our experience. We do not merely observe our actions. With the world as with language, we are agents rather than mere spectators. The other problem with the account in question is that it deprives the world of meaning. If actions are reduced to mere events, then the question of why they are performed, in the sense of what intention they embody, disappears. We could in that case trace causes and effects, perhaps, but not reasons or intentions in any non-causal sense.

A being whose world lacks intelligible order in this way sounds like a zombie, not a living being in the full(est) sense of the term. Thinking, willing, and action all require some kind of normative structure, as Christensen argues. The subject that thinks is not distinct from the subject that wills, as Friedlander brings out. Representation requires will, as Gómez-Alonso shows. And so, where there is life there is will and normativity or evaluation. Understanding this should help us when we come to evaluate the relative strengths of Anscombe's and Wittgenstein's views on the will. Before that, though, I turn to Schopenhauer as possibly helpful background to Wittgenstein's ideas.

11.2

I began with Anscombe's thoughts on 6.43. This is a passage that can easily remind one of Schopenhauer on altruism and egoism. Egoism concentrates, he says, while altruism expands:

> The *good conscience*, the satisfaction we feel after every unselfish deed, is the opposite of the pangs of conscience. … A good conscience comes from the fact that unselfish deeds, arising out of the immediate recognition of our own essence in other appearances, confirm the recognition that our true self does not exist only in the single appearance of our own person, but in every living thing. This makes the heart feel larger, in the same way that it contracts in egoism. … The egoist feels he is surrounded by alien and hostile appearances, and all his hopes rest on his own well-being. The good person lives in a world of friendly appearances: the well-being of each of these appearances is his own well-being. (Schopenhauer 2010: 400–401, emphasis in the original)

Schopenhauer implies that the egoist has a small heart but lives in a big world, a world populated by multiple individuals. The good person, on the other hand, has a big heart but lives in a happily small world, a world in which there is really only one inner being. Schopenhauer expresses a similar thought in the following passage:

> The good character … lives in an external world that is homogeneous with his own true being. The others are not a non-ego for him, but an "I once more." (Schopenhauer 2019: 211)

The felt world of the good and happy is a different world from that of the miserable egoist.

At least in his *Notebooks*, Wittgenstein's views on the will seem to be similar to Schopenhauer's. Schopenhauer (2010: 125) writes: "Willing and doing are different only for reflection: in actuality they are one. Every true, genuine and immediate act of will is instantly and immediately also the appearance of an act of the body." Similarly, Wittgenstein (Wittgenstein 1979: 87e) writes:

> The act of the will is not the cause of the action but is the action itself. One cannot will without acting. (4.11.16)

On the next page, on the same day, he writes that "wishing (*Wünschen*) is not acting. But willing is acting" and "The wish (*Wunsch*) precedes the event, the will accompanies it." The very early Wittgenstein, then, seems similar to Schopenhauer. In the *Notebooks*, Wittgenstein identifies willing with acting, as Schopenhauer does. And in the *Tractatus*, he appears to make at least a similar contrast to that made by Schopenhauer between the good and happy, on the one hand, and the egoistic and miserable, on the other. Anscombe, however, sees the *Tractatus* as taking a very different view. It is time now to look at what she says in more detail before finally assessing it.

11.3

Anscombe says that Schopenhauer identifies the world with my will and regards both as bad (see Anscombe 1971: 172fn), whereas Wittgenstein, she says, sees the world as good and independent of my will. Schopenhauer's idea of a good will is one that denies itself. Wittgenstein's good will is not concerned with how things are; it accepts the world as it is, however it is, "and in that sense is like Schopenhauer's good will" (Anscombe 1971: 172fn). The alleged similarity between Wittgenstein's view and Schopenhauer's on this point, I take it, is that neither asks for anything from the world. As far as her own view goes, Anscombe calls the will that alters the limits of the world but effects nothing in it "chimerical" (Anscombe 1971: 172). Will, like intention, she suggests, resides in what we do.[1]

This account of Anscombe's, it seems to me, could be misleading. This is because the contrast between Schopenhauer's regarding the world as bad

---

[1] See also Wittgenstein (2009: §644), which brings up a similar idea.

and Wittgenstein's regarding it as good sounds too strong. We have already seen some points of apparent agreement between Schopenhauer and the *Tractatus*. In addition to these, it is worth noting that, while Schopenhauer recommends turning away from the world and regarding it as nothing, he also clearly admires the saintly and holy of various religious traditions. He also believes that everything is beautiful.[2] So not everything (or everyone) in the world is bad, in his view.

To understand what Anscombe says about 6.43, it helps to back up a little. Before she condemns 6.43 as "obviously wrong" she quotes 6.422, where Wittgenstein says that "There must be a kind of ethical reward and ethical punishment, but these must reside in the action itself" (see Anscombe 1971: 171). She then asks what this "action itself" is. To answer this, she begins by quoting 6.373: "The world is independent of my will." She also refers to 6.374, where Wittgenstein writes that "Even if all that we wished happened, then this would still only, so to speak, be a gift of fate, since there is no *logical* connection between will and world that would guarantee this, and the assumed physical connection itself we could surely not in turn will." She concludes her account of Wittgenstein's position by saying that, according to him, "If one has reached a solution [to the task one has been set], this is made to be a solution ... by an alteration 'in the limits of the world' (6.43)." Then her verdict: "It is this part of the *Tractatus* that seems to me most obviously wrong" (Anscombe 1971: 171).

The problem she sees is that "the philosophy of the *Tractatus* could not allow" that "'What happens' includes 'actions', in the sense of the word in which 'good' and 'bad' are predicated of actions" (Anscombe 1971: 172). Because there is no value, no good or bad, in the world. And so we are left with "the chimerical 'will' which effects nothing in the world, but only alters the 'limits' of the world" (Anscombe 1971: 172). Although she says that what we ought to say instead of what the *Tractatus* says has not yet been discovered, despite having already published *Intention* (Anscombe 1957), which one might think of as offering her answer to this question, she clearly prefers Wittgenstein's implying in *Investigations* §644 that one's intention resides (at least partly) in what one does, and his consideration in

---

[2] See Schopenhauer (2010: 234–235): "Since on the one hand, every existing thing can be considered purely objectively and apart from all relation, and since on the other hand, the will appears in every thing on some level of its objecthood, making the thing an expression of an Idea; so it follows that everything is *beautiful* – Dutch still lifes, which we have already mentioned above (§38) in this connection, testify to the fact that even the most insignificant thing can be viewed in a purely objective and will-less manner, and hence prove to be beautiful."

the *Notebooks* of the idea that because some things are done by me and others not, one part of the world is closer to me than another (see Anscombe 1971: 172; Wittgenstein 1979: 88).[3]

11.4

We are now in a better position to decide whether Anscombe's criticism of Wittgenstein is justified. At least part of what Anscombe is complaining about seems to be that good and bad are not to be found in the world, according to the *Tractatus*, and that therefore actions, which can be good or bad, are not to be found in the world. Anscombe does indeed seem right and Wittgenstein wrong. At least at first sight. That is, good and bad actions surely are performed in the world, and yet Wittgenstein says that all value must lie outside the world. But when someone seems as obviously wrong as Wittgenstein does here it is, at least in cases like his, worth wondering whether their meaning has been fully understood.

Some of what Wittgenstein says is obviously *right*. As he observes, there is no logical connection between my wanting something to happen, or wishing it would happen, or trying to make it happen, and its actually happening. He also seems right to say that there is no ethical reward or punishment to be found in this world, at least not by any scientific investigation. And that it is a gift of fate that I can do anything at all.

Against Wittgenstein, though, there is a connection between what happens and what I do. Some of what happens *is* what I do. One wonders how Wittgenstein could have denied this, or failed to see it, if that is what he really did. Since the *Tractatus* seems so obviously wrong, as Anscombe says, it is worth looking at what else he wrote on the subject.

In the *Notebooks* (21.7.16), Wittgenstein imagines someone who cannot move his limbs and so in a sense has no will to exercise but who can nevertheless wish and communicate thoughts. Ethics would have validity for him, Wittgenstein says. At this point, he wonders whether there is a difference between this (ethical) will and the will that moves the body. And he asks whether the mistake here (a mistake therefore presumably has been made, as he sees it) lies in the fact that even wishing is an activity of the will, so that a man without will would not be alive. Someone who could not so much as wish would seem not to be an agent at all, and in that sense might be said not to be alive, as discussed in Part 1. Wittgenstein goes from this immediately to whether one could have representation or idea

---

[3] See Richter (2018) for a detailed discussion of Wittgenstein (2009: §§611–620).

but not will. "In some sense this seems impossible. But if it were possible then there could also be a world without ethics" (Wittgenstein 1979: 77e). Representation without will seems impossible partly because mere awareness without concern, without any kind of preference or evaluation, seems zombie-like, or almost non-awareness. Unconcerned or disinterested awareness seems like a kind of obliviousness, although it need not quite amount to that. However, representation or idea also surely requires concepts, and these need to be formed. Their formation seems to require at least the will to form concepts, if not also some sense of pertinence, of what matters and belongs with what else. So representation without will does indeed appear to be impossible. If, somehow, either as a miracle or because one first acquired concepts and then later became completely indifferent, one just did have concepts and awareness but not will, then, Wittgenstein says, there could be a world without ethics. One would, after all, do nothing at all except be aware of what was going on, neither approving nor disapproving of anything whatsoever. Such a being could not be good or evil. But this is not how we are, so even if such a being, and a world without ethics, could exist, that has little relevance to me. My world is not free of ethics. Ethics, as Wittgenstein here conceives of it, clearly has to do with the will, as Christensen and Friedlander explain. Whether what Wittgenstein thinks in the *Notebooks* is the same as what he thinks in the *Tractatus*, though, is open to doubt. So it may be as well to return to the *Tractatus*.

Michael Kremer argues that the problem Anscombe sees is more a result of Anscombe's reading of the *Tractatus* than of what Wittgenstein actually means. The conception of the will that we find in the *Notebooks*, and which Anscombe seems to like, is not explicit in the *Tractatus*, Kremer agrees, but it is implied by the book:

> The book itself undermines the conception of the relation between language, thought and world which it seemingly expresses, and shows the way to a quite different conception. In particular, the standard interpretation of the *Tractatus*' account of will is based principally on the 6.4's, which we have seen Wittgenstein deconstruct in the 6.5's. The "account" of the will in the 6.4's is more self-undermining nonsense. "Of the will that is the subject of the ethical we cannot speak" (6.423) is nonsense – to say "we cannot speak of x" is to speak of x. There is *nothing* of which we can say that we cannot speak of it. The solution of the problems of life lies in realizing this. But this is not to realize that "there is" the ethical will, which "shows itself." It is rather to realize that we have lives to live. There is no riddle; there is just life. (Kremer 2001, emphasis in original)

I will argue that Kremer is essentially right, but there is still something problematic about how he presents his point here, especially in the final sentence just quoted. Life itself can seem to be, if not a riddle, at least a kind of puzzle. What is it about? How should it be lived? Anscombe observes that the analogy in 6.4321 between life and a homework exercise was one that Wittgenstein still used at the end of his life (Anscombe 1971: 171). Given this, it seems implausible that he meant his readers to reject it as nonsense in the *Tractatus*, even if he perhaps expected them to come to a different understanding of the idea. As Friedlander points out, if one has been worrying for a long time about the meaning of life then "it would not be sufficient to say something like 'it was all nonsense, get over it'" (Friedlander 2017: 98). The point of Wittgenstein's ladder is surely to help people work their way out of their problems, rather than simply to show that they are wrong.

As an idea that is found in both the *Tractatus* and his later thought is unlikely to be one that Wittgenstein meant to reject in the *Tractatus*, so too a good idea that he held before and after the *Tractatus* is unlikely to be one that he meant to be thrown away by readers of that book. Anscombe notes that Wittgenstein took a more seemingly reasonable view of the will in both his notebooks and the *Philosophical Investigations* (see Anscombe 1971: 172), and it is unlikely that he seriously adopted the less reasonable, indeed "obviously wrong," view that he might appear to defend in the *Tractatus*. This is reason to believe that Kremer is right, but we need to see how and why he is right. Kremer provides useful help with this task.

He says, for instance, that the 6.5s deconstruct the 6.4s. If this is true, then ultimately the *Tractatus* does not offer an account of a metaphysical or ethical will of the kind that Anscombe finds objectionable. However, we might also wonder whether in this case we can rely on the ideas from Christensen, Friedlander, and Gómez-Alonso that I have discussed, since these are derived in part from remarks in the *Tractatus*. I think the answer is that we can, since there is much more than *Tractatus* exegesis going on in those papers. Among other things, Christensen builds on work by John McDowell, Friedlander focuses on Wittgenstein's *Notebooks*, and Gómez-Alonso thinks about the nature of representation. All argue, above all, on the basis of what seems to be true, and all, I argue, reach conclusions that are compatible with Kremer's reading of the *Tractatus*.[4] The question then is whether his reading is a good one.

It seems worthwhile to take a closer look at this part of the *Tractatus* to see whether he is right. The 6.4s make a number of metaphysical(-

---

[4] Indeed, Kremer himself notes the similarity between his view and Friedlander's in endnote 24 of his paper. He also points out some apparent differences, and he cites different works by Friedlander, but the point remains.

seeming) claims about value and the meaning of the world lying outside the world, about ethics being transcendental, about the non-phenomenal will as the bearer of the ethical, about altering the limits of the world, about immortality, about the riddle of life (whose solution lies outside space and time), about God and the mystical. It is surely reasonable to ask what "outside the world" means, what Wittgenstein means by "transcendental," what he means by "God," and what he means here by "the will." These are not nonsense words, but what does *he* mean by them in *this* context? There are doubtless other questions one could reasonably ask too.

Proposition 6.5 and the rest of the *Tractatus*, however, suggest that this is all problematic. "If a question can be put at all, then it *can* also be answered," Wittgenstein writes in 6.5. If Wittgenstein's obscure claims in the 6.4s are meant to be answers to questions, then perhaps those questions were themselves ill-conceived. Proposition 6.52 implies that all possible questions are questions of natural science. This would rule out questions about anything mystical or non-phenomenal or outside the world, unless these words are given a mundane sense. Proposition 6.53 confirms this anti-metaphysical stance, while also undercutting itself, since it does not itself belong to natural science (as pointed out by Kremer (2001: 57–58)) and implies a distinction between saying what can be said and saying something else. But there surely is no saying anything but what can be said. So metaphysics is apparently rejected but so too is the *Tractatus'* own explicit rejection of metaphysics. This is not, it seems, a defence of metaphysis via a double negative. Rather, 6.54 tells us that we must overcome these propositions – not turn back to the 6.4s or earlier. And then 7 is a (contentless) tautology that sounds like "shh." In short, I think that Wittgenstein himself rejects the chimaera to which Anscombe objects.

In the midst of the 6.5s, we find Wittgenstein saying, "There is to be sure the inexpressible. This *shows* itself, it is the mystical" (6.522). This refers back to 6.44, which tells us that the mystical is that the world is. So 6.522 seems to amount to the assertion that the world exists, or that there is the fact that the world exists. I take it that this needs to be understood in connection with such things as the question of why there is something rather than nothing and with Wittgenstein's talk about wondering at the existence of the world in the Lecture on Ethics (Wittgenstein 1965). In a sense, the kind of sense implied at times in the 6.5s, there is no problem here at all, because there is simply nothing to be either thought or said. "The world exists," like "Something exists," says nothing at all. The informational content of such sentences is zero. On the other hand, someone wondering at the fact that anything at all exists might feel as though "The world exists!" says *everything*. But, at least in the view of the early Wittgenstein (including the author of the Lecture on Ethics), sentences like this are nonsense. The fact that a sentence might say, or merely seem to say, everything that one wants to express does not mean that there is any *content* that one wants to express. The best one can do might still be nothing. The nonsense one then speaks can be seen as evidence of something good in the speaker, a certain kind of attitude, perhaps, but it is nonsense all the same. At least, this appears to be the early Wittgenstein's view. In other words, Kremer seems to be right.

Anscombe's complaint is that will resides in what we do, and that this belongs to, or lies within, the world. So the connection between will and world is that will is internal to the world, rather than something that in some sense alters the limits of the world. The *Tractatus*, as understood by Christensen, suggests that ethics (in Wittgenstein's sense) is a normative structure established by how we act and relate to our actions. It represents the possibility of having a particular view of what is right and wrong, but it is not any such view itself. It is something like the opposite of indifference with regard to action, and action is something like happening accompanied by will. Which seems to imply that will is indeed inside the world, just as Anscombe wants it to be. Will understood otherwise, the chimerical will that Anscombe rejects, I think must be rejected by Wittgenstein himself. It is, or ought to be, part of the nonsense that readers of the *Tractatus* are to overcome, as Kremer has argued. Certainly, the ethical will cannot be talked about, which makes it ineffable at best (see 6.423), if not simply nonsense.

What, though, about the will that we are trying to understand, if only to reject it? And why would anyone believe in it, to begin with? What Anscombe rejects as chimerical, or at least one thing that she rejects, is the will that effects nothing in the world. It seems to me both right and wrong to reject this idea as chimerical. Rejecting it seems wrong because, as Wittgenstein says, there is no logical or necessary connection between my (or anyone else's) wishing or wanting something, or even trying to make something happen, and that thing's happening. In this sense, it seems quite reasonable to deny that there is some thing called the will that effects events in the world. So if we are to talk about the will, it *should* be as something that effects nothing in the world. All it determines is what I want to happen or, rather (since one can will not to do what one wants, or is tempted, to do), what I will to do or to happen.

Anscombe seems right, though, to reject this idea of the will as a chimaera. There is no empirical evidence for it; it is outside the empirical world of causally interacting objects, and reason does not require us to believe in it. In other words, the will does effect nothing in the world, but this is for the simple reason that it (the will understood this way) does not exist, not because its powers are mysterious. It is at least possible, though, that Wittgenstein *meant* his readers to give up this idea of what the will might be, perhaps to return to ordinary uses of the idea.

So how is the idea of will used, if not to name some kind of dubious object? To will something is not to bring it about. It is more like wanting it or having a pro-attitude towards its happening, but it also involves trying to make it happen, or actually making it happen (willingly) (see Wittgenstein 2009: §§611–620). Doing something willingly is a kind of doing, though, not doing with a particular kind of cause (the will). To be an agent at all, even if one that only thinks, seems to involve will.

Perhaps, though, there could be a kind of saint who wills only that God's will be done and who is constantly satisfied, believing that all that happens is in conformity with God's will. Such a person is happy no matter what happens (and in that sense is indifferent) but is not indifferent about it (on the contrary, they are *happy*). This is something like the happy person whom Wittgenstein imagines in the *Notebooks* (Wittgenstein 1979: 77–78, 29.7.16). But, as Wittgenstein apparently demonstrates, it is hard to know what to say about such a person. Do they want good fortune for their neighbour, for instance? In which case, will they not be disappointed if their neighbour has bad fortune? Or do they want neither good nor bad for their neighbour? Do they perhaps want good fortune but without being attached to this altruistic desire? It seems they must want in a flexible manner, not rigidly insisting, even in thought or attitude, that things go as they want (however altruistically).

Questions along these lines lead Oskari Kuusela to the conclusion that Wittgenstein believes both that we should accept the world and that we need not accept injustices (or, presumably, other evils). Kuusela suggests that if we try to right a wrong (as we may do, on his understanding of Wittgenstein's ethics) and fail, then we must accept this. But we may then try again, perhaps the next day: "The fight against injustice may have been lost, and, rather than letting the pain incapacitate us, we must accept the outcome. But tomorrow we try again!" (Kuusela 2017: 49). It might be hard to see how behaviour such as this is *really* accepting the world as it is. I will try to explain later how it can be. Before that, however, let us return our focus to Anscombe's criticism of Wittgenstein.

What I think Anscombe objects to is the idea that it does not matter what one does. That "'action', in the ethical sense, is something independent of what happens" (Anscombe 1971: 171). But Wittgenstein does not quite say that. He says that if one has done as required then this is not because one has changed the world in this way or that, but because one has done something that he calls altering the limits of the world. What this means, though, is very obscure.

Anscombe clearly has in mind people who can bring about changes in the world, not the exceptional case of someone who can only think and want, and she wants to say that the actions of ordinary people can be good or bad. Wittgenstein's apparent denial of this separates physical events from willing in a way that makes events neither good nor bad in a moral sense and makes the will mysterious and elusive, if not completely chimerical. I think she is right about this, but I also think that we can read Wittgenstein as wanting his readers to reject the way of thinking that brings up these problems. Such thinking is part of the ladder that is to be climbed or overcome and then discarded.

How can we make sense of the fact that what happens includes actions? That the world I find myself in includes things that I (and others) do? And not in the sense that I find myself doing them, but in the sense that I do them?

The very question, or questions, can be resisted. How can we *not* make sense of the fact that what happens includes things I do? How could such a fact seem at all mysterious? One can wonder at it as one can wonder at anything whatsoever, but otherwise there is nothing inherently mysterious about it. It can come to seem mysterious, though, if we insist on framing things a certain way, on committing to a certain kind of metaphysical theory or picture. If we think of the subject as an object, at least potentially located in the world, then we will not find it. It alone would have to be left out of *The World as I Found It*. If we think of good and evil as absolutes somehow located in the world, then we will struggle to make sense of them. As Hume and Wittgenstein point out, where would we find them? (See Wittgenstein 1965: 6–7; Hume 1978: 468–469.) And if we think of the will as something that might give rise to good or evil actions, then we will struggle to say anything intelligible about it. Hence, we need to give up the problematic view of the will as a phenomenon or something somehow within the world, whose role as the link between ethics and events in the world then becomes utterly obscure or implausible as one tries to work out what exactly it might be. It is this that seems to get Wittgenstein into trouble. Giving up this view is what the *Tractatus* itself can be read as telling us to do, so that we then see the world aright.

Wittgenstein does not put a different metaphysical picture or theory in place of the one he rejects, but he does, the suggestion is, show that thinking of the will as something that the self knows leads to an implausible and unacceptable divorce between the self and one's actions.

Friedlander argues that Wittgenstein's thoughts on the will connect with questions about scepticism and "a fundamental ethico-religious attitude" (Friedlander 2017: 97). Friedlander offers a kind of summary of Wittgenstein's ethics, which brings us back to the problem of whether Wittgenstein thinks we should not will at all and, if so, what this could mean:

> It would indeed be precisely right to say that not *wanting* is the true attitude of the will. But ... the stance of "not wanting" can be understood in two different ways. We could imagine an attempt to "shut down" all wanting or desire (hopelessly, one should add, since this is tantamount to life itself). The other way not to remain with unfulfilled wanting would be to *concretize* the want into willing. To concretize want into will *is* to do away with wanting. (Friedlander 2017: 116, emphasis in the original)

Willing is concrete because it is acting. This is the difference between (really) willing and (merely) wanting: "An action is, one might say, the expression of a thought in the medium of reality" (Friedlander 2017: 111). To want in the sense of wishing is to be unhappy with the world but to do nothing about it. To will, on the other hand, is to act, thereby changing the world. Not in the sense that all actions achieve their goal, but in the sense that all actions are themselves events in the world, and therefore part of it. To act is to change the world, even if the act in question is only thinking a certain thought. A world in which that thought occurs is different from a world in which it does not. The recognition that thinking is a kind of action might blur the distinction between wanting and willing, but perhaps it is right to recognise a blur here. "It is in concretizing *meaning* that we move from want to will," Friedlander writes (2017: 112). Wanting and willing are not the same thing, but not wholly distinct either. The difference is that willing, being more closely connected to action, is more significant.

Here, I think, is the key to both making sense of Kuusela's reading of Wittgenstein and seeing that it is right after all. We cannot be sure that our efforts will end an injustice that we oppose, but we can be sure that the injustice will not go unopposed if we take action against it. By taking such action, we give up wanting in the sense of wishing, and thereby give up our unharmonious relationship with the world, but do not merely acquiesce to evil. We also, by neither idling nor going on holiday, ensure that our activity has meaning. If our goal is not so much achieving a certain end, such as ending a particular injustice, but acting in a certain way, then we can be guaranteed success. As Friedlander puts it, "Indeed, in taking the action *itself* as one's object, one can precisely introduce the possibility of agreement with the world, of happiness, irrespective of an action achieving its aim or purpose" (Friedlander 2017: 117). In this sense, the reward for ethical action lies in the action itself, as Wittgenstein suggests it should at 6.422.

Friedlander seems to provide a solution to the apparent tension between accepting an outcome and trying to change it. One does not accept the unjust situation. One accepts the world, which includes both that situation and one's own opposition to it. One does not *wish* that the situation would change, but does take action against it. Accepting the world, then, does not mean doing nothing about evil. On the contrary, it might well mean taking active steps to oppose evil. What it does not allow is merely wishing that the evil would go away.

In suggesting that one should not *want*, Wittgenstein is not, however, telling us what we ought to do instead. He does not tell us what to will. As Christensen observes, "he has carefully removed all such normative recommendations from the final version of the *Tractatus*" (Christensen 2011: 802). As a work of philosophy, the *Tractatus* can tell us nothing about how to live, much as Kremer suggests.

In short, Anscombe is right to reject the view of the will that she calls wrong, but it is at least possible that Wittgenstein intends his readers to reject it too. Working through his remarks about the will, with help from Kremer, Christensen, Gómez-Alonso, and Friedlander, helps us to see this, and to understand his views on ethics as well. The will, conceived as something distinct from our actions in the world, is indeed a chimaera. Will belongs to what we do. And it is not, as such, something that we can or should reject. If we are to reject anything in this neighbourhood, it is mere wanting.

References

Anscombe, G. E. M. 1957. *Intention*. Oxford: Blackwell.
  1971. *An Introduction to Wittgenstein's Tractatus*. 2nd ed. London: Hutchinson.
Anzengruber, Ludwig. 1872. "Die Kreuzelschreiber". In *Ludwig Anzengrubers Gesammelte Werke*. Stuttgart and Berlin: G. Cotta'sche Buchhandlung Nachfolger.
Appelqvist, Hanne. 2016. "On Wittgenstein's Kantian Solution of the Problem of Philosophy". *The British Journal for the History of Philosophy* 24 (4):697–719.
Aristotle. 1964. *Analytica Priora*. Edited by W. D. Ross. Oxford: Clarendon Press.
Barker, Peter. 1979. "Untangling the Net Metaphor". *Philosophy Research Archives* 5:182–199.
Bell, David. 1996. "Solipsism and Subjectivity". *European Journal of Philosophy* 4:155–174.
Black, Max. 1964. *A Companion to Wittgenstein's Tractatus*. Ithaca, NY: Cornell University Press.
Bradley, Raymond. 1992. *The Nature of All Being: A Study of Wittgenstein's Modal Atomism*. New York and Oxford: Oxford University Press.
Burnyeat, Myles. 1987. "Wittgenstein and Augustine De Magistro". *Proceedings of the Aristotelian Society Supplementary Volume* 61:1–24.
Butterfield, Jeremy. 2004. Between Laws and Models: Some Philosophical Morals of Lagrangian Mechanics, https://arxiv.org/pdf/physics/0409030.pdf.
Carnap, Rudolf. 1930. "Die Alte Und Die Neue Logik". *Erkenntnis* 1 (1):12–26.
  1983. "The Logicist Foundations of Mathematics". In *Philosophy of Mathematics: Selected Readings*, edited by P. Benacerraf and H. Putnam. Cambridge: Cambridge University Press, 41–52.
Cartwright, Richard. 1987. *Philosophical Essays*. Cambridge, MA: MIT Press.
  2003. "Russell and Moore, 1898–1905". In *The Cambridge Companion to Bertrand Russell*, edited by N. Griffin. Cambridge: Cambridge University Press, 108–127.
Child, William. 2013. "Does the Tractatus Contain a Private Language Argument?". In *Wittgenstein's Tractatus: History and Interpretation*, edited by P. Sullivan and M. Potter. Oxford: Oxford University Press, 143–169.
Christensen, Anne-Marie Søndergaard. 2011. "Wittgenstein and Ethics". In *The Oxford Handbook of Wittgenstein*, edited by O. Kuusela and M. McGinn. Oxford: Oxford University Press, 796–817.

Church, Alonzo. 1932. "A Set of Postulates for the Foundation of Logic". *The Annals of Mathematics* 33 (2):346–366.
　1941. *The Calculi of Lambda Conversion*. Princeton, NJ: Princeton University Press.
Chwistek, Leon. 1967. "Antinomies of Formal Logic". In *Polish Logic: 1920–1939*, edited by S. McCall. Oxford: Clarendon Press, 338–345.
Conant, James. 2000. "Elucidation and Nonsense in Frege and Early Wittgenstein". In *The New Wittgenstein*, edited by A. Crary and R. Read. London: Routledge, 174–217.
　2002. "The Method of the Tractatus". In *From Frege to Wittgenstein: Perspectives on Early Analytic Philosophy*, edited by E. H. Reck. Oxford: Oxford University Press, 374–462.
　2011. "Wittgenstein's Methods". In *The Oxford Handbook of Metaphysics*, edited by O. Kuusela and M. McGinn. Oxford: Oxford University Press, 620–645.
Copi, Irving M. 1958. "Objects, Properties and Relations in the Tractatus". *Mind* 67:145–165.
Diamond, Cora. 1991a. "The Face of Necessity". In *The Realistic Spirit*. Cambridge, MA: MIT Press, 243–266.
　1991b. "Throwing Away the Ladder: How to Read the *Tractatus*". In *The Realistic Spirit*. Cambridge, MA: MIT Press, 179–204.
　1991c. "What Nonsense Might Be". In *The Realistic Spirit*. Cambridge, MA: MIT Press, 95–114.
　2000a. "Does Bismarck Have a Beetle in His Box? The Private Language Argument in the Tractatus". In *The New Wittgenstein*, edited by A. Crary and R. Read. Abingdon: Routledge, 262–292.
　2000b. "Ethics, Imagination and the Method of Wittgenstein's *Tractatus*". In *The New Wittgenstein*, edited by A. Crary and R. Read. Abingdon: Routledge, 149–173.
　2002. "Truth before Tarski: After Sluga, after Ricketts, after Geach, after Goldfarb, Hylton, Floyd, and Van Heijenoort". In *From Frege to Wittgenstein: Perspectives on Early Analytic Philosophy*, edited by E. H. Reck. Oxford: Oxford University Press, 252–279.
　2018. "Commentary on José Zalabardo's 'the Tractatus on Unity'". *Australasian Philosophical Review* 2:272–284.
　2019. *Reading Wittgenstein with Anscombe, Going on to Ethics*. Cambridge, MA: Harvard University Press.
DiSalle, Robert. 1995. "Spacetime Theory as Physical Geometry". *Erkenntnis* 42 (3):317–337.
Dreben, Burton, and Juliet Floyd. 1991. "Tautology: How Not to Use a Word". *Synthese* 87 (1):23–50.
Drury, Maurice O'Connor. 1981. "Some Notes on Conversations with Wittgenstein". In *Ludwig Wittgenstein. Personal Recollections*, edited by R. Rhees. Totowa, NJ: Rowman and Littlefield, 76–96.
Dummett, Michael. 1959. "Truth". *Proceedings of the Aristotelian Society* 59:141–162.

1991. "Frege's Myth of the Third Realm". In *Frege and Other Philosophers*. Oxford: Oxford University Press, 249–262.

Eisenthal, Joshua. 2018. "Mechanics without Mechanisms". *Studies in History and Philosophy of Science Part B: Studies in History and Philosophy of Modern Physics* 62:42–55.

2021. "Hertz's Mechanics and a Unitary Notion of Force". *Studies in History and Philosophy of Science Part B: Studies in History and Philosophy of Modern Physics* 90:226–234.

2022. "Models and Multiplicities". *Journal of the History of Philosophy* 60 (2):277–302.

Engelmann, Mauro Luiz. 2021. *Reading Wittgenstein's Tractatus*. Cambridge: Cambridge University Press.

Fairhurst, Jordi. 2019. "The Ethical Subject and the Willing Subject in the Tractatus: An Alternative to the Transcendental Reading". *Philosophia* 47 (1):75–95.

Floyd, Juliet. 1995. "On Saying What You Really Want to Say: Wittgenstein, Gödel, and the Trisection of the Angle". In *From Dedekind to Gödel: Essays on the Development of the Foundations of Mathematics*, edited by J. Hintikka. Dordrecht: Kluwer 373–425.

1998. "The Uncaptive Eye: Solipsism in Wittgenstein's Tractatus". In *Loneliness*, edited by L. S. Rouner. Notre Dame, IN: University of Notre Dame Press, 79–108.

2000. "Wittgenstein, Mathematics and Philosophy". In *The New Wittgenstein*, edited by R. Read and A. Crary. London: Routledge, 232–261.

2001. "Number and Ascriptions of Number in the Tractatus". In *Future Pasts: Perspectives on the Analytic Tradition in Twentieth Century Philosophy*, edited by J. Floyd and S. Shieh. New York: Oxford University Press, 145–191.

2005. "Wittgenstein on Philosophy of Logic and Mathematics". In *The Oxford Handbook to the Philosophy of Logic and Mathematics*, edited by S. Shapiro. New York: Oxford University Press, 75–128.

2007. "Wittgenstein and the Inexpressible". In *Wittgenstein and the Moral Life*, edited by A. Crary. Cambridge, MA: MIT Press, 177–234.

2010. "On Being Surprised: Wittgenstein on Aspect Perception, Logic and Mathematics". In *Seeing Wittgenstein Anew: New Essays on Aspect Seeing*, edited by W. Day and V. J. Krebs. New York: Cambridge University Press, 314–337.

2018. "'Ultimate' Facts? Zalabardo on the Metaphysics of Truth". *Australasian Philosophical Review* 2 (3):299–314.

Fogelin, Robert J. 1987. *Wittgenstein*. 2nd ed. London: Routledge and Kegan Paul.

Frascolla, Pasquale. 1994. *Wittgenstein's Philosophy of Mathematics*. London: Routledge.

1997. "The Tractatus System of Arithmetic". *Synthese* 122:353–378.

2004. "On the Nature of Tractatus Objects". *Dialectica* 58 (3):369–382.

2007. *Understanding Wittgenstein's Tractatus*. London: Routledge.

2016. "Wittgenstein's Early Philosophy of Mathematics". In *A Companion to Wittgenstein*, edited by H.-J. Glock and J. Hyman. Hoboken, NJ: Wiley-Blackwell, 305–318.

Fraser, Craig. 1985. "D'Alembert's Principle: The Original Formulation and Application in Jean D'Alembert's Traité de Dynamique (1743)". *Centaurus* 28:31–61.

Frege, Gottlob. 1879. *Begriffsschrift, Eine Der Arithmetischen Nachgebildete Formelsprache Des Reinen Denkens*. Halle: L. Nebert.

1893. *Grundgesetze Der Arithmetik*. Vol. I. Jena: Verlag Hermann Pohle.

1906. "Über Die Grundlagen Der Geometrie I, II, III". *Jahresbericht der Deutschen Mathematiker-Vereinigung* 15:293–309, 377–403, 423–430.

1972. *Conceptual Notation and Related Articles*. Translated by T. W. Bynum. Edited by T. W. Bynum. Oxford: Clarendon Press.

1979a. "Logic in Mathematics". In *Posthumous Writings*, edited by H. Hermes, F. Kambartel and F. Kaulbach. Oxford: Blackwell, 203–250.

1979b. *Posthumous Writings*. Translated by P. Long and R. White. Edited by H. Hermes, F. Kambartel and F. Kaulbach. Oxford: Blackwell.

1980a. *The Foundations of Arithmetic*. Translated by J. L. Austin. Evanston, IL: Northwestern University Press.

1980b. "On Concept and Object". In *Translations from the Philosophical Writings of Gottlob Frege*, edited by M. Black and P. T. Geach. Oxford: Basil Blackwell, 42–55.

1984. *Collected Papers on Mathematics, Logic, and Philosophy*. Edited by B. McGuinness. Oxford: Blackwell.

2013. *Basic Laws of Arithmetic*. Edited by P. Ebert and M. Rossberg. Oxford: Oxford University Press.

Friedlander, Eli. 2017. "Logic, Ethics and Existence in Wittgenstein's *Tractatus*". In *Wittgenstein's Moral Thought*, edited by E. Dain and R. Agam-Segal. London: Routledge, 97–131.

Friedman, Michael. 2001. *Dynamics of Reason: The 1999 Kant Lectures at Stanford University*. Stanford, CA: CSLI Publications.

Gabriel, Gottfried. 2017. "Solipsism – The Leitmotif in Wittgenstein's Life and Philosophy". *Wittgenstein Studien* 8:1–14.

Gandon, Sébastien. 2002. *Logique Et Langage. Études Sur Le Premier Wittgenstein*. Paris: Vrin.

Georgallides, Andreas. 2021. "A Possible Resolution of the Tractarian Paradox". *Open Journal of Philosophy* 11 (1):148–158.

Glock, Hans-Johann. 1992. "Cambridge, Jena or Vienna? The Roots of the *Tractatus*". *Ratio* 5 (1):1–23.

1997. "Kant and Wittgenstein: Philosophy, Necessity and Representation". *International Journal of Philosophical Studies* 5 (2):285–305.

Goldfarb, Warren. 1997. "Metaphysics and Nonsense: On Cora Diamond's The Realistic Spirit". *Journal of Philosophical Research* 22:57–74.

Gómez-Alonso, Modesto. 2016. "Wittgenstein on the Will and Voluntary Action". In *Action, Decision-Making and Forms of Life*, edited by J. Padilla Gálvez. Berlin and Boston, MA: De Gruyter, 77–108.

Griffin, James. 1964. *Wittgenstein's Logical Atomism*. Oxford: Oxford University Press.
Griffin, Nicholas. 1985. "Russell's Multiple Relation Theory of Judgement". *Philosophical Studies* 47:213–248.
  ed. 1992. *The Selected Letters of Bertrand Russell, Vol. 1: The Private Years (1884–1914)*. Boston, MA: Houghton Mifflin Co.
Hacker, P. M. S. 1972. *Insight and Illusion: Wittgenstein on Philosophy and the Metaphysics of Experience*: Oxford: Clarendon Press.
  1986. *Insight and Illusion: Themes in the Philosophy of Wittgenstein*. Rev. ed. Oxford: Clarendon.
Hancock, Peter, and Per Martin-Löf. 1975. Syntax and Semantics of the Language of Primitive Recursive Functions. In *Research Reports in Mathematics*. Preprint 3. Stockholm: Department of Mathematics, University of Stockholm.
Hanslick, Eduard. 1986. *On the Musically Beautiful*. Translated by G. Payzant. Indianapolis: Hackett.
Hertz, Heinrich. 1894. *Prinzipien Der Mechanik*. Leipzig: J.A. Barth.
  1899. *The Principles of Mechanics Presented in a New Form*. London: Macmillan and Co.
Hume, David. 1978. *A Treatise of Human Nature*. 2nd ed. Oxford: Clarendon.
Hyder, David Jalal. 2002. *The Mechanics of Meaning: Propositional Content and the Logical Space of Wittgenstein's "Tractatus"*. Berlin: de Gruyter.
Hylton, Peter. 1990. *Russell, Idealism, and the Emergence of Analytic Philosophy*. Oxford: Clarendon.
Janik, Allan. 2000. *Wittgenstein's Vienna Revisited*. New Brunswick: Transaction Publishers.
Kannisto, Heikki. 1986. *Thoughts and Their Subject: A Study of Wittgenstein's Tractatus*. Helsinki: Philosophical Society of Finland.
Kant, Immanuel. 1977. *Prolegomena to Any Future Metaphysics*. Translated by P. Carus and J. W. Ellington. Indianapolis: Hackett.
  1998. *Critique of Pure Reason*. Translated by P. Guyer and A. Wood. Edited by P. Guyer and A. Wood. Cambridge: Cambridge University Press.
  2000. *Critique of the Power of Judgment*. Translated by P. Guyer and E. Matthews. Edited by P. Guyer. Cambridge: Cambridge University Press.
  2006. *Anthropology from a Pragmatic Point of View*. Translated by R. B. Louden. Edited by R. B. Louden. Cambridge: Cambridge University Press.
Kimhi, Irad. 2018. *Thinking and Being*. Cambridge, MA: Harvard University Press.
Kjærgaard, Peter C. 2002. "Hertz and Wittgenstein's Philosophy of Science". *Journal for General Philosophy of Science* 33 (1):121–149.
Kremer, Michael. 2001. "The Purpose of Tractarian Nonsense". *Noûs* 35 (1):39–73.
  2002. "Mathematics and Meaning in the *Tractatus*". *Philosophical Investigations* 25:272–303.
  2004. "To What Extent Is Solipsism a Truth?". In *Post-Analytic Tractatus*, edited by B. Stocker. London: Routledge, 59–84.

2007. "The Cardinal Problem of Philosophy". In *Wittgenstein and the Moral Life. Essays in Honour of Cora Diamond*, edited by A. Crary. Cambridge, MA: MIT Press, 143–176.

2012. "Russell's Merit". In *Wittgenstein's Early Philosophy*, edited by J. L. Zalabardo. Oxford: Oxford University Press, 195–241.

Kuhn, Thomas S. 2012. *The Structure of Scientific Revolutions*. Chicago, IL: University of Chicago Press.

Kuusela, Oskari. 2011. "The Development of Wittgenstein's Philosophy". In *The Oxford Handbook of Wittgenstein*, edited by O. Kuusela and M. McGinn. Oxford: Oxford University Press, 597–619.

2017. "Wittgenstein, Ethics and Philosophical Clarification". In *Wittgenstein's Moral Thought*, edited by E. Dain and R. Agam-Segal. London: Routledge, 37–65.

2019. *Wittgenstein on Logic as the Method of Philosophy. Re-Examining the Roots and Development of Analytic Philosophy*. Oxford: Oxford University Press.

2023. "Wittgenstein's *Tractatus* and the Epistemology of Logic". In *Wittgenstein's Tractatus at 100*, edited by M. Stokhof and H. Tang. Cham, Switzerland: Palgrave Macmillan, 35–56.

Lanczos, Cornelius. 1962. *The Variational Principles of Mechanics*. Toronto: University of Toronto Press.

Lebens, Samuel. 2017. *Bertrand Russell and the Nature of Propositions*. London: Routledge.

Lewy, C. 1967. "A Note on the Text of the *Tractatus*". *Mind* 76:416–423.

Longuenesse, Béatrice. 2017. *I, Me, Mine; Back to Kant, and Back Again*. Oxford: Oxford University Press.

Lützen, Jesper. 2005. *Mechanistic Images in Geometric Form: Heinrich Hertz's 'Principles of Mechanics'*. Oxford: Oxford University Press.

MacBride, Fraser. 2013. "The Russell-Wittgenstein Dispute: A New Perspective". In *Judgement and Truth in Early Analytic Philosophy and Phenomenology*, edited by M. Textor. Basingstoke: Palgrave Macmillan, 206–241.

Malcolm, Norman. 1984. *Ludwig Wittgenstein. A Memoir with a Biographical Sketch by G.H. Von Wright and Wittgenstein's Letters to Malcolm*. Oxford: Oxford University Press.

Marion, Mathieu. 1998. *Wittgenstein's Finitism and the Foundations of Mathematics*. Oxford: Clarendon Press.

2011. "Wittgenstein on the Surveyability of Proofs". In *The Oxford Handbook on Wittgenstein*, edited by M. McGinn and O. Kuusela. Oxford: Oxford University Press, 138–161.

Marion, Mathieu, and Mitsuhiro Okada. 2018. "Wittgenstein, Goodstein and the Origin of the Uniqueness Rule for Primitive Recursive Arithmetic". In *Wittgenstein in the 1930s. Between the Tractatus and the Investigations*, edited by D. Stern. Cambridge: Cambridge University Press, 253–271.

McGinn, Marie. 2006. *Elucidating the Tractatus: Wittgenstein's Early Philosophy of Language and Logic*. Oxford: Clarendon.

McGuinness, Brian. 1966. "The Mysticism of the Tractatus". *Philosophical Review* 75 (3):305–328.
  2002a. *Approaches to Wittgenstein. Collected Papers*. London: Routledge.
  2002b. "Solipsism". In *Approaches to Wittgenstein. Collected Papers*. London: Routledge, 131–139.
  2005. *Young Ludwig: Wittgenstein's Life, 1889–1921*. Oxford: Oxford University Press.
  2006. "Wittgenstein and Ramsey". In *Cambridge and Vienna: Frank P. Ramsey and the Vienna Circle*, edited by M. C. Galavotti. Vienna and New York: Springer, 19–28.
  ed. 2008. *Wittgenstein in Cambridge. Letters and Documents 1911–1951*. Oxford: Blackwell.
McGuinness, Brian, and G. H. von Wright, eds. 1995. *Ludwig Wittgenstein: Cambridge Letters*. Oxford: Basil Blackwell.
Monk, Ray. 1991. *Ludwig Wittgenstein: The Duty of Genius*. London: Vintage.
Moore, Adrian W. 1987. "On Saying and Showing". *Philosophy* 62 (242):473–497.
  2003. "Ineffability and Nonsense". *Aristotelian Society Supplementary Volume* 77 (1):169–193.
  2013. "Was the Author of the Tractatus a Transcendental Idealist". In *Wittgenstein's Tractatus: History and Interpretation*, edited by P. Sullivan and M. Potter. Oxford: Oxford University Press, 239–255.
  2020. "The Bounds of Nonsense". In *Wittgenstein and the Limits of Language*, edited by H. Appelqvist. New York: Routledge, 27–45.
Moore, G. E. 1901. "Truth and Falsity". In *Dictionary of Philosophy and Psychology*, edited by J. M. Baldwin. New York: The Macmillan Company, 716–18.
Munz, Regine. 1995. "Wittgensteins Ehrfurcht". In *Culture and Value / Philosophie Und Die Kulturwissenschaften. Pre-Proceedings of the 18th International Wittgenstein Symposium in Kirchberg Am Wechsel*, edited by K. S. Johannessen and T. Nordenstam. Vienna: Hölder-Pichler-Tempsky, 68–74.
Myhill, John. 1974. "The Undefinability of the Set of Natural Numbers in the Ramified Principia". In *Bertrand Russell's Philosophy*, edited by G. Nakhnikian. London: Duckworth, 19–27.
Narboux, Jean-Philippe. 2009. "Négation et totalité dans Le Tractatus De Wittgenstein". In *Lire Le Tractatus De Wittgenstein*, edited by C. Chauviré. Paris: Vrin, 127–176.
  2014. "Showing, the Medium Voice, and the Unity of the Tractatus". *Philosophical Topics* 42 (2):201–262.
Newton, Isaac. 2004. *Issac Newton: Philosophical Writings*. Cambridge: Cambridge University Press.
Nir, Gilad. 2021. "The Tractatus and the Riddles of Philosophy". *Philosophical Investigations* 44 19–42.
Okada, Mitsuhiro. 2007. "On Wittgenstein's Remarks on Recursive Proofs: A Preliminary Report". In *Essays in the Foundations of Logical and*

Phenomenological Studies, edited by M. Okada. Tokyo: Keio University Press, 121–131.

Oz, Amos. 2003. *Sipour Al Ahava Vehoshekh [A Tale of Love and Darkness]*. Jerusalem: Keter Publishing House.

    2017. *A Tale of Love and Darkness*. Translated by N. de Lange. London: Vintage.

Pascal, Blaise. 1958. *Pensées*. New York: E. P. Dutton & Co.

Peano, Giuseppe. 1967. "The Principles of Arithmetic, Presented by a New Method". In *From Frege to Gödel. A Sourcebook in Mathematical Logic. 1879–1931*, edited by J. van Heijenoort. Cambridge, MA: Harvard University Press, 85–97.

Pilch, Martin. 2016. Wittgenstein Source Prototractatus Tools (PTT). In *Wittgensteinsource* (www.Wittgensteinsource.org), edited by A. Pichler and J. Kathrein. Bergen: Wittgenstein Archives, University of Bergen.

Plato. 1985. "Sophista". In *Platonis Opera*, edited by J. Burnet. Oxford: Clarendon Press.

Potter, Michael. 2000. *Reason's Nearest Kin. Philosophies of Arithmetic from Kant to Carnap*. Oxford: Oxford University Press.

    2009a. "The Logic of the Tractatus". In *Handbook of the History of Logic. Volume 5. Logic from Russell to Church*, edited by D. M. Gabbay and J. Woods. Amsterdam: North Holland, 255–304.

    2009b. *Wittgenstein's Notes on Logic*. Oxford: Oxford University Press.

    2020. *The Rise of Analytic Philosophy, 1879–1930: From Frege to Ramsey*. Abingdon, Oxon: Routledge.

    2021. "How Substantial Are Tractarian Objects Really?". *Disputatio (Spain)* 10:93–107.

Preston, John. 2008. "Hertz, Wittgenstein and Philosophical Method". *Philosophical Investigations* 31 (1):48–67.

Proops, Ian. 1997. "The Early Wittgenstein on Logical Assertion". *Philosophical Topics* 25 (2):121–144.

Quine, Willard Van Orman. 1960. *Word and Object*. Cambridge, MA: MIT Press.

Ramsey, Frank. 1926. "The Foundations of Mathematics". *Proceedings of the London Mathematical Society* 25:338–384.

Rhees, Rush. 1947. "Review of Cornforth, Science and Idealism". *Mind* 56:374–392.

Richter, Duncan. 2018. "Augustine and Wittgenstein on the Will". In *Augustine and Wittgenstein*, edited by K. Paffenroth, A. R. Eodice and J. Doody. Lanham, MD: Lexington Books, 169–184.

Ricketts, Thomas. 1996. "Pictures, Logic, and the Limits of Sense in Wittgenstein's Tractatus". In *The Cambridge Companion to Wittgenstein*, edited by H. Sluga and D. G. Stern. Cambridge: Cambridge University Press, 59–99.

    2002. "Wittgenstein against Frege and Russell". In *From Frege to Wittgenstein: Perspectives on Early Analytic Philosophy*, edited by E. H. Reck. Oxford: Oxford University Press, 227–251.

Rogers, Brian, and Kai Wehmeier. 2012. "Tractarian First-Order Logic: Identity and the N-Operator". *Review of Symbolic Logic* 5 (4):538–573.

Russell, Bertrand. 1903. *The Principles of Mathematics*. Cambridge: Cambridge University Press.

——— 1904. "Meinong's Theory of Complexes and Assumptions". *Mind* 13:204–219, 336–354, 509–524.

——— 1905. "On Denoting". *Mind* 14:479–493.

——— 1908. "Mathematical Logic as Based on the Theory of Types". *American Journal of Mathematics* 30 (3):222–262.

——— 1912. *The Problems of Philosophy*. London: Williams & Norgate.

——— 1914. *Our Knowledge of the External World*. London: George Allen & Unwin.

——— 1918a. *Mysticism and Logic and Other Essays*. London: Allen & Unwin.

——— 1918b. "The Philosophy of Logical Atomism. Lectures I–II". *The Monist* 28:495–527.

——— 1919a. *Introduction to Mathematical Philosophy*. London: George Allen & Unwin.

——— 1919b. "The Philosophy of Logical Atomism. Lectures III and IV". *The Monist* 29 (1):32–63.

——— 1927. *The Analysis of Matter*. London: Kegan Paul, Trench, Trubner & Co.

——— 1959. *My Philosophical Development*. London: Allen & Unwin.

——— 1984. "Theory of Knowledge: The 1913 Manuscript". In *The Collected Papers of Bertrand Russell. Vol 7*, edited by E. R. Eames and K. Blackwell. London: Allen & Unwin.

——— 1994. "Necessity and Possibility". In *Collected Papers of Bertrand Russell, Vol. 4, Foundations of Logic, 1903–05*, edited by A. Urquhart and A. C. Lewis. London: Routledge, 507–520.

Schlick, Moritz. 1930. "Die Wende Der Philosophie". *Erkenntnis* 1 (1):4–11.

Schopenhauer, Arthur. 2010. *The World as Will and Representation*. Edited by C. Janaway, A. Welchman and J. Norman. Cambridge: Cambridge University Press.

——— 2019. *On the Basis of Morality*. Translated by E. F. J. Payne. Indianapolis: Hackett.

Shapiro, Stewart. 2000. *Thinking About Mathematics. The Philosophy of Mathematics*. Oxford: Oxford University Press.

Shieh, Sanford. 2014. "In What Way Does Logic Involve Necessity?". *Philosophical Topics* 42 (2):298–337.

——— 2015. "How Rare Is Chairman Mao?". In *Dummett on Analytical Philosophy*, edited by B. Weiss. London: Macmillan, 84–121.

——— 2019. *Necessity Lost: Modality and Logic in Early Analytic Philosophy, Vol. 1*. Oxford: Oxford University Press.

——— 2021. "What Could Be the Great Debt to Frege? Or, Gottlobius Ab Paene Omni Naevo Vindicatus". *Disputatio. Philosophical Research Bulletin* 10 (18):5–62.

——— 2022. "On Attempting to Solve the Direction Problem". *Russell: The Journal of the Bertrand Russell Research Centre* 42:132–168.

In press-a. *Necessity Regained: Modality and Logic in Early Analytic Philosophy*, Vol. 2. Oxford: Oxford University Press.

In press-b. *Wittgenstein and Russell, Elements of the Philosophy of Ludwig Wittgenstein*. Cambridge: Cambridge University Press.

Skolem, Thoralf. 1967. "The Foundations of Elementary Arithmetic Established by Means of the Recursive Mode of Thought, without Use of Apparent Variables Ranging over Infinite Domains". In *From Frege to Gödel. A Sourcebook in Mathematical Logic. 1879–1931*, edited by J. van Heijenoort. Cambridge, MA: Harvard University Press, 303–333.

Sölle, Dororthee. 1997. *Mystik Und Widerstand: "Du Stilles Geschrei"*. Hamburg: Hoffmann und Campe.

Somavilla, Ilse, ed. 1997. *Ludwig Wittgenstein, Denkbewegungen: Tagebucher 1930–1932, 1936–1937 (Ms 183)*. Innsbruck: Haymon.

ed. 2006. *Wittgenstein – Engelmann: Briefe, Begegnungen, Erinnerungen*. Innsbruck: Haymon.

Spinoza, Baruch. 1992. *Ethics. Treatise on the Emendation of the Intellect and Selected Letters*. Translated by S. Shirley. Edited by S. Feldman. Indianapolis: Hackett.

Stebbing, Susan. 1933. "Logical Positivism and Analysis". *Proceedings of the British Academy* 19:53–87.

Stegmüller, Wolfgang. 1966. "Eine Modelltheoretische Präzisierung Der Wittgensteinschen Bildtheorie". *Notre Dame Journal of Formal Logic* 7 (2):181–195.

Stein, Edith. 1959. *Die Frau. Ihre Aufgabe Nach Natur Und Gnade*. Freiburg: Herder.

Stenius, Erik. 1960. *Wittgenstein's Tractatus. A Critical Exposition of Its Main Lines of Thought*. Oxford: Basil Blackwell.

Sullivan, Peter. 1994. "The Sense of 'a Name of a Truth-Value'". *Philosophical Quarterly* 44:476–481.

1996. "The 'Truth' in Solipsism, and Wittgenstein's Rejection of the a Priori". *European Journal of Philosophy* 4 (2):195–219.

2011. "Synthesizing without Concepts". In *Beyond the Tractatus Wars: The New Wittgenstein Debate*, edited by R. Read and M. A. Lavery. New York and Abingdon: Routledge, 171–189.

2013. "Idealism in Wittgenstein: A Further Reply to Moore". In *Wittgenstein's Tractatus: History and Interpretation*, edited by P. Sullivan and M. Potter. Oxford: Oxford University Press, 256–270.

Sundholm, Göran. 1992. "The General Form of the Operation in Wittgenstein's Tractatus". *Grazer philosophische Studien* 42:57–76.

Sullivan, Peter, and Colin Johnston. 2018. "Judgments, Facts, and Propositions: Theories of Truth in Russell, Wittgenstein, and Ramsey". In *The Oxford Handbook of Truth*, edited by M. Glanzberg. Oxford: Oxford University Press, 150–192.

Tang, Hao. 2011. "Transcendental Idealism in Wittgenstein's Tractatus". *The Philosophical Quarterly* 61 (244):598–607.

Tejedor, Chon. 2015. *The Early Wittgenstein on Metaphysics, Natural Science, Language and Value*. London: Routledge.
Trybus, Adam. 2020. "Two of a Kind: Setting the Record Straight on Russell's Exchange with Ladd-Franklin on Solipsism". *Russell* 39:101–120.
Urquhart, Alasdair. 2003. "The Theory of Types". In *The Cambridge Companion to Bertrand Russell*, edited by N. Griffin. Cambridge: Cambridge University Press, 286–309.
van der Schaar, Maria. 2018. "Frege on Judgement and the Judging Agent". *Mind* 127:225–250.
   forthcoming, "Russell on Judgment and the Judging Subject". In *Early Analytic Philosophy: Origins and Transformations*, edited by J. F. Conant and G. Nir. New York: Routledge.
von Wright, Georg Henrik. 1982. "Modal Logic and the *Tractatus*". In *Wittgenstein*. Oxford: Basil Blackwell, 185–200.
Waismann, Friedrich. 1965. "Notes on Talks with Wittgenstein". *The Philosophical Review* 74 (1):12–16.
   1979. *Wittgenstein and the Vienna Circle*. Oxford: Blackwell.
   1986. "The Nature of Mathematics: Wittgenstein's Standpoint". In *Ludwig Wittgenstein. Critical Assessments*, edited by S. Shanker. London: Croom Helm, 60–67.
Weiner, Joan. 2001. "Theory and Elucidation: The End of the Age of Innocence". In *Future Pasts: Perspectives on the Analytic Tradition in Twentieth Century Philosophy*, edited by J. Floyd and S. Shieh. New York: Oxford University Press, 43–66.
Weininger, Otto. 1903. *Geschlecht und Charakter. Eine Prinzipielle Untersuchung*. Vienna and Leipzig: Wilhelm Braumüller Verlag.
   1906. *Sex and Character*. New York and Chicago, IL: A.L. Burt Company Publishers.
Weiss, Max. 2017. "Logic in the Tractatus I: Definability". *Review of Symbolic Logic* 10 (1):1–50.
White, Roger M. 2006. *Wittgenstein's Tractatus Logico-Philosophicus: Reader's Guide*. London and New York: Continuum.
Whitehead, Alfred North, and Bertrand Russell. 1910. *Principia Mathematica*. Cambridge: Cambridge University Press.
   1925. *Principia Mathematica*. 2nd ed. Cambridge: Cambridge University Press.
Williams, Bernard. 1974. "Wittgenstein and Idealism". In *Understanding Wittgenstein, Royal Institute of Philosophy Lectures, Vol. 7, 1972–73*, edited by G. Vesey. London: Macmillan, 76–95.
Winch, Peter. 1972. *Ethics and Action*. London: Routledge & Kegan Paul.
Wittgenstein, Ludwig. 1921. "Logisch-Philosophische Abhandlung". In *Annalen der Naturphilosophie*, edited by W. Ostwald. Leipzig: Verlag Unesma, 185–262.
   1922. *Tractatus Logico-Philosophicus*. Translated by C. K. Ogden. London: Routledge and Kegan Paul.
   1929. "Some Remarks on Logical Form". *Aristotelian Society Supplementary Volume* 9:162–171.

1965. "A Lecture on Ethics". *The Philosophical Review* 74 (1):3–12.
1967. *Zettel*. Translated by G. E. M. Anscombe. Edited by G. E. M. Anscombe and G. H. von Wright. Berkeley: University of California Press.
1969a. *The Blue and Brown Books*. 2nd ed. Oxford: Basil Blackwell.
1969b. *Briefe an Ludwig Von Ficker*. Edited by G. H. von Wright and W. Methlagl. Salzburg: Otto Müller Verlag.
1971. *Prototractatus. An Early Version of Tractatus Logico-Philosophicus*. Translated by D. Pears and B. F. McGuinness. Edited by B. McGuinness, T. Nyberg and G. H. von Wright. London: Routledge & Kegan Paul.
1973. *Letters to C. K. Ogden with Comments on the English Translation of the Tractatus Logico-Philosophicus*. Oxford: Basil Blackwell.
1974a. *Philosophical Grammar*. Translated by A. Kenny. Edited by R. Rhees. Oxford: Blackwell.
1974b. *Tractatus Logico-Philosophicus*. Translated by D. F. Pears and B. McGuinness. 2nd ed. London: Routledge and Kegan Paul.
1975. *Philosophical Remarks*. Translated by R. Hargreaves and R. White. Edited by R. Rhees. Oxford: Blackwell.
1976. *Wittgenstein's Lectures on the Foundations of Mathematics, Cambridge, 1939, from the Notes of R. G. Bosanquet, Norman Malcolm, Rush Rhees, and Yorick Smythies*. Edited by C. Diamond. Ithaca, NY: Cornell University Press.
1979. *Notebooks, 1914–1916*. Translated by G. E. M. Anscombe. Edited by G. H. von Wright and G. E. M. Anscombe. 2nd ed. Oxford: Blackwell.
1989. *Logisch-Philosophische Abhandlung. Tractatus Logico-Philosophicus. Kritische Edition*. Edited by B. McGuinness and J. Schulte. Frankfurt am Main: Suhrkamp.
1993. *Ludwig Wittgenstein. Philosophical Occasions 1912–1951*. Edited by J. Klagge and A. Nordmann. Indianapolis and Cambridge: Hackett.
1999. *Culture and Value*. Translated by P. Winch. Edited by G. H. von Wright. 2nd ed. Oxford: Blackwell.
2000. *Wittgenstein's Nachlass: Text and Facsimile Version*. The Bergen Electronic Edition. Oxford: Oxford University Press.
2005. *The Big Typescript. Ts 213*. Translated by C. G. Luckhardt and M. A. E. Aue. Edited by C. G. Luckhardt and M. A. E. Aue. Oxford: Blackwell.
2009. *Philosophical Investigations*. Translated by G. E. M. Anscombe, P. M. S. Hacker and J. Schulte. Edited by P. M. S. Hacker and J. Schulte. 4th ed. Oxford: Blackwell.
2016. *Wittgenstein: Lectures, Cambridge 1930–1933 from the Notes of G. E. Moore*. Edited by D. Stern, B. Rogers and G. Citron. Cambridge: Cambridge University Press.
Zalabardo, José L. 2015. *Representation and Reality in Wittgenstein's Tractatus*. Oxford: Oxford University Press.
2018a. "Response to Commentaries on 'The *Tractatus* on Unity'". *Australasian Philosophical Review* 2:343–354.
2018b. "The *Tractatus* on Unity". *Australasian Philosophical Review* 2:250–271.

Index

aesthetics, 9, 71, 77, 80–81, 187–193, 195
analysis, 5, 7, 25, 32, 37–39, 46, 48, 51–53, 56, 59–63, 66–68, 70, 75, 85, 114, 129, 135
Anscombe, G.E.M., 9, 19, 50, 113, 159, 201, 203, 205, 207–215, 218
arithmetic, 8, 108, 145–146, 148, 158, 165
assertion, 6, 74, 90, 96–99, 101–105, 107–108, 127
assertion sign, 91–93, 99, 101–104, 108, 127
atomism, 6, 112–114, 116, 121–122
  logical, 112, 120
axiom
  of infinity, 8, 149–150
  of reducibility, 8, 149–150

belief, 27–31
Blue Book, 7, 119, 121, 123

Carnap, R., 25, 50, 146–147
causality, 183–184, 186
  law of, 9, 75, 168, 183, 185–186
Christensen, A.-M. S., 205–207, 211–212, 214, 218
Church, A., 8, 155–157
clarification, 5, 11, 17, 19, 50–51, 58–61, 66–68, 151, 156, 196
complex, 28–32, 34, 63, 127

Diamond, C., 2, 4, 24–26, 37, 39, 41, 44, 117, 141, 159, 201
direction, 28, 30–31
Dummett, M., 98–99, 113

ethics, 1, 8–10, 71, 120, 126, 133, 143, 166, 187–189, 193–202, 205–206, 211, 213–216, 218

fact, 12, 26–27, 32–37, 48, 85, 134
  negative, 33–34, 37, 134
  picturing, 36–37, 40, 114
falsity, 5, 26–27, 33–34, 36–38, 40, 99
first person, 126, 130–138, 140–144

Floyd, J., 5, 17, 36, 39, 42, 46, 48, 120
form, 24, 32, 34–37, 39–40, 44, 70, 73, 79, 82, 85, 87, 114–115
  logical, 7, 24, 37, 40–41, 51, 54–56, 58, 60, 63, 69–76, 79, 81–82, 84, 86, 88, 114, 116, 118, 121, 129, 134, 138, 188
formal procedure, 46, 48
Frascolla, P., 73, 146, 148, 155
Frege, G., 1, 6, 36, 38, 50–56, 60–61, 63–64, 90–108, 111–113, 116–117, 127–128, 136, 138, 140, 145–146, 148, 157
Friedlander, E., 206–207, 211–212, 217–218

Gómez-Alonso, M., 206, 212, 218

Hancock, P., 146, 154
Hertz, H., 8, 78, 136, 147, 151, 166–176, 178–179, 181, 184–185

idealism, 116–117
  transcendental, 6, 73, 83, 120, 126, 138
ineffable, 9, 80–81, 83, 159, 194–196, 198, 202, 214

judgment, 6–7, 26–28, 31, 90–98, 100–103, 105–108, 129–135, 137–141
  multiple relation theory of, 5, 26–29, 31, 129, 134

Kannisto, H., 71, 73, 77, 79, 83
Kant, I., 7, 70–76, 78–79, 81–83, 85, 88, 126, 138, 140
Kremer, M., 12–14, 63, 141, 143, 158, 201, 211–214, 218
Kuusela, O., 12, 50, 53, 55–58, 60–61, 64, 67, 143, 204, 215, 217

lambda-calculus, 8, 155, 157
language, 13, 15, 19, 38, 47–48, 62, 69–71, 77–79, 83–84, 86, 88, 112–113, 115–118, 122, 125–126, 132–133, 136, 138–140,

143–144, 187–188, 195, 201, 204–205, 207
completely analyzed, 55, 58, 62, 64, 66, 68
limits of, 20, 83–86, 88, 112, 132–133, 137, 140, 187–188, 194–195, 198, 200–201
logical, 5, 50–51, 58–59, 61, 66
ordinary, 50–55, 58, 60–61, 63–68, 75, 112, 158, 175, 195
limits, 4–5, 9, 13, 18–23, 26, 63, 74, 82–89, 121, 125, 133, 137, 139–141, 146, 156, 187, 189–190, 195, 197, 203–205, 208–209, 213–214, 216
of language. *See* language, limits of
logic, 1, 7–8, 12, 15, 24, 26, 36, 38–42, 44–48, 54–58, 60, 62, 71, 73–74, 79, 81–83, 87–88, 96, 113, 117, 126–128, 130, 132, 139, 142, 144, 146, 148, 150–151, 161, 166, 177, 186–187, 189–190, 199
transcendental, 70–74, 139
logical space, 36, 138–139, 190
logicism, 8, 145–146

Martin-Löf, P., 146, 154
mathematics, 1, 25, 72, 80, 82, 87, 145–146, 151, 158, 160–161, 166
McGuinness, B., 10, 18, 116–117, 137, 154, 168, 199
mechanics, 9, 138, 170–185
modality, 5, 24, 26, 36, 38, 41
Moore, A.W., 77, 80, 88
Moore, G.E., 27, 31, 34, 130, 142
mystical, 9, 81, 124, 187–199, 213
mysticism, 189, 198–200

Narboux, J.-P., 13–14, 22, 34, 41
necessity, 12, 24–27, 39–40, 45–46, 74, 78–79, 86, 88, 169, 186, 189, 192
negation, 5, 14, 26, 33, 90, 103, 128, 160
neo-Kantianism, 7, 138
Nir, G., 13
nonsense, 2–4, 8, 18–22, 24, 51, 64, 67, 80–83, 85, 87–88, 131–132, 134, 144, 159–160, 165, 187–188, 194–195, 201, 204, 211–214
number
cardinal, 147, 164
natural, 8, 145–146, 148–156, 161, 165

operation, 8, 14, 17, 142, 145, 152–155, 160

Peano, G., 145, 148, 150, 161
phenomenalism, 110–111
philosophy, 1–4, 11–13, 15–18, 54, 56, 60–62, 64, 67, 83, 121, 128, 133, 137, 139, 141, 166, 188–189, 195–196, 198, 201
cardinal problem of, 4, 11–15, 19, 22–23

picture, 5, 15, 18, 34–44, 47, 70, 72, 79, 82, 84–86, 97, 115, 126, 134–138, 142, 188
logical, 38, 72, 135
picture theory, 4, 7, 34, 50, 69, 114–116
picturing, 5, 25, 34–38, 40–47, 70, 77, 82, 86, 97, 107, 114, 135, 138, 142, 169–170
possibility, 5, 24, 73
Potter, M., 6–7, 113, 124, 127, 146
principle
context, 63, 136
vicious circle, 147–149
Proops, I., 101–102
proposition, 12–14, 16–19, 27, 38–39, 42, 46–48, 63, 77, 84, 86, 127, 135–136, 139–140, 142, 160, 188
elementary, 14, 17, 19–21, 24, 43, 46–48, 51, 61–62, 84, 122, 160, 166
general form of, 19–21, 46, 83, 86, 160–161, 166
logical, 11, 15, 42, 46, 48, 90, 107
non-elementary, 5, 43
pseudo-proposition, 8, 82, 87, 149, 151, 156, 158, 160
psychologism, 7, 126–128, 133

quantification, 46, 111, 113, 122, 163–164

Ramsey, F.P., 10, 113, 122, 148, 150, 154, 161, 167
realism, 117, 130, 141, 150, 205
relation
external, 130, 132–134, 206
internal, 8, 18, 37–38, 44–45, 47–48, 75, 81, 115, 130, 135, 141–142
religion, 9, 192, 194, 196, 199–201
Russell, B., 1, 4–8, 11–14, 17, 20, 22, 26–32, 34, 38, 41–42, 50–68, 102–103, 106, 110–115, 119, 122–123, 125, 127–134, 137, 145–152, 160, 189, 199

saying-showing distinction, 12, 22, 158–160, 164, 187, 195, 201
Schopenhauer, A., 118, 138, 189, 191, 193, 200, 203–204, 207–209
self, 1, 88, 117–118, 120–121, 123–124, 217
sentence, *See* proposition
Sheffer stroke, 46, 160
showing, 4–5, 8, 11–15, 19, 21, 26, 36, 40–41, 158, 189, 198–199
sign, *See* symbol vs. sign
propositional, 18, 20
silence, 9, 187, 189, 195, 197–198, 201
Skolem, T., 154, 157, 161–164
solipsism, 6–7, 13, 110, 112–114, 116–124, 126–127, 137, 140–141, 199, 205

Spinoza, B., 189–192, 200
state of affairs, 25, 27, 36–40, 71–72, 74–75, 77, 79, 82, 84–86, 88, 126, 132, 134–135, 138–139, 142–143, 188
state-of-things, *See* state of affairs
Stenius, E., 25, 71–73, 83, 86
structure, 6, 24, 34–40, 61, 73, 76–78, 80, 85–86, 115–117, 139, 207
sub specie aeternitatis (sub specie aeterni), 9, 187, 189–192, 202
subject, 84, 106, 126, 129–130, 132–133, 138, 204–206, 216
  metaphysical, 6, 70, 83, 85, 87–89, 121, 140, 204–205
  thinking, 7, 118, 120–121, 123, 206
  transcendental, 126, 140
substitution, 8, 151, 155–158, 165
Sullivan, P., 20, 27, 70–71, 75, 83–88, 100, 120, 139, 141
symbol, 6, 142
  vs. sign, 52, 61, 63–67, 116

tautology, 11, 18, 25, 42, 46, 76–77, 79–80, 82, 87, 142, 158, 161, 166, 186, 188, 213

thought, 5, 11, 19–23, 25, 27, 37–41, 47, 63, 70, 72, 74, 77, 79, 83, 86, 88, 95–96, 99, 101–104, 107, 118, 130, 133–137, 139–141, 169, 187, 210, 217
  musical, 69–70, 76–79, 81–82, 88, 115
transcendental aesthetic, 70–74, 76
truth, 5–6, 26–28, 34, 36–38, 40, 42, 48, 79, 95–99, 104–108, 138, 142
  logical, 25, 42, 46
truth operation, 160
truth-condition, 28, 47–48, 97, 99, 101, 117, 136
truth-function, 19–20, 41–43, 61–62, 160, 166
truth ground, 48
truth-possibility, 24, 45, 47–48
truth-table, 18, 47–48
type theory, 8, 148, 150

uniqueness rule, 8, 161–164

White, R., 20–22
will, 1, 9, 191–192, 196, 199–200, 203–205, 207–211, 213–218
  ethical, 204–205, 211–212, 214
Winch, P., 133, 143
world-soul, 137, 200

CAMBRIDGE CRITICAL GUIDES

Titles published in this series (continued):

Kant's *Metaphysics of Morals*
EDITED BY LARA DENIS
Spinoza's *Theological-Political Treatise*
EDITED BY YITZHAK Y. MELAMED, MICHAEL A. ROSENTHAL
Plato's *Laws*
EDITED BY CHRISTOPHER BOBONICH
Plato's *Republic*
EDITED BY MARK L. MCPHERRAN
Kierkegaard's *Concluding Unscientific Postscript*
EDITED BY RICK ANTHONY FURTAK
Wittgenstein's *Philosophical Investigations*
EDITED BY ARIF AHMED
Kant's *Critique of Practical Reason*
EDITED BY ANDREWS REATH, JENS TIMMERMANN
Kant's *Groundwork of the Metaphysics of Morals*
EDITED BY JENS TIMMERMANN
Kant's *Idea for a Universal History with a Cosmopolitan Aim*
EDITED BY AMÉLIE OKSENBERG RORTY, JAMES SCHMIDT
Mill's *On Liberty*
EDITED BY C. L. TEN
Hegel's *Phenomenology of Spirit*
EDITED BY DEAN MOYAR, MICHAEL QUANTE